Matthew

A Parascriptural Gospel Narrative

DENNIS CORNISH

WESTBOW
PRESS®
A DIVISION OF THOMAS NELSON
& ZONDERVAN

WestBow Press books may be ordered through booksellers or by contacting:

WestBow Press
A Division of Thomas Nelson & Zondervan
1663 Liberty Drive
Bloomington, IN 47403
www.westbowpress.com
1 (866) 928-1240

ISBN: 978-1-9736-9584-4 (sc)
ISBN: 978-1-9736-9583-7 (hc)
ISBN: 978-1-9736-9585-1 (e)

Library of Congress Control Number: 2020912454

Print information available on the last page.

WestBow Press rev. date: 07/20/2020

This book is in reverence of and to point to the glory of my Lord and Savior, Jesus Christ

CONTENTS

PREFACE

The following commentary is based upon personal journal entries made and edited over several years. As I study through scripture, I write down my thoughts and ideas so that I can more clearly come to an understanding of what God's Word is teaching me. I supplement my thoughts with direct quotes, paraphrasing, and other means of coming to a better understanding of a particular chapter or verse, and where used, they are cited as footnotes. Some of my journal entries and completed commentaries have been shared with the pastoral staff at my church, the church small group that I facilitate, and as the basis for a weekly men's Bible study. They have also been used to teach numerous adult classes on several books of the Bible or portions of the Bible, such as the beatitudes. For several years now, I have been encouraged by my lead pastor, executive pastor, and many others to publish, and after much prayerful consideration, I have decided to write this book.

The version of the Bible quoted in my work (unless otherwise noted) is the King James Version as it is in the public domain. I tend to read the ESV Study Bible and have used quotes from it, but copyright requirements restrict the number that can be used without written permission. As you read the following commentary, it would be useful to have your favorite version of the Bible next to you as a ready reference to the wording you are most familiar with and compare them with what I have written.

Throughout my writings, I reference several study Bibles and many different commentaries, with authors ranging various spans of time, some being contemporary and others being early church fathers, some reformers, and some puritans as well as many others. I also refine my thinking with extra biblical sources, such as, but not limited to, theological dictionaries, the Apostle's Creed, and the Westminster Confession of Faith, as well as quotes from ancient historians, such as Josephus. This is not an exhaustive list but an overview of the types of sources that have been used in my studies. With that having been said, the final arbiter is God's Holy Word, Sola Scriptura, and each of you are to be good Bereans (Acts 17:11) and satisfy yourselves that what I have written is scripturally sound.

Matthew 7:13–14 tells us to enter through the narrow gate, and as I write, I am cautioned in my spirit not to stray from that path. I say this in that God's Word is a complex mixture of near-future fulfillment and the more long-term fulfillment that will come at the end of the age. Historically there have been ongoing councils and theological debates over the issues you and I will grapple with in this book. Pray that you will be given the wisdom that is required to have the right understanding of scripture as a whole, and especially what the Holy Spirit and the rest of scripture (in its entirety) leads you to conclude as you read and study what has been set before us. Of course, this is true of any study of scripture that one endeavors as one moves closer to Christlikeness through the process of sanctification. My prayer is that the following study will enhance your own efforts at understanding God's Word and that it will prompt you to further deepen your own relationship with Jesus.

A final wish of mine is that, whether you are new to the study of the gospel message or have been faithfully reading your Bible for years, each person follows the advice that J. C. Ryle gives in his book, *Holiness.* He says that we should

> cease to regard the Gospel as a mere collection of dry doctrines. Look at it rather as the revelation of a mighty living Being in whose sight you are daily living. Cease to regard it as a mere set of abstract propositions and abstruse principles and rules. Look at it as the introduction to a glorious personal friend.

INTRODUCTION

Matthew's personal calling is chronicled in each of the three synoptic gospels. Luke calls him "Levi the tax-gatherer," Mark refers to him as "Levi, the son of Alphaeus," and Matthew names himself as Matthew but further identifies himself as "the tax collector" when listing the twelve apostles in verse 3 of chapter 10.

Matthew wrote primarily for a Jewish audience, and this is evident by the fact that when he cites Jewish customs, he does so without the need for explaining them. He was also respectively cautious and even guarded when referring to the name of God. As an example, he would say "the kingdom of heaven" instead of saying "the kingdom of God" like the other New Testament writers did. Matthew also quotes extensively from Old Testament prophetic passages in order to link the promises of the coming Messiah to the reality of the fulfillment of them in Jesus. Another difference is in the way he wrote his gospel. He did so by giving his readers firsthand accounts as he was an eyewitness to the events that took place surrounding Jesus during His earthly ministry.

Traditionally, the writing of Matthew has been set within the time of AD 50–70. It is often speculated that Matthew leaned heavily on the writings of Mark as he prepared his own gospel presentation. However, John MacArthur tells us in his commentary that "the nearly unanimous testimony of the church until the nineteenth century was that Matthew was the first Gospel written. Such a consistent and impressive chorus cannot be ignored." He goes on to list numerous bullet points refuting Matthew's dependence on the book of Mark, finally stating,

> The traditional view that the Gospel writers were inspired by God and wrote independently of each other, except that all were moved by the same Holy Spirit, remains the only plausible view.

CHAPTER 1

GENEALOGY AND BIRTH OF JESUS

VERSE 1

This verse describes the genealogy of Jesus, which is an important proof text to Jesus's right to claim the throne of David.

As mentioned, Matthew wrote his gospel for a Jewish audience, and for them, the Hebrew name for Jesus was *Joshua,* which means "Yahweh saves" or "the Lord is salvation." *Christ* is derived from the Greek word *Christos,* which in Hebrew was *Messiah (mashiakh)* or "Anointed." This Hebrew word pointed back to the anointed king of Israel, David. The designation of Messiah came to be linked to the Old Testament expectations of the promise of an Anointed One who would righteously rule God's people. The designation as the Son of David expressly connected the Messiah with a royal lineage that would reestablish the throne and kingdom of Israel. And finally, He was called the son of Abraham, the patriarch of the Jewish nation that arose out of the Abrahamic covenant.

It should be noted that Matthew's listing of Jesus's genealogy is not exhaustive and that he intentionally did not list every generation. As a sort of shorthand, he skipped over some to highlight the better-known persons within the lineage. This was a common practice and would have been both acceptable and understood by his Jewish readers.

Because genealogy was so important to the Jewish people, and they often referred to themselves as the children of Abraham, Matthew's genealogy traces Jesus's ancestry back only as far as Abraham. Luke's gospel account goes all the way back to Adam, and in R. C. Sproul's commentary, he tells us that this indicates that Christ is not simply the Savior of the Jews but that the scope of Jesus's redemptive work is universal. There are other differences in these two genealogies that are beyond the scope of this commentary, but with study, those differences can be harmonized. Matthew traced the lineage through Joseph and Luke through Mary, both of whom could trace their genealogy back to David. However, for Matthew's Jewish readers, and for the legal consideration of the genealogical record, Joseph's lineage, even though he was Jesus's stepfather, would have been of the utmost importance.

In John Calvin's comments on this genealogy, he expresses that Matthew's order of linage was a "legal" genealogy, whereas Luke's is laid out in a "natural" genealogy. Matthew lists Solomon after David because a legal genealogy is defined as one that traces Christ's right to the throne. Luke lists Nathan after David because he was the elder of the sons born to David and would be listed in a natural genealogy.

Calvin's comments were

> Matthew has exhibited the legal order because, by naming Solomon immediately after David, he attends, not to the persons from whom in a regular line, according to the flesh, Christ derived his birth, but to the manner in which he was descended from Solomon and other kings, so as to be their lawful successor, in whose hand God would "establish the throne of his kingdom forever." (2 Samuel 7:13)

Verses 2–16

These verses contain the long but extremely important lineage of Jesus's ancestry. In the comments on verse 1, I gave the reasoning behind Matthew's genealogical account, but a few more points might be helpful.

> The Jews kept extensive genealogical records and the religious leaders had every opportunity to disprove Jesus' claim to be Messiah by substantiating that He was not a descendent of David, but they could not use their own records to refute His being in the line of David. Finally, we should remember Paul's warnings about striving or arguing over genealogies and other controversies, calling them unprofitable and worthless. (1 Timothy 1:4 and 6:4; Titus 3:9)[1]

Another notable point is that Matthew's genealogy contains the subtle fact that Joseph was not the father of Jesus by specifically calling Joseph the husband of Mary and specifically refraining from calling Him Joseph's son.

Also of interest is that besides Mary, four other women are listed, a rarity in ancient Near Eastern genealogical records. Not only are they mentioned, but we find that two were prostitutes: Tamar, who sold herself to her father-in-law, and Rahab, a Gentile prostitute. One was an enemy of Israel: the Moabite Ruth. And the fourth was Bathsheba, the adulteress whose husband David had arranged to be killed.

Charles Spurgeon said,

> These four women have an important place in the genealogy of Jesus to demonstrate that Jesus identifies with sinners in His genealogy, even as He will in His birth, baptism, life, and His death on the cross. "Jesus is heir of a line in which flows the blood of the harlot *Rahab*,

---

[1] Paraphrased from www.blueletterbible.org study notes on Matthew 1 by David Guzik.

and of the rustic *Ruth*; he is akin to the fallen and to the lowly, and he will show his love even to the poorest and most obscure."

VERSE 17

This verse splits the number of generations into three distinct groups; each contains fourteen generations, which include from Abraham to David, from David to the Jewish deportation to Babylon, and finally, from the time of the deportation to Jesus, who is specifically called the Christ.

I have already covered the common practice of skipping certain generations and that Matthew had done so; therefore, his listing is not inclusive of all generations from Abraham to Christ. We also reviewed some of the differences between Matthew's and Luke's listings. Matthew left another of the royal line off his list, and that was Jehoiakim (2 Chronicles 36:5–8). He was so wicked that the prophet Jeremiah, as God's spokesperson, promised that no blood descendant of his would sit on the throne of Israel (Jeremiah 36:30–31). Therefore, if someone was a blood descendant of David through Jehoiakim, he could not sit on the throne of Israel and be the king and the Messiah because of this curse. But if Christ was not descended through David, He could not be the legal heir of the throne because of the promise made to David and the nature of the royal line.

This is where we come to the differences in the genealogies of Matthew and Luke. Matthew recorded the genealogy of Joseph, Mary's husband (Matthew 1:16). He began at Abraham and followed the line down to Jesus, through Joseph. Luke recorded the genealogy of Mary, and it is worded within Luke's genealogy that Jesus is the *supposed* son of Joseph (Luke 3:23). He began with Jesus and followed the line back up, all the way to Adam, starting from the unmentioned Mary.

Each genealogy is the same as it records the line from Adam (or Abraham) all the way down to David. But at David, the two genealogies become separated. According to Matthew 1:6, Joseph's line went through Solomon (and therefore Jehoiakim, the cursed one). Jesus was the legal son of Joseph but not the blood son of Joseph, so the curse on Jehoiakim did not affect

Him. Joseph did not contribute any of the "blood" of Jesus, but he did contribute his legal standing as a descendant of the royal line to Jesus. *Mary's* line—the bloodline of Jesus—did not go through Solomon but through a different son of David, Nathan (Luke 3:31). Mary was therefore not part of that blood curse on the line of Jehoiakim.[2] No detail is too small for our mighty God, and in this way, Jesus had every right to the throne of David, not only legally through Joseph but by blood through Mary.

VERSES 18–21

These verses tell of Mary's Immaculate Conception prior to her being married to Joseph. They tell of Joseph's doubts and concerns, of his being a just man and wanting to quietly divorce Mary without putting her to shame, but that an angel of the Lord came to him and intervened, telling him not to fear. He was to take her as his wife, and she would have a son that they would name Jesus because He would be the Savior of His people.

Matthew doesn't speak to the events that surround the actual birth experience of Jesus. His focus is where Jesus came from and how He came about. He tells us that after she was betrothed to Joseph, and before they had a physical union, Mary was found to be with child through the supernatural power of the Holy Spirit while remaining a virgin and unknown to any man.

The betrothal of a man and a woman during this time in Jewish history was the second of three parts of the marriage. The first was an engagement between the two, often arranged by the parents while the couple were still young; the second was the betrothal, which made the engagement binding. They were then known to be husband and wife for a period of about a year before they were actually married, which was the final stage during which they were wed.

This period of betrothal, with Mary being pregnant, was an extremely difficult time for this young couple. Many believed that Mary had

---

[2] Paraphrased from www.blueletterbible.org study notes on Matthew 1 by David Guzik.

become pregnant by a Roman soldier, and sexual unfaithfulness during the betrothal was an adulterous act. Joseph was understandably troubled, and in his doubt, he resolved to secretly put her aside through divorce. Although they were still in the betrothal stage of their marriage, the only way out of their binding relationship was by obtaining a divorce. Joseph was an honorable man and did not want Mary to be subjected to any more public scandal than was already upon her. That is why he thought to divorce her privately and as quietly as possible.

While he was contemplating how to best go about the divorce, an angel of the Lord appeared in a dream and told him to lay his fear aside and to take Mary as his wife. The angel went on to tell him that the child within her was conceived from the Holy Spirit.

The angel Gabriel (Luke 1:26) addressed Joseph as the son of David, a reference to his legal lineage to the throne. His being called by this title was significant and pointed forward to Christ's right to the throne. Joseph was to name his son Jesus, which means "the Salvation of Yahweh" or "Yahweh Is Salvation." Jesus was a common name during the time, but Christ was divinely appointed from eternity past to fulfill His mission as Lord and Savior of those who have been chosen as the elect. Jesus was and is the long-prophesized Immanuel that Isaiah wrote about, "God with us." The angel specifically tells Joseph that Jesus will save His people from their sin. Jesus's people would include Jew and Gentile alike. Salvation from sin was an often-repeated promise of the Old Testament prophets. It also raises the question of who Christ's atonement was intended for. Gabriel's words here tell Joseph that Jesus will save His people from their sins. Jesus's own words tell us that His sheep hear His voice and that He knows them. He goes on to say that He gives them eternal life and that they will never perish, and that God the Father has given them to Him (John 10:27–30). This is clearly not the view of the adherents of Universalism, who claim that there is no hell and that all people will be eventually saved from God's righteous yet wrathful judgment. Jesus died for a particular people, not to atone for every person who will ever live, and this doctrine is known as limited atonement or particular redemption. This is a substitutionary atonement with Jesus offering Himself as the perfect sacrifice and taking upon Himself the sins of His people, the elect, and imputing His righteousness to them. The atonement guarantees the salvation of those for whom it was offered, ensuring that they will trust in Christ. This is the gift of faith that we receive at regeneration. It is at this point that the Holy Spirit indwells us, and we begin the lifelong process of sanctification.

It should be noted that there are "only a few angelic visitations in the New Testament and most are associated with Christ's birth."[3]

VERSES 22–23

We are told that this was in fulfillment of what the Lord had spoken through the prophet, that a virgin would conceive and give birth to a son, and that they would name Him Immanuel, which means "God with us."

Matthew knew of and recognized that the supernatural conception of Jesus had been prophesized in Isaiah 7:14, and in this verse, he is pointing to the fulfillment of that prophecy. Historically, there has been some controversy about Isaiah's use of the Hebrew word *almah*, which can be translated either as "virgin" or "young woman"; however, Strong's Lexicon H5959 shows that in the context Isaiah used the word, it meant virgin. This, in conjunction with Mary's statement to the angel in Luke 1:34 that she had never known a man, which is a Jewish idiom for sexual intercourse between a man and a woman, should be sufficient to disavow this weak argument of their denial of a virgin birth. The angel Gabriel told Mary, and scripture reminds us, that there is nothing impossible for God to accomplish (Luke 1:37).

Additionally,

> 200 years before the birth of Christ the Septuagint translators, who took the Hebrew Scriptures and translated them into Greek, combined the Hebrew *"almah"* with the

---

[3] John MacArthur, *The MacArthur Bible Commentary* (Nashville, TN: Thomas Nelson Inc, 2005), 1120.

Greek "*parthenos*" to properly render the word virgin as a maiden who was sexually chaste.[4]

The name *Jesus* specifies what He does: saves His people from their sins. Immanuel is the messianic title of Jesus and specifies who He is, "God with us." Charles Spurgeon said, "If Jesus Christ be 'God with us,' let us come to God without any question or hesitancy. Whoever you may be, you need no priest or intercessor to introduce you to God, for God has introduced Himself to you."

VERSES 24–25

Joseph awoke in the full realization of the truth that the angel had revealed to him, and in obedience to that realization, he did what the angel commanded of him. He took Mary as his wife, yet they did not consummate their marriage until after the birth of Jesus.

---

[4] Paraphrased from the footnotes in the ESV Study Bible (Wheaton, IL, Crossway, 2008) 1821.

CHAPTER 2

WISE MEN VISIT AND FLIGHT TO EGYPT

VERSES 1–2

Matthew tells us little about the birth of Jesus, and in this chapter, he begins by telling us that the period of time that he is now referring to was after the birth of Jesus. He picks up his narrative from there. He includes where Jesus was born, and that Herod was the reigning king, because they are important historical facts. Jesus the Christ was a descendant of King David of Israel. Both were from the tribe of Judah, and both were born in Bethlehem, which was a small and insignificant town about six miles south of Jerusalem. Unlike David, Jesus's birth, as well as the exact place of birth, had been foretold by many of the Old Testament prophets (e.g., Micah 5:2). Although the exact date of Jesus's birth is unknown, the fact that he was born before the death of Herod the Great in 4 BC gives us a chronological reference point to approximate Christ's birth.

Matthew tells us that wise men came from the east in search of Jesus, and they refer to Him as having been born as the King of the Jews. They were from the east, but they were not kings, and more than likely, they were a part of a larger group of men who had been looking for the newborn Messiah. There are Old Testament passages that say kings will come and worship the Messiah, and this probably led to them being referred to as kings (Psalm 68:29; 72:10–11; Isaiah 49:7; 60:1–6).

As Matthew tells us, they were wise men, or magi, "a term that covered a variety of men who were interested in dreams, astrology, magic, and books thought to contain mysterious references to the future."[5] They may have been part of the larger Jewish contingent who had formerly been exiled into captivity. Matthew tells us that they had seen Christ's star when it rose and had come to worship Him. They may have remembered Balaam's prophecy about a star coming out of Jacob and a scepter rising out of the nation of Israel (Numbers 24:17). The movement of the star and its coming to rest (verse 9) suggest that this star was not a natural phenomenon, such as a comet, a supernova, an alignment of several planets, or any other speculative theory that points away from the supernatural event that it was. If it were to be compared to anything, it could be viewed as similar to the Shekinah that had led Moses and the Israelites through the wilderness during the exodus.

VERSES 3–6

When Herod heard the news that the wise men had come to worship Jesus, it troubled him, and when Herod was troubled, all in Jerusalem were troubled. This king, like many others, was jealous for his throne and saw this as a direct threat. He had already killed his wife and sons and anyone else he deemed to be less than loyal. Herod was an Edomite whom Rome had recognized as the king over Judea. History tells us that as soon as he came to the throne he began annihilating the Sanhedrin and killed over three hundred court officials. He was hated by the Jews, but his massive building projects, including the restoration of the temple, were admirable and kept them at bay. All Jerusalem was aware that Herod would stop at nothing to ensure that his kingdom remained firmly in his grasp. The people were troubled because they didn't know what to expect from him after he had heard the news that the magi had spoken of, that of a new rival, a legitimate heir to the Davidic throne who had been born King of

---

[5] Paraphrased from www.blueletterbible.org study notes on Matthew 2 by David Guzik.

the Jews. Herod was the king, and it was he who ruled over the Jews; this news did not set well with him.

Herod summoned the chief priests, including those who had held the office of High Priest, as well as the scribes. The scribes were experts and teachers of the Old Testament. They told Herod that they were fully aware of the passage in Micah (5:2) that prophesized that the Messiah would be born in Bethlehem of Judea and would be the shepherd of God's people Israel, but somehow they had not connected that knowledge with the events that were going on right in front of them. They specialized in the explanation and application of scripture to one's life. They were filled with knowledge, but because they were not filled with the Spirit, not even one of them bothered to go with the wise men on the short journey to Bethlehem.

VERSES 7–8

Herod calls the wise men to him, and he does so in secret. The Bible, as well as the commentaries that I have read, are silent as to why he summoned them secretly, but there is the potential that it may have been his intention to find and kill Jesus. During his questioning of the magi, he finds out when the star first appeared to them. Once he had gathered all the facts, he surmises that Jesus had been born about a year before. After their having met, he sends them to Bethlehem and further tells them that when they have found Jesus to send word back to him. He feigns a desire to go and worship Jesus, but it was murder that was in his heart. Charles Spurgeon commented, "Mark that the wise men never promised to return to Herod; they probably guessed that all this eager zeal was not quite so pure as it seemed to be, and their silence did not mean consent."

VERSES 9–12

After they had met with Herod, the wise men continued their journey in search of the Messiah. Matthew uses the word "behold" to draw our attention to the importance of what he was about to say. They once again saw the star that had appeared to them earlier while they were yet in the east. It now continued to guide them until it came to rest over the exact place where the child was. These verses again speak to the supernatural aspect of this "star" in its appearance, movement to guide them, disappearance while the wise men were in Jerusalem, and then its reappearance to once again lead them onward before finally stopping and standing still over the place where Jesus was located. They rejoiced at seeing the star and how it led them to their destination. Scripture points out that they not only rejoiced but did so with an exceedingly great joy. This stands in stark contrast to the religious elite who had stayed behind in the comfort of their homes in Jerusalem; those who had an intellectual knowledge of prophetic events but did not follow through with their own worshipful obedience and submission to the coming of their Messiah.

Once the magi had arrived, they entered the house and saw Jesus with his mother, Mary, and they fell before Him and worshipped Him. Even in his writing, Matthew gives deference to Jesus by mentioning the child before his mother; the inverse would have been the customary practice. They followed their worship by opening their gifts and offering them to Him, and among those offered were gold, frankincense, and myrrh. In their culture, when one appeared before royalty or a person of importance, it was customary to bring them gifts, and the preciousness of the gifts that they had brought before Him was in recognition of who they believed Him to be. The abundance of their gifts also fulfilled several Old Testament prophecies that spoke of many kings rendering Him tribute and bringing gifts to Him (Psalm 72:10). And in Isaiah 60:6, we read about those from Sheba who will come bringing good news while praising the Lord, lavishing Him with gifts of gold and frankincense.

There are many who have a misconception of where the magi found the Christ child, and this is more than likely based upon artist's renderings of the nativity. However, a careful reading shows us that they arrived at, and then entered, a house and not a stable, with their arrival having potentially been up to a year or more after Christ's birth.

Herod had asked the wise men to return to him with a message as to where Jesus could be found, but they had been warned in a dream not to return to Herod and instead traveled back home in a different direction. We too should be obedient to God's divine authority, which always supersedes that of mere men.

VERSES 13–15

As soon as the magi departed, an angel of the Lord appeared to Joseph in a dream. The timing suggests an urgency to the message, which was punctuated by Joseph being told to arise and to flee to Egypt because Herod's intention was to search for Jesus and to kill Him.

The family fled by night to Egypt, which at the time had a population of about 1 million Jewish settlers. R. C. Sproul tells us that Egypt was a classic place of refuge for Jews who were fleeing oppression in that they would find community among their own people. Egypt was a Roman province about ninety miles from Bethlehem, and it was well beyond Herod's jurisdiction. They stayed in Egypt as the angel of the Lord commanded them until after Herod's death, at which time they returned. Matthew viewed this as a further fulfillment Hosea's prophecy (11:1) through whom God had proclaimed that His Son would come out of Egypt. John MacArthur says that Israel's exodus from Egypt was a pictorial prophecy rather than a specific verbal prophecy and that these pictorial prophecies are always fulfilled in Christ. Where Israel had failed to be the light of the world and fulfill the calling of God, Christ Jesus fulfilled this call by bringing into the body of His church men and women from every tribe and every nation.

VERSES 16–18

Herod was furious at the wise men having gone home without coming back to report to him all that they had seen. In his anger, he sent his troops to kill all the male children two years and younger, not only in Bethlehem but within the entire region. He based the age of his genocide upon the timing he had ascertained from his earlier meeting with the wise men.

Some critics point to a lack of nonbiblical historical evidence or reports of Herod having perpetrated this atrocity, but this act of cruelty shouldn't be surprising to anyone. Herod was notoriously ruthless, and it is well-known that he had his own wife and sons murdered. Contemporary historians had many examples of Herod's murderous violence that they could report on, which were generally on a much larger scale than the killing of perhaps a dozen or two male children in Bethlehem. (The sum of those murdered has been extrapolated based upon the total population at the time). What should mark this atrocity as exceedingly heinous is Herod's knowledge that his intent was to specifically target the Lord's Anointed One, the long-awaited Messiah. Herod, in his cold-heartedness, would have considered the other children merely as collateral damage.

Matthew quoted Jeremiah's account (31:15) to invoke the imagery of the wailing and mourning of the mothers in the tribes of Benjamin and Judah for their children who were murdered or carried away in captivity to Babylon. Rachel's name and her grief-stricken condition are being used as a descriptive representation, or a personification if you will, of the sorrow of Bethlehem's mothers, and all the mothers of Israel throughout history who have or will have to go through a similar experience.

Matthew tells us that this brutal event and the ensuing sorrow that was perpetrated by Herod were the fulfillment of Jeremiah's prophecy and we should understand that the term "fulfill," as used in the New Testament, often had the meaning of "bringing something to completion" or "showing the full significance of." Matthew uses this second meaning as he demonstrates that

> although the Jews had long been back in their homeland, their exilic condition and their persecution still persisted and that faithful men and women in Palestine still awaited "the consolation of Israel," namely, God's promised restoration, and that can only be found in Christ Jesus (Luke 2:25).[6]

---

[6] Paraphrased from *Tabletalk Magazine* (Sanford, FL, Ligonier Ministries, Inc., August 6, 2013).

VERSES 19–21

Herod has now died and any danger from him was no longer to be feared. An angel of the Lord appeared once again to Joseph in a dream and told him to take the young Child and His mother and that they could leave Egypt and go back to the land of Israel. Each time an angel of the Lord addresses Joseph, the first person mentioned is the young Child, and this was an unusual method of addressing the members of a family. Under normal etiquette, the children would be mentioned last, if at all. Jesus being given first place in these various accounts demonstrates the extraordinary supremacy of this Child.

Matthew goes on to tell us that in obedience, Joseph immediately arose and took the Child and His mother back to Israel.

VERSES 22–23

Archelaus was the son of Herod the Great and succeeded him on the throne over Judea, Samaria, and Idumea. Many study Bibles say that he was hated by the Jews and displayed the same type of cruelty that characterized his father. At the plea of the Jews of Judea, the Romans finally deposed him and banished him to Gaul.

At some point, Joseph had another dream, and fearing Archelaus, he turned aside and went into the region of Galilee. John Calvin's commentary tells us that "the governor of Galilee was Philip, a man of gentle disposition, and almost like a private individual. Joseph complied with the suggestion of the angel, because, under a prince who had no delight in shedding blood, and who treated his subjects with mildness, there was less danger."

This area was also outside the more religious regions of Jerusalem and had a significantly larger population of Gentiles than Judea or Jerusalem. And so, Joseph took Jesus and Mary back to Nazareth; scripture tells us that this was in fulfillment of the prophecy that He would be called a Nazarene. Interestingly, although in Acts 22:8 Jesus identified Himself to Paul on the road to Damascus by saying, "I am Jesus of Nazareth," there is no specific Old Testament prophecy that Matthew is quoting, but it is thought that he is "referring to a general theme in the Old Testament prophets which foretold that the Messiah would be despised much in the same way that the town of Nazareth was despised in Jesus' time."[7] Others view this as a play on words by Matthew because *Nazareth* sounds like the word for branch in Hebrew, which was a designation for the Messiah. Therefore, "if there was a specific passage that Matthew had in mind, it may likely have been Isaiah 11:1, where we read, There shall come forth a shoot from the stump of Jesse, and a branch from his roots shall bear fruit."[8]

---

[7] Paraphrased from the footnotes in the ESV Study Bible (Wheaton, IL, Crossway, 2008) 1823.

[8] Paraphrased from Frederick F. Bruce's reference to Jerome as cited from www. blueletterbible.org study notes on Matthew 2 by David Guzik.

CHAPTER 3

JOHN THE BAPTIST

VERSES 1–2

The Bible is silent on the formative years of Jesus, and the last we hear about Him, prior to the beginning of His earthly ministry, He was twelve years old. His parents had searched for Him for three days after the Feast of the Passover. When they found Him, He was in the temple and He questioned why they were looking for Him. He indicated that they should have known that He was in His Father's house and conducting His Father's business (Luke 2:49). Matthew, in introducing us to John the Baptist, begins to unfold the events that led up to the beginning of the now grown man, Jesus, and His ministry.

Matthew begins with the phrase "In those days," a general statement about the timing of John's ministry, which would have been a historical event that was well-known to his Jewish audience. Near the Jordan River, in an area just west of the Dead Sea, was the Judean wilderness, and it was here that John the Baptist preached an urgent message of repentance. It was an appeal to sinners that through this means, by God's mercy and grace, they might be saved. This is not to imply that repentance is the cause of regeneration but that it is the fruit of being born again. Furthermore, repentance is not a one-time event; it is an act of contrition that must take place daily. Jesus taught if any man would truly follow Him, then that man must deny himself and daily take up his cross (Luke 9:23).

Repentance is a turning away from sin, a prayerful confession and renunciation of your sin. It is the decisive, life-changing event that Paul speaks about in the book of Romans when he tells us that we are to renew our minds and to no longer be conformed to the world. In his first epistle, John tells us that if we confess our sins, Christ, in His faithfulness and His justice, will forgive our sins and cleanse us from all our unrighteousness (verse 9).

The concept of repentance is so important we find the word itself to be at the forefront of many significant events of the gospel books, as well as in Acts. David Guzik's commentary or study guide tells us that

> · *repent* was the *first word* of John the Baptist's gospel (Matthew 3:1–2)

> ·*repent* was the *first word* of Jesus's gospel (Matthew 4:17)

> · *repent* was the *first word* in the preaching ministry of the twelve disciples (Mark 6:12)

> · *repent* was the *first word* in the preaching instructions Jesus gave to His disciples after His resurrection (Luke 24:47)

> · *repent* was the *first word* of exhortation in the first Christian sermon (Acts 2:38)

> · *repent* was the *first word* in the mouth of the apostle Paul through his ministry (Acts 26:20)

While many Bibles differ from the word *repent* as being the very first word in these verses, Guzik is making a valid point regarding the importance of repentance.

John the Baptist's exhortation for his hearers to repent was because the kingdom of heaven was at hand, the long-awaited advent of the Messiah was imminent, and it was soon to be revealed. John MacArthur tells us in his commentary,

> The kingdom is now manifest in heaven's spiritual rule over the hearts of believers (Luke 17:21), and one day it will be established in a literal earthly kingdom (Revelation 20:4–6).

VERSES 3–4

Matthew quotes Isaiah 40:3 to show that John the Baptist is the fulfillment of this prophetic word. The Baptist's calling was to lay the groundwork and to prepare the way of the Lord. He was to prepare the hearts and minds of Israel by making their sin known to them in such a way as they would see their need for the salvation that the coming Messiah would offer them.

Matthew tells us that the Baptist was to make the Messiah's paths straight. Adam Clarke, a British Methodist theologian, in his commentary on this passage, wrote, "The idea is taken from the practice of eastern monarchs, who, whenever they entered upon an expedition, or took a journey through a desert country, sent harbingers before them, to prepare all things for their passage; and pioneers to open the passes, to level the ways, and to remove all impediments." The impediments in the case of the Israelites, and for us, are our sinful and disobedient hearts. Charles Spurgeon, in agreement with Clarke, said this: "Men's hearts were like a wilderness, wherein there is no way; but as loyal subjects throw up roads for the approach of beloved princes, so were men to welcome the Lord, with their hearts made right and ready to receive him."

In Luke 1:14–17, we read what the angel of the Lord told Zacharias regarding their yet unborn son John.

> And thou shalt have joy and gladness; and many shall rejoice at his birth. For he shall be great in the sight of the Lord and shall drink neither wine nor strong drink; and he shall be filled with the Holy Ghost, even from his mother's womb. And many of the children of Israel shall

> he turn to the Lord their God. And he shall go before him
> in the spirit and power of Elias, to turn the hearts of the
> fathers to the children, and the disobedient to the wisdom
> of the just; to make ready a people prepared for the Lord.

John was the last of the Old Testament prophets, and his mission in life was predestined that he be the harbinger for Jesus's earthly ministry. He was crying out in the wilderness, his voice the first of its kind, coming after four hundred years of silence since the Old Testament prophet Malachi last spoke God's words.

The ESV Study Bible footnotes indicate that garments he wore were common to nomadic desert dwellers and that locusts and wild honey were not unusual as food for these same inhabitants. Jesus said of him, "For John the Baptist came neither eating bread nor drinking wine …" (Luke 7:33). John was the promised prophet who was to come "in the spirit and power of Elijah." In his dress and in the simplicity of every aspect of his being, he was living out his destiny to make ready a people prepared for the Greater One to come.

Verses 5–6

Earlier I defined true repentance, and it shouldn't surprise anyone that John the Baptist's message of repentance and baptism bristled the sensibilities of the religious elite. For them, repentance and baptism were something that the Gentiles were required to do as proselytes converting to Judaism. The Pharisees could not conceive of themselves as sinners. After all, they were children of Abraham and felt no personal necessity to repent or to be baptized. These verses demonstrate that the Pharisees were out of touch with the people and the heartfelt needs of these great masses of people who heard the call to repent and to be baptized. As they stood on the banks of the Jordan River and listened to the proclamation that the kingdom of heaven was at hand, the people recognized their sinfulness, confessed their sins, and acknowledged their need for a Savior.

VERSES 7–12

John calls out to the Pharisees and the Sadducees, two discrete religious groups who had banded in the common cause of protecting what they saw as their right of religious leadership. The Pharisees, or separated ones, intently maintained a focus on the Mosaic law and even more so on their unbiblical interpretations known as the traditions of the elders. The Sadducees were a small group who derived authority from the work they performed in the temple in Jerusalem. They sought to preserve the identity, religion, and the culture of the Jewish people. They also rejected human tradition, scorned legalism, and the only scriptural authority that they accepted was the Pentateuch (Genesis through Deuteronomy).

These two factions disagreed on many issues, including the resurrection of the dead. In Acts 23:6–8, Paul used this fact during his defense in front of the high priest.

> But when Paul perceived that the one part were Sadducees, and the other Pharisees, he cried out in the council, Men and brethren, I am a Pharisee, the son of a Pharisee: of the hope and resurrection of the dead I am called in question. And when he had so said, there arose a dissension between the Pharisees and the Sadducees: and the multitude was divided. For the Sadducees say that there is no resurrection, neither angel, nor spirit: but the Pharisees confess both.

These two groups of men may have come to show those watching that they too were ready for and anticipating the coming Messiah; however, in their hypocrisy, they had not repented. Other commentators say that they were there as critics, onlookers, and spies. John called them a brood of vipers and asked who had warned them to flee from the wrath to come. If they had repented, John asks them where the fruit of their repentance was, how it was demonstrated in their lives, and if their mere outward conformity to the law was insufficient. In anticipation to their often-used self-defense of their being Abraham's children, he tells them that God could easily raise up children of Abraham out of stones that were lying all around them and that their Jewish heritage wasn't enough. He goes on to tell them that if a tree doesn't bear good fruit, it will be chopped down and thrown into the fire. Not only that, but that the axe was ready to be wielded at any moment; irreversible judgment was imminent. Charles Spurgeon said, "No mere pruning and trimming work did John come to do; he was the handler of a sharp axe that was to fell every worthless tree."

He goes on to tell them that he will baptize them with water, but that One was coming that would be mightier than him, so much so that John didn't consider himself worthy to carry His sandals. In this saying, John was humbling himself and taking a position that was lower than a normal rabbi's disciple. He who was to come would be no mere rabbi. He would be the Messiah. He knows that the position, power, and work of the coming Christ would be far superior to any other ever known.

John tells them that the One to come would baptize them with the Holy Spirit and with fire.

> The baptism of the Holy Spirit represents the outpouring of the Spirit that was promised in Ezekiel 37:14 where we read, "I will put my Spirit within you, and you shall live, and I will place you in your own land. Then you shall know that I am the LORD; I have spoken, and I will do it, declares the LORD."[9]

Further, just as the axe was ready to fell unproductive trees, the coming Messiah's winnowing fork was in His hands and ready to gather the wheat (His chosen people), and like chaff, the others would be burned in the unquenchable fire of hell. John Calvin said of this verse that it represents "a dreadful torment, which no man can now comprehend, and no language can express." This message would have been both puzzling and thought-provoking to the Jewish leaders. Their interpretation of the Messiah coming in judgment meant a judgment against Israel's enemies. They tenaciously clung to their heritage as Abraham's descendants and

---

[9] Paraphrased from www.blueletterbible.org study notes on Matthew 3 by David Guzik.

were blind to their need for repentance, but John assures them that the cup of wrath was not just for Israel's enemies but for all who were at enmity with God.

VERSES 13–15

Jesus's coming from His home in Galilee to the Jordan to be baptized was the inauguration of His public ministry, a definitive break from His life as others had previously seen Him. The fact that Jesus, the sinless One, had come to be baptized was puzzling to John because he knew who Jesus was: the One who would baptize with the Holy Spirit and fire. We know from the gospel of John (1:29) that when the Baptizer, the last old covenant prophet, saw Jesus approaching, he declared to those at the Jordan, "Behold, the Lamb of God, who taketh away the sin of the world!"

John's water baptism was symbolic of a sinner's repentance in preparation for the coming Messiah, and in his reluctance over Jesus's desire to be baptized, John openly said that it was he who needed to be baptized by Jesus. Jesus did not dispute what John said, but in His understanding about John's confusion and God's greater purpose, Jesus told him that this act would fulfill all righteousness. Jesus, in perfect obedience to His Father, knew that this was a necessary step in His identification with the fallen and sinful. This act was another example of Jesus standing in the place of sinful man, just as He would on the cross, which He described as a greater form of baptism in Luke 12:50. At Jesus's words, John consented and baptized Him.

VERSES 16–17

This is one of the clearest examples of the Trinity in all the Bible. We have God the Son, who had just received a water baptism, we have the Spirit of God in the form of a dove descending and coming to rest upon Jesus, and we have God the Father proclaiming from heaven that Jesus is His Son and that He was extremely pleased with Jesus's act of obedience in His water baptism. This was a baptism unlike any ordinary baptism because it wasn't a baptism of repentance but a righteous identification of Jesus with sinners.

In John 1:32–34, we read what John the Baptist saw and what he had to say about this phenomenal experience.

> And John bare record, saying, I saw the Spirit descending from heaven like a dove, and it abode upon him. And I knew him not: but he that sent me to baptize with water, the same said unto me, Upon whom thou shalt see the Spirit descending, and remaining on him, the same is he which baptizeth with the Holy Ghost. And I saw, and bare record that this is the Son of God.

This was not a private meeting such as Gabriel had with Mary. It was a very public display of God's loving and audible approval of Jesus's life and ensuing ministry, which also included a physical manifestation of the Holy Spirit, who descended upon Jesus in an anointing of His earthly ministry. "The veil that hides the glory of heaven from human eyes had been removed."[10]

---

[10] R. C. Sproul, *St. Andrew's Expositional Commentary on Matthew* (Wheaton, IL, Crossway, 2013), 47.

CHAPTER 4

TEMPTATION OF CHRIST AND DISCIPLES ARE CALLED

VERSES 1–2

Scripture, in telling us that Jesus was being led[11] by the Spirit, is another way in which He, in His humanity, identifies with us as we too are led by the Spirit. Satan himself was the instigator of the temptations that Jesus endured in the wilderness. This was an all-out assault upon God's plan for our salvation, but God used Satan's evil intent to strengthen Jesus through His trust and dependence upon scripture in combating the devil. Although these temptations were more severe than ours, they link Jesus to the lesser sufferings that we undergo when we too are tempted. Hebrews 2:18 clearly tells us this: "For because he himself has suffered when tempted, he is able to help those who are being tempted." The author of Hebrews repeats this idea in 4:15, where we read, "For we do not have a high priest who is unable to sympathize with our weaknesses, but one who in every respect has been tempted as we are, yet without sin."

---

[11] Mark is more emphatic about the prompting of the Holy Spirit. Mark doesn't say that the Holy Spirit led Jesus but that He drove Jesus into the wilderness.

During His time in the wilderness, Jesus had fasted forty days and forty nights, and He was hungry.

> Scripture often associates forty days and nights with difficult circumstances. As an example, Elijah endured the same period without food while on the run from Ahab and Jezebel: "and went in the strength of that food forty days and forty nights to Horeb, the mount of God" (1 Kings 19:8).[12]

Another would be Moses when he was on Mount Sinai.

> So he was there with the LORD forty days and forty nights. He neither ate bread nor drank water. And he wrote on the tablets the words of the covenant, the Ten Commandments. (Exodus 34:28)

This period of fasting was extreme, and throughout it, Jesus was wholly dependent upon God the Father; it was only due to the power of the Holy Spirit that Jesus was able to be physically sustained.

VERSES 3–4

Scripture says that the tempter came, and because Jesus was led into the wilderness for this purpose, the fact that Satan came to tempt Him shouldn't surprise anyone. Other versions of the Bible say, "when the tempter came." And in this instance, this difference in wording may help us in understanding our own periods of temptation. It is never a question of *if* temptation will come but *when* it will come. Our temptation is an ongoing struggle and one that will consistently be with us on this side of glory. Although we too are children of God, Charles Spurgeon had this to say about the inevitability of temptation: "God had one Son without sin, but he never had a son without temptation."

---

[12] *Tabletalk Magazine* (Stanford, FL, Ligonier Ministries, Inc., February 1, 2008).

Satan knew of Jesus's great hunger and said that if He was "the Son of God, command these stones to become loaves of bread." Jesus rebuffed the tempter by quoting scripture. "Man shall not live by bread alone, but by every word that comes from the mouth of God." Jesus did not surrender Himself to sin as the first Adam had and wasn't about to abandon His trust in His Father by using the divine prerogative that He had set aside in His humanity just to satisfy His hunger. He knew that He was being tested and that the Father's purpose was higher than His mere hunger as a man. John MacArthur tells us that Christ's use of this passage from Deuteronomy fed Him spiritually, which from an eternal perspective is of greater advantage than the satisfying of our physical needs.

VERSES 5–7

Satan took Jesus to Jerusalem and stood upon a pinnacle of the temple, which is said to be somewhere between two hundred and three hundred feet above the floor of the Kidron valley. Josephus, the ancient Jewish historian, maintained that this was a drop of nearly four hundred and fifty feet. No matter which number is believed, it was a tremendous height to fall from.

Satan, in response to Jesus having used scripture, tries to entice Jesus by saying "it is written" and proceeds to partially quote Psalm 91:11–12. Satan is the great deceiver and will use scripture, both in and out of context, to accomplish his evil intentions. In this misuse of scripture, he left out a very important aspect, and that was the fact that the purpose of this command to the angels was to "guard you in all your ways." Jesus fully understood the whole counsel of God and the pretext that Satan was trying to foist upon Him. Whereas Psalm 91 is an exhortation to trust in God, the devil twisted its meaning for his own purpose of testing Jesus, while at the same time intentionally leaving verse 13 out of his quote. It says, "Thou shalt tread upon the lion and adder: the young lion and the dragon shalt thou trample under feet."

Satan uses this same type of manipulation today, and we hear it from the false teachers who stand behind pulpits every Sunday and misquote scripture to make a case for whatever personal agenda they are peddling, whether it be asking those in their audience for some seed money, ostensibly to help them grow their faith, or some other prosperity gospel. These are different gospels altogether from the message of the new covenant. "People say that the Bible is the Word of God but still take that Word and twist it to support what they want to do, and this violates the hermeneutic principles that govern how scripture should be interpreted."[13] The very first principle is that scripture interprets scripture, which means that His Word is immutable and that we must always consider the entire canon of scripture, and we are to do so within the context of its writing. John Calvin exhorts us to remember that scripture has been ordained by God for our salvation. We must not be ignorant of God's truth if we are to resist temptation and to recognize the deceit of the devil and his legions.

In full confidence of His Father's redemptive plan, Jesus relied solely on "the sword of the Spirit, which is the word of God" (Ephesians 6:17), to counter Satan's seductive lies. His succinct reply to Satan was "It is written again, 'Thou shalt not tempt the Lord thy God.'" In the same way, we who are followers of Christ are to humbly submit to God's guidance, and without doing so, we cannot expect to rely upon His promises.

VERSES 8–11

Through Adam's fall Satan has had dominion and power over this world, it will once again come under Jesus's rule at the end of the age. Satan wanted God to worship him, and in a desperate venture the devil offered Jesus all the kingdoms of the world if He would prostrate Himself at his feet. This hopelessly reckless scheme did not fit into the Triune God's plan for our redemption. Jesus had to go to the cross as the perfect sacrifice, and besides, He had no need to worship Satan to obtain the kingdoms that were rightfully His and that He would claim again at the end of the age. John Calvin says that Satan's ploy was intended to be a means for Christ to obtain the inheritance that was already His, but to do so in a manner that was not in the way that the Father had intended. Jesus had

---

[13] Slightly paraphrased from R. C. Sproul, *St. Andrew's Expositional Commentary on Matthew* (Wheaton, IL, Crossway, 2013), 57.

no desire to commit an idolatrous act and thereby dishonor His Father. In Jesus's resistance to this temptation, and in obedience to His Father's will, He commanded Satan to be gone. Quoting scripture again, Jesus had forcefully rebuked Satan's latest attempt by saying, "Thou shalt worship the Lord thy God, and him only shalt thou serve." We are to glorify God and Him alone. Anything else robs Him of the honor that is His and we profane Him.

At this, the devil left Him, and the angels came down to comfort and minister to Christ's physical needs. I am sure there was a gloriously jubilant chorus in the heavenly hosts at Jesus's major victory over the temptations that He had faithfully endured. The first Adam had failed the test of temptation; the second Adam was triumphant over Satan's attempts to overpower His resolve to do His Father's will. Jesus in His humanity had suffered in the wilderness, and in His suffering, He is able to help us when we are tempted (Hebrews 2:18). "In order for us to be saved, Jesus had to succeed where Adam failed. Where Adam as a man broke God's covenant, Jesus as a man had to keep God's covenant if we were to be redeemed."[14]

A cursory glance at the news, or the cover of magazines that are strategically located near the check stand at the grocer, will reinforce "that fame, power, and authority are so enticing that many people embrace wickedness in their drive to be known and followed.[14]" Matthew Henry said that "the glory of the world is the most charming temptation to the unthinking and unwary and that by which men are most deceived. The pride of life is the most dangerous snare."

God's truth, as revealed in scripture, was Jesus's weapon of choice. It was effective for Him and can be effective for us. That is why it is so important to be in God's Word and to have it locked securely in our hearts and minds, ready to be used in our defense against the temptations that will surely be ours.

---

[14] *Tabletalk Magazine* (Stanford, FL, Ligonier Ministries, Inc., March 27, 2014).

VERSES 12–17

In fulfillment of another prophecy by Isaiah (9:1–2), Jesus went into the region of Galilee, which is an area of about thirty miles by sixty miles. Josephus, the ancient Jewish historian, indicated that there were 204 villages, with each hosting a population of at least 15,000 people, which extrapolates to a population in that area which totaled more than 3 million people. There was a large contingent of Jewish settlers in this area, but it was predominately populated by Gentiles. Isaiah called this area "Galilee of the Gentiles."

Zebulun and Naphtali, while under Assyrian control, had experienced a great deal of turmoil, and the Jews of that area had longed for liberation from Gentile rule. Along with this, we must also remember that the book of Judges tells us that God was angry because His people had failed to drive out the pagans from the land, and He told them that these pagans would be a snare to them.

With the arrival of Jesus in their midst, those in the darkness that prevailed saw the dawning of a great light. John Calvin's comments were that

> the commencement of this light, and, as we might say, the dawn, was the return of the people from Babylon. At length, Christ, "the Sun of Righteousness" (Malachi 4:2), arose in full splendor, and, by His coming, utterly abolished the darkness of death.

Because it was on a major trade route, it became a strategically important center for Roman occupation. Galilee's tetrarch, or ruler, was Herod who had imprisoned John the Baptist, and it was here that Jesus chose to continue preaching what John had been proclaiming, and that was for the people to repent, for the kingdom of heaven is at hand. Capernaum, located on the northern shores of the Sea of Galilee, became the central base of operations from which Christ's Galilean ministry was disseminated, and Jesus's gospel message would soon go far beyond that of the Baptist's.

From that time, Jesus began to preach, saying, "Repent, for the kingdom of heaven is at hand." Although Jesus's initial ministry in Jerusalem and Judea briefly overlapped that of John's, after the Baptist's arrest, Jesus's ministry now could be said to be marked by a new phase, or one that could be regarded as the earnest beginning of His public ministry. John was the last of the Old Testament prophets and Jesus the first of the New, yet both the old covenant and the new speak of same kingdom and the need for a heartfelt and contrite repentance, which was foundational to both covenants.

Verses 18–22

Jesus went along the shore of the Galilee and saw two brothers casting a net, but this was not His first encounter with Peter and his brother Andrew. Andrew was a follower of John the Baptist, who had said to him, "Behold, the Lamb of God," and he began to follow Jesus and then told Peter that he had found the Messiah. They had apparently resumed their trade working as fishers, and John 1:35–42 and Luke 5:3 give us a fuller account. But it was now, in God's timing, that they were being called into a long-term discipleship. Jesus beckoned them to leave behind their normal occupation and to follow Him, saying that He would make them fishers of men, whereupon they immediately left their nets and their lucrative business.

A little further down the shore, Jesus again called another set of brothers, James and John, the sons of Zebedee, to follow Him, and they too followed Jesus and left behind their father and his hired servants (Mark 1:20). James, John, and their father were business partners with Peter and Andrew (Luke 5:10), and this being the case, because of the obedience of these four new disciples to follow their teacher, their combined business venture took a big hit from a manpower and leadership perspective.

These men knew who Jesus was, and their willingness to follow was in obedience to their Lord and Master; the Baptizer had already told them that Jesus was the Lamb of God. As Charles Spurgeon said, they were following an imperial command. This was the effectual calling of God, an internal and irresistible call that comes from the Holy Spirit, who pierces your soul and "changes the disposition of your heart so that you are made willing and eager to come to Him. God's effectual call works a life-changing effect in the hearts of those who hear it."[15]

The disciple Judas was called, but it was not an effectual calling to be a true follower. His was a calling that was meant to serve God's own purpose, to betray Jesus at the hands of men. He was called for the appointed purpose to deliver Jesus to His destiny with death for our salvation.

VERSES 23–25

Growing up and living in a Jewish community had the advantage of being able to go to the synagogue and to hear God's Word. It also gave itinerate rabbis the opportunity to teach in them during their travels. Jesus took these opportunities to teach the gospel message of the kingdom of God, and at the same time, He received all who were in need and healed every affliction among them, including those who were demon possessed. This is the first mention of demon possession found in the New Testament. These miracles were the signs that the Pharisees continually asked for through Jesus's earthly ministry, but in their spiritual blindness, they never correlate the truth and the power behind them as a testimony to, and an ongoing demonstration of, Jesus as being Messiah.

These miracles attracted great multitudes from many diverse areas, and this increased the number of people Jesus could minister to through the preaching of His message. Many who followed needed healing for themselves or for friends and family. Others followed Him just to see the miracles that they had heard rumor of, but all who followed were given the gospel message so that those who had ears could hear.

---

[15] Paraphrase of R. C. Sproul and Charles Spurgeon as cited by R. C. Sproul, *St. Andrew's Expositional Commentary on Matthew* (Wheaton, IL, Crossway, 2013), 71.

CHAPTER 5

SERMON ON THE MOUNT/BEATITUDES

The first part of this chapter deals with the beatitudes, and I want to clarify an issue that is often paraded out by those who are unbelievers, and that is a perceived difference in the two accounts that we will be looking at. In Matthew's version of these teachings, Jesus is giving what is known as the Sermon on the Mount. The mountain itself is not specifically identified so it is unclear precisely where this sermon was preached. In Luke's description of the events, he writes that Jesus "went out to the mountain to pray and continued all night in prayer to God." Luke's narrative doesn't identify the mountain either. Luke tells us that after this night of prayer, Jesus called together His disciples and chose the twelve and designated them as apostles (Luke 6:12–13).

In verse 17, Luke writes, "And he came down with them, and stood in the plain, and the company of his disciples, and a great multitude of people out of all Judaea and Jerusalem, and from the seacoast of Tyre and Sidon …" This mention of a plain or a level place is one example that unbelievers point to when they say that the Bible is inconsistent, but I don't see any inconsistency. Both accounts talk about a mountain experience, and it is easily conceivable that a level place, or a plain, could be found on a mountain, such as some type of plateau. Matthew, in the section of his gospel outlining the beatitudes, doesn't say that "he came down with them, and stood in the plain," as Luke says in his account; nor does Matthew concurrently speak about Jesus designating His choice of the twelve apostles, yet Luke's does. What we do have are two men relaying the teachings of Jesus, each from their own perspective, although one was an eyewitness while the other relied on what he had been told by other eyewitnesses. To be clear, Matthew does talk about Jesus selecting the twelve apostles in a prior section of his gospel, just before he gets into the beatitudes. As already mentioned, Matthew's account of the events is a longer narrative, and we know that none of the biblical authors used chapter and verse when they wrote.

An additional factor to keep in mind is that in matters that are important, teachers frequently teach them on more than one occasion, and often in more than one place. In the larger scheme of things, it shouldn't matter where, or how often, Jesus spoke these truths. They remain the Word of God, and they should be venerated for what they are.

It seems that the issue that unbelievers raise is just another opportunity for them as naysayers to once again try to pick the fly specks out of the pepper versus it being a topic of any real concern for anyone who is interested in the truth of God's Word. They are overlooking the importance of what Jesus is teaching while they focus on ways to discredit scripture instead of hearing and perceiving what God's Word has for them.

Calvin said it this way:

> The design of the Evangelist was to collect into one place the leading points of the doctrine of Christ, which related to a devout and holy life. Pious and modest readers ought to be satisfied with having a brief summary of the doctrine of Christ placed before their eyes.[16]

Scholars still debate whether Matthew and Luke's accounts were written based upon the exact same teaching event or if they were based upon the

---

[16] Calvin's Commentary on Matthew 5 at www.studylight.org/commentaries/cal.html.

same teachings given on two different occasions. They do, however, agree that the teachings themselves were the same, regardless of where or when they were taught. Although Luke's account is sometimes referred to as the "'Agenda of God's Kingdom," in most Bibles, we see that the teachings found in Luke 6 as well as in Matthew 5 still fall under the heading of the beatitudes.

Apart from any form of academic argument, in both books, we find Jesus pronouncing the various types of blessings that will be bestowed upon those believers who find themselves categorized as being in one condition or another, and these blessings all come under the heading of the beatitudes.

To define what a beatitude, is we'll go back to the Vulgate, the Latin version of the Bible that was compiled by Jerome, an early theologian and historian who lived in the fourth century. Here we find the word *beati,* which is translated as "blessed."[17] With this definition, we can easily see that this simply means that those who are classified within the categories that Jesus describes will be blessed.

One commentator cleverly defined the beatitudes as "the Blessings" but then went on to say that Christ gave the believers the "attitudes" that they should "be" in possession of, or what their *"be*-attitudes" should be comprised of.[18]

John MacArthur says that the beatitudes speak at a much deeper level than a mere surface emotion. He goes on to say that

> Jesus was describing the divinely bestowed well-being that belongs only to the faithful. The beatitudes demonstrate that the way to heavenly blessedness is antithetical to the worldly pattern normally followed in the pursuit of happiness. The worldly idea is that happiness is found in riches, merriment, abundance, leisure, and such things.

---

[17] *Vine's Expository Dictionary* online at www.blueletterbible.org/search/Dictionary.
[18] www.blueletterbible.org study notes on Matthew 5 by David Guzik.

> The real truth is the very opposite. The beatitudes give
> Jesus' description of the character of true faith.

In the beatitudes, Jesus instructs us on what are to be considered as the most fundamental principles of what it is to be a Christian. If we are Christians, the beatitudes outline who we are in Christ presently as opposed to a checklist of what we are to become. Jesus is telling us of the blessedness of what we are when we abide in Him as they are descriptions of the characteristics of God's people. Jesus Himself is represented in each of them, and He is the supreme example of what it means to have obtained them.

This final definition of the beatitudes is probably the most succinct yet the most accurate of any. Simply put, they are a description of Jesus, and they reveal to us what, or who, we are in Him.

There are Bible versions that use the word "happy" instead of "blessed," but *happy* lacks the depth of meaning that we have in the word *blessed*. Happy conveys, or at least suggests, more of an emotional condition that can be viewed as situational, versus the state of being blessed with all the eternal implications of God's bestowing His grace upon us as His children.

There is a great number, perhaps even the majority, of people who feel that to be happy is to find oneself free from all external annoyances, having plenty of money, and everything else that society tells us that we should have in order to lead a comfortable, carefree, and leisurely life. The innumerable instances of depression, substance abuse, and suicide among the rich and famous should easily dispel this myth.

It isn't the present life that we live or the state of our current condition that counts toward the blessings that we will receive if we follow Christ's teaching. This can be illustrated by the difference between joy and happiness. We may not be happy with our current job, our financial situation, our health, or any number of things, but we can still be joyful in our spirit. This joy is because we know, as followers of Christ, that we are blessed by our obedience to His Word. This is a joy that has the quality of serenity, an intangible condition that is beyond all that life brings to our doorstep. This joy is linked to the peace that surpasses all understanding that we read about in Philippians 4. Furthermore, we are admonished in James 1 to "count it all joy, my brothers, when you meet trials of various kinds, for you know that the testing of your faith produces steadfastness."

Our hope and joy are in salvation, and that is only ours through the grace of God. This is our eternal blessing and has little to do with the temporal and fleeting happiness that the unsaved strive for. Happiness is certainly a part of being blessed by God, but divine blessing goes far beyond mere happiness. To be blessed by God is to receive from Him spiritual benefit that lasts forever. To be blessed by our Creator is to find that we are within the sphere of His approval, and what more approval or blessing can we desire than to have God claim us as His children? Blessing in the highest sense involves God's favor, His willingness to come near and dwell among His people.

It is this concept that is the chief meaning of the Aaronic blessing that we find in Numbers 6:22–26, where we read,

> The Lord spake to Moses, saying, "Speak unto Aaron and his sons, saying, on this wise ye shall bless the children of Israel, saying unto them, The Lord bless thee and keep thee; the Lord make his face to shine upon thee and be gracious unto thee; the Lord lift up his countenance upon thee and give thee peace."

The Aaronic blessing was the hope of Israel, and it should be ours too, which is that God would shine His face upon us and that we would have a close and intimate relationship with Him.

This same viewpoint is spoken of, and slightly expanded upon, in the New Testament passages that are known as the beatific vision. In 1 Corinthians 13:12, we read, "For now we see through a glass [mirror], darkly; but then face to face: now I know in part; but then shall I know even as also I am known." And in 1 John 3:2, he tells us, "Beloved, now are we the sons of God, and it doth not yet appear what we shall be: but we know that, when he shall appear, we shall be like him; for we shall see him as he is."

In these two verses is encompassed all that we hope for in Christ, the face-to-face communion with God and His glory for all eternity. This vision, once realized, will flood our souls with the utmost measure of blessedness imaginable.

Although we are focusing on the New Testament, and specifically the beatitudes, as you are all aware, God's blessings are found throughout the Bible. I can't help but quote one of my favorite Old Testament psalms (1:1–6), where we read,

> Blessed is the man that walketh not in the counsel of the ungodly, nor standeth in the way of sinners, nor sitteth in the seat of the scornful. But his delight is in the law of the LORD; and in his law doth he meditate day and night. And he shall be like a tree planted by the rivers of water, that bringeth forth his fruit in his season; his leaf also shall not wither; and whatsoever he doeth shall prosper. The ungodly are not so: but are like the chaff which the wind driveth away. Therefore the ungodly shall not stand in the judgment, nor sinners in the congregation of the righteous. For the LORD knoweth the way of the righteous: but the way of the ungodly shall perish.

In these verses, the fruit that is to be had in its season, and the prospering that this blessed man obtains, is not from his own effort or merit, nor is it something that he ever could earn. They are heavenly gifts. His devotion to the Word of God, and his obedience in the shunning of the wicked, are the fruit of his being saved. This fruit is evidenced by his living in, and depending upon, God's will and graces, and again, they are not as a result of anything that he has done on his own.

Shifting gears slightly, in the Bible, we have two antithetical terms that are frequently used, one for blessing and one for judgment. For judgment, the term is "woe," such as in Matthew 23:13, when Jesus used this term as He addressed the sinfulness of the Pharisees and said, "Woe unto you, scribes and Pharisees, hypocrites …" For blessings, such as in the beatitudes as Matthew outlined them, we find the word "weal." The term *weal* is identified by a literary form that is used to describe the divine favoring of individuals when they are said to be blessed. We see examples of both woe and weal in Luke's rendering of the beatitudes, as well as find Jesus's pronouncements of woe and weal in the book of Revelation, and of course they are scattered throughout scripture.

There are a lot of people who believe that Jesus's message found in the beatitudes is for all men, and although the instructions and lessons gleaned from His preaching are of worthy note for humankind as a whole, they were being taught to believers, as will be evident when we get to verse 11. This was a message preached to those who belong to God's kingdom, both then and now, to the believing community, the followers of Christ. This is not to say it was originally taught only to those who were the twelve chosen as apostles but that it was taught to all those of His disciples who were present, and they were comprised, in a broad sense, of all who "followed" Him and heard Him. As we know, many of these later fell away when Jesus began to preach what has become known as the hard sayings of Jesus, which is beyond the scope of this teaching and better suited for another time. At any rate, the blessings that Jesus taught include promises for Christians, for those who daily take up their crosses and follow Christ.

VERSE 1

We have already briefly reviewed the minor differences in Matthew's and Luke's accounts, so I want to focus on the last portion of this verse that says, "and when He was set," which is to say when He sat down. Sitting is the normal posture or position that a rabbi takes when he is teaching. One detail that I found to be interesting was the fact that when teachers sit to teach, it doesn't matter what they are physically sitting on; they are said to be seated on "Moses' seat." Jesus Himself used this term in Matthew 23:2, where we read, "The scribes and the Pharisees sit in Moses' seat." Jesus then tells them to do whatever they say to do, but they are not to do what they do because they are hypocrites, saying one thing yet practicing another.

Jesus's followers became attentive based upon the fact that they were fully aware that once He sat down, He was about to teach. At this time, His disciples and others who were about to receive His teachings would gather and sit on the ground near His feet to be close to Him. You may have even heard a common expression when listening to someone who tells about a teaching that they learned while they sat at the feet of their pastor or spiritual leader.

The source of this idea comes from the Mishnah, which is a collection of rabbinic thoughts that still form the core of Jewish belief today. The following quotation is from Yose ben Yoezer. He was one of the earliest members of the rabbinic movement and lived about two centuries before Jesus. He said, "Let thy house be a meeting-house for the wise; and powder thyself in the dust of their feet; and drink their words with thirstiness."

The overall idea was to encourage people to make their homes places of Bible study and to welcome itinerant teachers as well as to eagerly learn from them. The middle line of this quote is sometimes translated as "sit amid the dust of their feet" and was understood as humbly sitting at the feet of one's teacher to learn from him. This is because it was customary to honor a teacher by sitting on the floor while he taught while seated in a chair.

From this arose a widely used phrase for studying with a rabbinic teacher: that you "sat at his feet." Paul even says that he was educated "at the feet of Gamaliel" (Acts 22:3). We also read in Luke 10:39 that while her sister Martha busied with preparations, Mary, forsaking all else, "sat at Jesus' feet" eager to hear every word that Jesus had to say. In the commentaries on this passage, Matthew Henry said, "If we sit with Him at His feet now, we shall sit with Him on His throne shortly."

I find it interesting that in Luke 4, just after Jesus returned from His forty days in the wilderness, enduring the temptations of Satan, He began His ministry, and the Bible tells us that He taught in their synagogues and was glorified by all. Jesus then went to Nazareth, and on the Sabbath, He stood and read from a scroll that was handed to Him. The scroll contained a passage from Isaiah 61:1. Jesus unrolled it until He found the place where it was written, "The Spirit of the Lord God is upon me; because the Lord hath anointed me to preach good tidings unto the meek; he hath sent me to bind up the brokenhearted, to proclaim liberty to the captives, and the opening of the prison to them that are bound."

First, we are awestruck by the way that God moves, and the fact that it was preordained that this specific scroll would be given to Jesus to read from. Little did those who handed Him that scroll know or realize how this incident was being used by God as a teachable moment for them as they were about to hear from Jesus Himself who He really was.

We need to take note of one more thing before we get to that unambiguous teachable moment. We know that during the reading of the scrolls it was customary for them to be read from a standing position, and once the reading was finished, the reader took his seat in order to signify that the recital had been completed. The point that I am driving at is that Jesus's teachable moment with these men, and for the rest of us, didn't occur until He sat down. Up to this point, He was merely reading from a text that most of those present more than likely already knew by heart. Scripture tells us that as soon as He sat down, He announced to them, "Today this Scripture has been fulfilled in your hearing." And with those few words, the Rabbi of all rabbis taught them a truth that they were not ready to hear.

VERSE 2

The word usage in this verse may sound a little peculiar in the way that this sentence is formed. It seems to us to be unnecessary to add the fact that He opened His mouth to teach them, but this was another way of signaling to those who were present that a teacher, rabbi, or prophet was about to declare a word from God.

Charles Spurgeon commented on this verse by saying, "It is not superfluous to say that He opened his mouth, for He had taught them often when His mouth was closed." Spurgeon meant that Jesus had taught them by His perfect, holy, and exemplary life. Spurgeon also said,

> He began to speak to them with freedom, so as the multitude might hear. Jesus spoke like a man in earnest; He enunciated clearly and spoke loudly. He lifted up His voice like a trumpet, and published salvation far and wide, like a man who had something to say which He desired His audience to hear and feel.

John Calvin said that this phrase would be faulty in other languages but that it is used frequently in the Hebrew. He goes on to tell us that the use of this mode of expression was generally used to draw attention to anything important and remarkable that had been or would be said.

VERSE 3

The poor are blessed.

We can also see that Luke's account in chapter 6, verse 20, is very similar where we read, "Blessed be ye poor, for yours is the kingdom of God." There are subtle differences in these two verses. One item of note is in how they identified who would be blessed. Luke used the personal pronoun "you" when describing who would be blessed, whereas Matthew more broadly directed the conferral of the blessing by using the term "the poor." MacArthur points out that Christ's concern for the poor and outcast is one of Luke's favorite themes, and that by his word usage, Luke was underscoring the tender and more personal sense of Christ's words.

Another subtlety is in the use, or absence, of God's name. As we pointed out earlier, in deference to his Jewish readers, Matthew was sensitive to using God's name, choosing instead to use the words "kingdom of heaven," while Luke had no qualms about the use of God's name in his writings.

The meaning of being poor in spirit is to be empty of oneself. It is to be humble and lowly in our own eyes. Steven Lawson, in one of his lectures, pointed out that the Greek word used here for "poor" is *ptochos* and carries with it the idea of being an empty-handed beggar, to be one of the least of the lowly, and that is the posture we are to take when we come to Christ in repentance. This does not mean that a person is without value or insignificant. It just means we are destitute of the fullness of Christ and the eternal riches that come with salvation and ongoing repentance. It is the heartfelt contrition that brings us to the confession that we are sinful and rebellious and woefully lacking in the characteristics of God, with nothing to offer to Him but our repentance. We as men have no spiritual assets of our own. In light of the perfection of God, we are spiritually bankrupt, with no righteousness or virtue of our own; we are totally dependent on God's mercy and grace. To be poor in spirit, we must be broken and be willing to set aside our pride and to respect the wisdom that we read in Psalm 51:17: "a broken and contrite heart, O God, thou wilt not despise."

Even the setting aside of all our pride is something we are powerless to do on our own. Recognizing the need to let go of everything that keeps us from all which God would have for us is something that can only come about through the work of the Holy Spirit within our hearts. This activity of the Holy Spirit is often imperceptibly subtle, but it is only through His work that we can respond to God in a way that is fittingly contrite.

Christians have the greatest example of humility in what Jesus did for us, and we need to fully embrace the fact that we are blessed beyond description in the fact that Jesus, the Son of God, humbled Himself in the incarnation in order to reconcile us to His Father.

While we are talking about the poor in spirit, it is worth mentioning that one problem with those who possess earthly riches is that it is very difficult for them to be humble and therefore to be poor in spirit. This may be one of the reasons that Jesus told His disciples, right after His discussion with the rich, young ruler, "It is easier for a camel to go through the eye of a needle than for a rich person to enter the kingdom of God" (Matthew 19; Mark 10; Luke 18).

One commentator said that humility, or poverty in spirit, is a prerequisite for worship and for receiving the kingdom of heaven. He went on to say that if we continue to harbor illusions about our own spiritual resources, we will never receive from God what we absolutely need in order to be saved.[19]

Those who come to the realization that they are only a mere breath, a quickly fading flower, that they are nothing compared to God, and that they are deserving of punishment and death can be called poor in spirit. They must come to fundamentally know that they cannot depend upon their own righteousness to be saved. Without the righteousness we have in Christ, we have no righteousness. In Isaiah 64:6, we are told, "We are all as an unclean thing, and all our righteousnesses are as filthy rags; and we all do fade as a leaf; and our iniquities, like the wind, have taken us away." To make sure we are all know how lowly our righteousness is viewed, we need to understand that the use of the term "filthy rags" is a euphemism for menstrual cloths, and from scripture, it is unmistakable that these would have been deemed as unclean.

Those who are poor in spirit know that they cannot trust in their own strength to overcome the obstacles, trials, afflictions, and the temptations of life. They cannot trust in themselves or in anything that they are able to offer, but they must trust entirely in Christ for the very breath that they breathe and for every beat of their hearts. Poverty in spirit is the emptying of our self-reliance and any false claims that we mistakenly believe that we have on God and His mercy. It is finally our concluding that we are utterly dependent on His grace and totally undeserving of His favor. To be poor in spirit requires an acute consciousness of being lost and hopeless without Christ at the center of our lives.

Matthew Henry said,

> To be poor in spirit is to have humble thoughts of ourselves, of what we are, and have, and do. It is to shun all confidence in our own righteousness and strength; that we may depend only on the merit of Christ and the spirit

---

[19] Paraphrased from www.blueletterbible.org study notes on Matthew 5 by David Guzik.

and grace of Christ. The kingdom of grace is composed of such; the kingdom of glory is prepared for them.

When one has humbled oneself to the point of total surrender to our Lord and begins to live in obedience to His will, forsaking one's own, one will be blessed. Scripture tells us that they will be exalted in heaven and given a place of honor in Christ's kingdom. Jesus is teaching us that the kingdom of God is a gracious gift to those who sense their own poverty in spirit and recognize that on their own they are lost.

Another commentator made the following observation on the order in which Jesus taught the beatitudes:

> The call to be poor in spirit is placed first for a reason, because it puts the following commands into perspective. No one is meek toward others until he has a humble view of himself. If you don't sense your own need and poverty you will never hunger and thirst after righteousness, and if you have too high a view of yourself you will find it difficult to be merciful to others.[20]

None of the beatitudes, which should be looked at as commands for those who would be in God's will, can be fulfilled in our own strength. It is for this reason that Jesus put being poor in spirit at the top of the list.

VERSE 4

Those who mourn are blessed.

Luke's account says, "Blessed are ye who weep now, for ye shall laugh."

Jesus isn't speaking of a casual sorrow for the consequences of our sin but a deep grief before the face of God (Coram Deo) over our fallen state. Ancient Greek grammar indicates an intense degree of mournfulness, it

---

[20] Paraphrased from www.blueletterbible.org study notes on Matthew 5 by David Guzik.

is the word that is used when mourning for the dead; it is the passionate lament for one who was loved. Not only are we to mourn for our sin, but we are to mourn for sin in general and the effect that it has had on the entire world. True mourning over sin, either individual or corporate sin, is to be focused on God and in acknowledgment that we can only find comfort from Him. It is the holiness of the Lord and the work of the Holy Spirit that reveal our desperation, and it is His grace which offers us forgiveness.

John Calvin says that this statement regarding mourning is closely connected with being poor in spirit, and he sees it as an appendage or confirmation of it. He says that nothing is supposed to be more inconsistent with blessedness or happiness than mourning, but by this verse, Christ shows that their very mourning contributes to a happy life by preparing them to receive eternal joy and the true comfort in God alone.

There are times in our lives when we experience, through the work of the Holy Spirit, the deep conviction of our sin and we mourn for the offense of our disobedience to our Holy Creator. We see biblical examples of this in 2 Samuel and Psalm 51 with David's repentance for his sin with Bathsheba, as well as in Acts 2, where we read the pilgrim's response to Peter's Pentecostal sermon when they were "pricked in their heart." They cried out to Peter, "Men and brethren, what shall we do?" Then Peter said to them, "Repent, and be baptized every one of you in the name of Jesus Christ for the remission of sins, and ye shall receive the gift of the Holy Ghost."

Matthew Henry's take on this beatitude is that this is a mourning of repentance and a sorrow according to God, a sorrow for our sin with an eye to Christ. He says that this includes a sympathetic mourning for the sin and afflictions of others, those who look with compassion on perishing souls. Jesus was a "Man of Sorrow," and as an example of this, He mourned for the wickedness of the Israelites and suffered for His people.

We can also mourn for other believers who are suffering, not just for their sins but for the suffering that is being experienced through their being persecuted for the work that they are doing and the life that they are living for the kingdom.

Those who mourn out of regard for God's honor mourn over their sin and the sin of others. As we read in Ezekiel 9:4, there are those who "sigh and that cry for all the abominations that be done in the midst thereof." They grieve over sin because they are sensitive to the dishonor it brings to the name of God. And if you read that passage, you will find that if they have a mark placed upon them, they are "passed over," whereas those who are unrepentant and don't have a mark on their forehead are wiped out by an executioner in white linen. Many believe that this executioner was the Angel of the Lord, the preincarnate Christ (a Christophany).

If you want to see a good example of the depth of mourning over sin that we have been talking about, take some time to read Daniel 9:3–19.

We see in this beatitude that those who mourn in repentance over their sin are promised comfort. In 2 Corinthians 7:10, Paul tells us, "For godly sorrow worketh repentance to salvation …" This verse shows us that God allows us to experience a mournful, godly grief over the sin in our lives as a path toward salvation, but it is a path that must include repentance and forgiveness. God's path for us, through our grief, does not bring us to a place for us to continue wallowing in self-pity, anguish, and guilt. With true repentance and forgiveness, God's path leads us to our final destination and to our promised blessing; it leads us to our heavenly home.

This promise of comfort in God's heavenly home consists of a perfect and eternal state of well-being. The comfort that we will receive is the comfort of forgiveness and salvation. Isaiah 40:1–2 tells us, "Comfort ye, comfort ye my people, saith your God. Speak ye comfortably to Jerusalem, and cry unto her, that her warfare is accomplished, that her iniquity is pardoned …" The word "warfare" used here can also be translated as "hardship." With that translation, we can see that through the mourning and sorrow for the hardships that we have brought upon ourselves, as well as how we have dishonored our Lord, He still pardons us. What a comfort it is that we have such a gracious and forgiving Father in heaven.

With this mourning over our sin and the repentance and the forgiveness that follows, we can begin to experience the joy and comfort that will be fully ours on the day that we are glorified before our Lord and Savior, Jesus Christ.

One observation that has been made is that the first two beatitudes, being poor in spirit and being mournful, point mostly to the inward man, but that the next beatitude, meekness, points outwardly and deals with how one relates to one's fellow man.

Another interesting note is that the New Geneva Study Bible says that this beatitude resembles, and is perhaps based upon, Psalm 37:11, where we read, "But the meek shall inherit the earth and delight themselves in the abundance of peace." Again, we see God's truth repeated and woven throughout scripture. Because of the consistent and unwavering declaration of these truths, we often find New Testament writers, and Jesus Himself, quoting from the Old Testament to highlight or emphasize their point.

VERSE 5

The meek are blessed.

When we are openly confronted in some way that is representative of, or at least thought on our part to be aggression, most people tend to lash back and to wholeheartedly defend themselves. We fail to take on the attitude of meekness because we are so wrapped up in only thinking about ourselves that we immediately go into a self-protective mode, putting up walls between ourselves and those who have provoked us into feeling this way. During all of this, we don't stop to consider why the other person has come off the way that they have, whether there has been some tragedy or loss that has caused their behavior toward us. In that moment, our default position is usually overly defensive, and it is so because of the selfishness that is born out of our sin nature. The problem with this is that the Lord has commanded us to meekness, to put ourselves last, to be humble and gentle before Him, as well as before those who have been hurtful and unjust toward us. Obviously, according to this beatitude, following our gut reaction to fight back wouldn't qualify us for a blessing.

Scholars tell us that it is almost impossible to translate the ancient Greek word for meek *(praus)* with just one English word. In the original Greek, there is the idea of a proper balance between anger and indifference; of a powerful personality properly controlled; and of humility. In their language, the meek person was not passive or easily pushed around, with the idea again being that the word meek represented strength under control. Jesus was the perfect example of meekness, but His strength of leadership and courage are more than evident throughout His incarnation.

When He had to, He responded with strength, such as when He was dealing with the Pharisees or even the money changers in the temple court, but on the other hand, when He encountered people who were lowly and broken by their sin, He ministered to them with compassion and gentleness.

Meekness is a quality that is frequently manifested by exceedingly strong people who do not use their strength or power to abusively crush others or to be mean-spirited toward them in some way.

To be meek means to show a willingness to submit to and work under proper authority. Meekness, when it comes to our relationship with others, shows a willingness to set aside and disregard one's own rights and privileges. Again, Christ's teachings are our greatest example. In Philippians 2:3, we read, "Let nothing be done through strife or vainglory; but in lowliness of mind let each esteem other better than themselves."

It should go without saying that the meekness we show before our Holy God is in humble recognition of who we are; therefore, we are to be submissive to His will and to conform to His Word.

Quoting Calvin again, he says, "By the meek he means persons of mild and gentle dispositions, who are not easily provoked by injuries, who are not ready to take offense, but are prepared to endure anything rather than do the like actions to wicked men." He goes on to say, "We must believe that Christ alone is the guardian of our life, all that remains for us is to "hide ourselves under the shadow of His wings. We must be sheep if we wish to be reckoned a part of His flock."

Basically, Calvin is saying that the meek are those who submit themselves to God in humble reliance upon Him and in reverence of His authority. They submit themselves to His Word, His commands, and His discipline, and they honor His sovereignty. Meekness is defined by an ultimate control that can only be achieved because it is empowered within us by the Holy Spirit.

The concept of meekness and how it is lived out is confirmed once again in Titus 3:1–2, where we read, "Put them in mind to be subject to principalities and powers, to obey magistrates, to be ready to every good work. To speak evil of no man, to be no brawlers, but gentle, shewing all meekness unto all men."

In the year 1859, Charles Spurgeon preached a sermon about meekness. He said that meekness was

> the Spirit which is necessary if we would become Christ's scholars. We can learn nothing, even of Christ himself, while we hold our heads up with pride, or exalt ourselves with self-confidence. We must be meek and lowly in heart, otherwise we are totally unfit to be taught by Christ. Empty vessels may be filled; but vessels that are full already can receive no more. The man who knows his own emptiness can receive abundance of knowledge, and wisdom, and grace, from Christ; but he who glories in himself is not in a fit condition to receive anything from God.

If we are to become true disciples of Christ, we must empty ourselves and become the unfilled vessels that Spurgeon talked about. This emptying of ourselves, this taking on the mantle of meekness, with the help of the Holy Spirit, is what it will take for us to be able to inherit the earth. We must deconstruct who we think we are and empty ourselves of who and what we think we are. Only through this radical emptying of ourselves is there room for us to be filled. It is then that Jesus can pour into us the life of abundance He came to give us (John 10:10).

In Matthew Henry's commentary, he has this to say regarding meekness:

The meek are those who quietly submit themselves to God and show true humility to all men; who can bear provocation without being inflamed by it; are either silent or return a soft answer; who keep possession of their own souls. They are the meek, who would rather forgive twenty injuries than revenge one.

The promise, or blessing, for those who are meek is that "they shall inherit the earth." Some Bible translations read this as "they shall inherit the land." The inheritance spoken of is symbolized by the land of Canaan, the Promised Land, which has long been representative of heaven itself. This promise gives us the confidence that God is watching over us and will deliver on this promise if we abide in Him in our meekness. We are under His divine protection, and on the day when we enter into His presence in our glorified bodies, we will take possession of the inheritance of the world, just as He has promised us.

R. C. Sproul in his commentaries on Matthew sums up the inheritance as follows:

> We are told that we are heirs of God, joint heirs with Christ. All things in this world have been given to Jesus, and the redemption He brings is not simply for the sins of people but for a fallen planet. At the present time, the whole creation groans together waiting for the redemption of the sons of God, but at the consummation of His kingdom the Lord will usher in a new heaven and a new earth, and that earth will be owned by the meek.

VERSE 6

Those who hunger and thirst after righteousness are blessed.

Sitting here in the comfort of our surroundings, many of us have already had a meal or two today, and there is a strong probability that none of us are facing the hunger or thirst that Jesus alludes to in this beatitude. People in the culture that He was speaking to knew what it was like to really be hungry or thirsty, and many may have even witnessed or experienced true famine in their lives. They "got it" when Jesus spoke of the profound intensity of hunger and the powerful need to be able to quench a thirst that so parched their throats that they could barely swallow. These irresistible forces are representative of the drive that should be behind our passion for His righteousness. For this blessing to be acquired, a man must long for the holiness of God, long to be sanctified, and long to be clothed in Jesus's righteousness. This intensity of craving for God's Word endures throughout the whole process of sanctification and is never completely satisfied on this side of heaven.

In book 1 of *The Confessions of St. Augustine,* he captured the urgency that we must have in our hungering for Christ.

> Behold, Lord, my heart is before Thee; open Thou thy ears thereof, and say unto my soul, I am thy salvation. After this voice let me haste and take hold on Thee. Hide not Thy face from me. Let me die—lest I die—only let me see Thy face.

The language Augustine used is archaic to us, but we can see the fervor in his prayerful desire for the Lord to be his salvation and for him to be able to respond to God as he ought to. He says that if he must die, so be it, and that his only wish is to see God's face. Augustine's plea is for the Aaronic blessing that we talked about earlier.

Jesus uses hunger and thirst because they are such powerful physical needs and they instinctively compel us to obtain that which is necessary for our survival. He wants us to understand that righteousness is just as necessary for our ultimate and eternal survival. It is because of this compelling necessity that hungering and thirsting for righteousness should be viewed as our most basic need. Without our passionate quest for righteousness before God, we cannot hope to inherit eternal life. But if we pursue it in the right spirit, we will find that we can hold fast to the promise that we have in this verse, which is that our hunger will be satisfied and that our thirst will be quenched.

Martin Luther wrote about hungering and thirsting for righteousness.

> In order to attain it one must have great earnestness, a yearning eagerness and incessant diligence: that where there is a lack of this hunger and thirst, all will amount to nothing.

We know as Christians that there is nothing we can do on our own to merit Jesus's righteousness, but we further know that He has imputed that same righteousness to all who call on His name and to those who through faith earnestly work out their salvation with fear and trembling. This too is only accomplished through the work of the Holy Spirit, with whom we cooperate in the process of our sanctification. If we truly hunger and thirst for righteousness, then we will put aside all evil and ungodly pursuits and begin to wholeheartedly live for Christ and follow what is written in Philippians 4:8.

> Finally, brethren, whatsoever things are true, whatsoever things are honest, whatsoever things are just, whatsoever things are pure, whatsoever things are lovely, whatsoever things are of good report; if there be any virtue, and if there be any praise, think on these things.

This verse outlines the personal righteousness that all Christians need to develop, and this is what begins to take place during the process of our sanctification. Within this ongoing practice and our progressive development, we are becoming more Christlike in our thoughts and our actions. Even though in our quest for holiness we know our own righteousness will never justify us, we nevertheless recognize that the fruit of our efforts is evidenced by the growth we experience in the advancement of our Christian character.

Again, the promise of this beatitude is that all who hunger and thirst after righteousness, who truly desire to have it, will not go without it; they will be filled. We will find that as we are satisfied in God and His everlasting sufficiency, He will be satisfied in our sincere yearning and earnest striving to be in His will. Jesus is faithful, and His promises will be fulfilled.

When we hunger after God and His righteousness, we are reminded of what God's Word tells us in Psalm 34:8. "O taste and see that the LORD is good: blessed is the man that trusteth in him." Jesus Himself told us, "But whosoever drinketh of the water that I shall give him shall never thirst; but the water that I shall give him shall be in him a well of water springing up into everlasting life" (John 4:14). Our Lord's Word is true, and this repeated promise is no exception.

VERSE 7

The merciful are blessed.

To be merciful is to be compassionate, and this compassion can be in word or deed, and it is especially beneficial if it is based upon a divinely inspired grace. Mercy is marked by a godly concern and kindness for others, an empathy for where they find themselves in their daily lives, and above all in their walk with the Lord. It is to have pity on someone. Not a pity that suggests any low, shameful, or derogatory sense of the word but in the meaning of having a loving sympathy and compassion for their situation. The very character of Christians, by virtue of calling themselves Christians, should manifest the spirit of mercy. To no one's surprise, and to our shame as Christians, this is not always the case

One who is merciful will be forgiving of other people and always looking for ways to restore a broken relationship. King David was just this sort of man. How many times did King Saul try to kill him, and how many times did David forsake the opportunity to kill Saul? Each time David was encouraged by those around him to seize the chance and to go ahead and kill Saul and to claim the kingship. David repeatedly told them that he could not because God had anointed Saul as king and David would not dishonor God's choice of who would reign. David was merciful, and therefore God was merciful to David. Through all his sin, God's mercy was extended to David and all future generations of his family linage. We know, of course, that linage includes our Lord and Savior, Jesus Christ, who reigns eternally.

We are merciful when we give to a godly charity, when we support the missionary field, when we take care of the widows and orphans, or when we give a gift through the compassion offering at church. We see a need, and our hearts recognize the truth in the old adage "There by the grace of God go I." When this occurs, we willingly take part in the distress of others. There is no outside source of prompting needed because it is what God would have of us as He gently nudges us to action.

John Calvin comments that "Christ says that those are happy, who are not only prepared to endure their own afflictions, but to take a share in the afflictions of others; who assist the wretched; who willingly take part with those who are in distress."

There are countless ways that we can show mercy, and when we do, many of them take place without the awareness of others within the church or community. They are really transactions between us and God, with any reward or mercy coming directly from God Himself. We may be on one side or the other of a merciful act, a benefactor, or the beneficiary, but it is God who orchestrates it all, and all the glory is His.

Mercy is another of the inevitable fruits that are produced out of an authentic faith in Jesus. If we love our Lord and Savior, we will extend the hand of compassion to those who are in need, as well as forgive those who have offended us. We should stop and consider how often we expect, and even demand, mercy from others, yet we are slow to show it ourselves. We must always remember that mercy does not deny that wrong has been done, nor does it make light of sin. What mercy requires is not to forget what has happened but to extend forgiveness despite the sin and despite that the person we are forgiving deserves judgment for the wrong that was done. We fail to remember that within our willingness to forgive others their trespasses is to be found an inherent sign of our own forgiven heart, a new heart that rests in Jesus alone for salvation. In contrast, in Matthew 18:35, Jesus tells us that we will be condemned if we do not forgive those who sin against us and who ask us for mercy.

Colossians 3:12–13 tells us,

> Put on therefore, as the elect of God, holy and beloved, bowels of mercies, kindness, humbleness of mind, meekness, longsuffering; Forbearing one another, and forgiving one another, if any man have a quarrel against any: even as Christ forgave you, so also do ye.

Another source that I read said,

> William Shakespeare understood the depth and treasure of mercy when he wrote in *The Merchant of Venice* that mercy is an attribute of God Himself, and that it blesses both him who gives and him who receives. He described it as holding back the power and dread of the scepter, a scepter that can be wielded rightfully in judgment and punishment. But mercy stays the hand of the monarch and softens the heart of the king. And though all the power of heaven could be brought against those who transgress, it is mercy that holds back well-deserved destruction.[21]

This parallels what we read in Esther 4:16 and the fear she had when she went uninvited to her husband, the king, to plead for Mordecai and her people. Although she knew that it was against the law to appear before the king without an invitation and that her life was in peril if she did so, she nevertheless had the courage to go before him after saying, "And if I perish, I perish." Of course, the king was delighted to see her and held out the golden scepter toward her, granting her the mercy of an audience.

All Christians are obligated to show mercy because we have been forgiven much. The same mercy that we show, we will receive from our King. We as sinners deserve His judgment and destruction, yet He loves us. Our praise should be given to our God, because through our repentance, He will grant us His forgiveness, His mercy, and His grace.

---

[21] *Tabletalk Magazine* (Stanford, FL, Ligonier Ministries, Inc., December 1998).

VERSE 8

The pure in heart are blessed.

Earlier we reviewed the Aaronic blessing (Numbers 6:24–26), which says in part, "The LORD bless thee and keep thee: The LORD make his face shine upon thee and be gracious unto thee." We also looked at the beatific vision (1 Corinthians 13:12; 1 John 3:2) which tells us, "For now we see through a glass, darkly; but then face to face: now I know in part; but then shall I know even as also I am known" and "But we know that, when he shall appear, we shall be like him; for we shall see him as he is."

This sixth beatitude tells us that the pure in heart shall see God, and we can only imagine being enraptured by the vision of God's face for all eternity as His beauty will be far more glorious than anything we could ever conceive of with our limited minds.

In stark contrast, we can turn in our Bibles to Isaiah 59:2, where we are told, "But your iniquities have separated between you and your God, and your sins have hid his face from you, that he will not hear." Isaiah is plainly telling us that those who are unrepentant and without a pure heart will not be able to see God, nor will God hear their cries.

In the ancient Greek, the phrase *pure of heart* had the idea of straightness, honesty, and clarity. In a similar line of thinking, John Calvin says, "Christ pronounces those to be blessed who take no delight in cunning, but converse sincerely with men, and they express nothing, by word or look, which they do not feel in their heart."

Psalm 24:3–5 is a similar or parallel verse to this beatitude.

> Who shall ascend into the hill of the LORD? or who shall stand in his holy place? He that hath clean hands, and a pure heart who hath not lifted up his soul unto vanity, nor sworn deceitfully. He shall receive the blessing from the LORD, and righteousness from the God of his salvation.

Once again, we discover that if we study the whole council of God, we will find the same truths woven throughout scripture. Another example that I referenced, when we were going through the beatitude on mourning, was Psalm 51 and the earnest prayer of David. During that same prayer, David pleaded that God would give him a pure heart and that he would be washed of all unrighteousness.

The pure hearted are those who have embraced Christ and are wholly devoted to our Father in heaven. They have been washed by His blood, and this cleansing leaves them uncontaminated from the corruption of the world.

We all desire what David desired, which is to walk before God clothed in the righteousness of Jesus and to enjoy God's fellowship unburdened by the weight of our sin. The heaviness of sin for a Christian is both an emotional and physical reality. It weighs down the mind to the point of it affecting not only the pattern of our thinking but includes a feeling of heaviness or sluggishness in our bodily movements, a similar condition to the one we find in someone that is chronically depressed. This is why when we go to our knees to confess and are truly repentant of our sin, we can accept Jesus's offer when He says to us, "Come unto me, all ye that labour and are heavy laden, and I will give you rest." Until we repent and lay our sins at Jesus's feet, we will remain heavy under the burden of our sin. It is only when we confess our sins and turn away from them can we find rest in Him, purified, righteous and restored.

The blessings of a purified heart are an unfettered prayer life and the resultant deepening of our relationship with our God. We no longer need to hide from Him because of our nakedness in the garden, we will be clothed in the righteousness of Christ, walking openly again, basking in the radiance of His glory. For us today to see God is a figure of speech used in hopeful anticipation because we trust in Jesus's promise that the pure in heart will see God. As it stands now, we see Him in faith and in knowing that Jesus said that anyone who has seen Him has seen the Father, and that the apostles walked with Him, ate with Him, laughed with Him, and cried with Him. They heard His promise of going to prepare a place for them in His Father's house and that He would come back for them and for us.

An intimate relationship with God must become our greatest motivation for purity if we are to stand before our Maker and hear the words "Well done, good and faithful servant."

Even though our purity has been imputed, or assigned to us by Christ, it is guaranteed to us in fullness by the completed work of our Savior, so we who are in Christ know without question that we will one day experience perfect happiness and inner peace; we know with confidence that we will one day see God as He is.

First John 3:2 says that it is not yet revealed to us what we shall be, but we know that when He is revealed, we shall be like Him, for we shall see Him as He is.

We have no concept or imaginings of what He looks like because He is Spirit, but it goes beyond that. It has to do with not only our visual and outward perception of Him but to seeing in a way that is much deeper than a mere visual pattern of Him that is a result of our optic nerves sending a signal to our brains. It is a perception of Him that permeates our whole being, a perception that is beyond mere sight.

Jonathan Edwards wrote a great deal about this experience of seeing not just outward appearances but in seeing the very essence of God and His character. Such seeing includes an immediate and deeply profound recognition formed by a direct perception that is wholly experienced by one's mind, body, and spirit, resulting in a fuller, although incomplete, understanding of the majesty of God. This knowing is not dependent on physical sensations. This is what those with a pure heart can expect in heaven when they see God as He is.

VERSE 9

The peacemakers are blessed.

We know as Christians that first and foremost the Son of God came to reconcile sinners to God the Father (Romans 5:1). Reconciliation was and is needed because after the Fall, humankind was cursed and has been at enmity with God. We can be in one of two camps: at war with God or at peace with God. On this point, Jesus told the Pharisees, "He that is not with me is against me; and he that gathereth not with me scattereth abroad" (Matthew 12:30). These are the only two options we have, and as His chosen, we are to be solidly in His camp. It is one more example of the love God has for us that He reached out to us while we were yet sinners and brought peace to us while we were His enemies.

Our Father's plan for our salvation has been sealed through the obedience of His Son, Jesus the Christ. Believers have been saved from the wrath of God, and in this, we find true peace in our hearts and souls as we are no longer estranged from Him. Since peacemaking is so firmly connected to the finished work of Christ, the peacemakers in this beatitude cannot be separated from the peace that Christ bought for us on the cross.

Matthew Henry said that the peacemakers are blessed when they are first and foremost pure, and then peaceful. They are pure toward God and peaceful toward men. They are industrious to preserve the peace that is not yet broken and to recover it when it is broken. He says that the peacemakers will be called sons of God because He will acknowledge them as such. He goes on to say that if the peacemakers are blessed, woe be to the peace breakers.

We, as Christians, are called to be united in the Spirit and to maintain peace. In fact, Romans 12:18 tells us, "If it be possible, as much as lieth in you, live peaceably with all men."

Those who are peacemakers work together with the Holy Spirit to proclaim peace on earth. They do this by having a peaceable disposition that flows from a quiet tranquility in their souls and a love toward others. This inevitably goes back to forgiveness as those who are considered peacemakers do everything that they can to reconcile with those they have offended, as well as with those who have offended them.

Another way we are to become peacemakers is through the spreading of the gospel. In 2 Corinthians 5, God gave, and entrusted to us, the ministry of reconciliation. When in obedience we respond to this command and take on this ministry of evangelism, and when through the Holy Spirit we bring peace between those who have been sinning against our God, we have engaged in peacemaking.

In addition, when striving for truth when there is church discipline being brought to bear because of heresy, the peace we are to bring about is a true peace that is made by clearly articulating the situation without compromising integrity, truth, or justice, and to do so without contentiousness but in a spirit that is seasoned in grace and all humility. None of this is to say that we are to whitewash or skirt the issues, but that they are to be handled with certainty and within the guidelines of scripture.

God is a God of peace, and His Spirit is the Spirit of peace. He drives away the turmoil and chaos in fallen hearts and soothes them with His oil of gladness (Psalm 45:7; Hebrews 1:9). By His grace, He reconciles sinners to Himself, and He calls those who have been saved from their sin to live at peace with others.

One of the benefits that we derive from being peacemakers is the enormous privilege of being rewarded. This magnificent reward is almost more than we can comprehend—that of our being recognized as true children of God, being called sons of God, and being adopted into His family as coheirs with Christ.

John Owen (1616–1683) said that to contemplate all the privileges of communion with Christ would be enough work for a man's whole life. Yet he goes on to say that all of them are summed up within the highest privilege of all, and that is in the adoption into the family of God with all the rights and privileges of knowing Him as our heavenly Father. Owen further tells us that that this adoption is the unswerving transfer of a believer, by the finished work of Jesus Christ, from the family of the world and Satan, into the family of God, with the induction into all the privileges and advantages of that family.[22]

VERSE 10

Those persecuted for righteousness's sake are blessed.

Luke 6:22–23 is the parallel scripture and goes beyond Matthew's verse 10 and into Matthew's verses 11 and 12 as well.

> Blessed are ye, when men shall hate you, and when they shall separate you from their company, and shall reproach you, and cast out your name as evil, for the Son of man's sake. Rejoice ye in that day, and leap for joy: for, behold, your reward is great in heaven: for in the like manner did their fathers unto the prophets.

The last two beatitudes as outlined by Matthew have a common theme with respect to persecution. These last several verses should give us pause and call us to contemplation because the promise we are given in them is somewhat unexpected in that those who go through and endure such persecution don't usually consider this type of experience as a blessing to them. Each of the beatitudes highlights what can be thought of as a type of countercultural transformation in the lives of Christians, and they culminate in these final beatitudes where we find that because of our faithfulness we will inevitably find conflict and persecution.

In the New Testament book of John, he wrote that darkness hates the light (John 3:20), and this being the case, evil men detest those who embody the qualities described in the beatitudes. Their hateful response is to persecute those walking in the light. God says we are to be salt and light, and if we obey His command, then it should go without saying we can expect persecution. In fact, Jesus told His disciples, "And ye shall be hated of all men for my name's sake: but he that endureth to the end shall be saved."

---

[22] A paraphrase from Sinclair B. Ferguson, *The Trinitarian Devotion of John Owen* (Sanford FL, Reformation Trust Publishing, 2014) 95.

Christ is the light of the world, and His righteousness is what the darkness hates about Christians. We as followers reflect His light, not as dramatically as Moses's face reflected the glory of God when he came down from Mount Sinai. Nevertheless, because we reflect the light of Christ, we have, as His disciples and representatives, been targeted.

Jonathan Edwards said the following regarding the light that we reflect when we are in Christ:

> The soul of a saint receives light from the Sun of Righteousness, in such a manner that its nature is changed, and it becomes properly a luminous thing; not only does the sun shine in the saints, but they also become little suns, partaking of the nature of the Fountain of their light.

Christians should consistently be discerning, having an ever-present awareness that those who are living in darkness and sin hate being reminded that Christ is the Sovereign Lord of all. They especially hate being told that they need His grace and mercy. They can't bear being reminded of their sin nature as they delude themselves in the belief that they are in total control of their own destiny. They constantly reassure themselves that they aren't as bad as their neighbor and that they really are good people. The Pharisees were prime examples of this because of their public pretense of a righteousness that wasn't real; it had no depth or substance. That is why Jesus said they were like whitewashed tombs on the outside but held within them the corruption of the grave. "When true righteousness appeared in the person of Jesus, the false righteousness of the Pharisees was exposed for what it was, and they hated it."[23]

Jesus tells us in Matthew 5:44–47,

> But I say unto you, Love your enemies, bless them that curse you, do good to them that hate you, and pray for

---

[23] R. C. Sproul, *St. Andrew's Expositional Commentary on Matthew* (Wheaton, IL, Crossway, 2013), 92.

them which despitefully use you, and persecute you; That ye may be the children of your Father which is in heaven: for he maketh his sun to rise on the evil and on the good, and sendeth rain on the just and on the unjust. For if ye love them which love you, what reward have ye? do not even the publicans the same? And if ye salute your brethren only, what do ye more than others? do not even the publicans so?

God extends His love to everyone, even those who are His enemies, and this is referred to as common grace. For this reason, all people can enjoy God's blessings in the most familiar events that we all share in, such as the sun and the rain, sunrises, and sunsets, and all the other wondrous events of everyday life.

MacArthur said, "The universal love of God is manifest in the blessing which God bestows on all people indiscriminately." These indiscriminate blessings MacArthur mentions are what I referred to above as common grace, but they are still to be separated and must be distinguished from the everlasting love God has for those who are His elect.

We will be persecuted when we speak the truth, because we do the right thing, because we defend the helpless, or because we try to make peace where others only want to tear down. We will be persecuted because we are different from the world and the fact that this is not our home. We will be persecuted especially because we speak the Word of God in the name of Jesus Christ with a boldness and confidence that is of the Holy Spirit.

VERSES 11–12

When, for Christ's sake, men revile and persecute you, you are blessed.

Luke's verses 22–23 cover this same material, and as mentioned earlier, the last two beatitudes in Matthew's gospel are essentially, or at least nearly, the same. This repetition should cause us take special notice, not only because Jesus repeated Himself, which accentuates importance, but because Jesus doesn't say "if" we are persecuted. He says "when" we are persecuted. This highlights persecution as an inevitable fact that has been or will be a very real part of our union with Christ. Jesus tells us that following Him as Lord will bring us many trials and tribulations.

John Calvin tells us,

> Satan, the prince of the world, will never cease to fill his followers with rage, to carry on hostilities against the members of Christ. It is no doubt, monstrous and unnatural, that men, who study to live a righteous life, should be attacked and tormented in a way which they do not deserve.

It should go without saying, if we are being persecuted for our sin, then any idea of receiving a blessing for this type of persecution is beyond reason on our part. It is not suffering in general that will bring about the blessing; it is the suffering of persecution for the Son of Man's sake that brings the promise of reward.

Conversely, if we are subject to oppression and persecution for doing the right thing, for following our convictions in Christ, we are assured that the kingdom of heaven is ours. This is the very same promise that was given in verse 3, the first beatitude, which speaks of those who are poor in spirit, and that is the promise of the kingdom of heaven.

Paul tells us that he was willing to face persecution, and to face it in joy. He said that I "…rejoice in my sufferings for you, … for his body's sake, which is the church, (Colossians 1:24)". He could say this and to live it out in the strength of Christ and for Christ's honor. He allowed Jesus's power to shine through Him, even in his own weaknesses.

The prophets were persecuted because they stood for truth, and we as Christians, if we stand firm in our convictions, will be persecuted as well. We will only endure in our suffering if we rely on the strength of Christ in our lives, and in order to rely on His strength, we must keep our eyes and hearts focused on Him and Him alone. If we do this, we will honor Christ, and a part of that honoring is facing what comes our way with humility and with rejoicing. Luke 6:23 addresses this rejoicing when it tells us, "Rejoice ye in that day, and leap for joy: for, behold, your reward is great in heaven: for in the like manner did their fathers unto the prophets."

We are to triumph in what becomes glory to God through the reality of our persecutions so that we may be counted as worthy to share in the ordeals of prophets and the saints who were treated in the same way. We find an example of this in Acts 5:41, where we see that after the apostles were beaten for their testimony, they left rejoicing at being considered worthy to suffer for their witness in Jesus's name.

It has been further said that the idea of true faith and persecution are inseparably linked, and this should not be a surprise to us as this has been the experience of the church throughout the ages. Martin Luther said that there is always opposition when the gospel is preached plainly and accurately.

We shouldn't limit our view of persecution to the physical aspects of it. Jesus's use of the term "revile" in verse 11 clearly includes slander, insults, and other spoken taunts into the overall definition of persecution. The early church was greatly maligned by mischaracterization of their beliefs and practices. They were said to practice cannibalism because of the gross misrepresentation of the sacrament of the Lord's Supper. They were considered treasonous because their allegiance was to Christ and they refused to honor the Roman gods or participate in emperor worship. These are but a few of the types of things that went on and would be considered persecution under the subheading of reviling. I am sure we could all list some form of this type of persecution in our own lives, whether it be at work, on the golf course, or just being excluded because we might spoil the fun of excessive drinking and licentiousness.

To get a good picture of persecution, we need only to read Hebrews 11:36–38, where we find this description of what some of the heroes of the faith endured.

> And others had trial of cruel mockings and scourgings, yea, moreover of bonds and imprisonment: They were

stoned, they were sawn asunder, were tempted, were slain with the sword: they wandered about in sheepskins and goatskins; being destitute, afflicted, tormented; (Of whom the world was not worthy:) they wandered in deserts, and in mountains, and in dens and caves of the earth.

Quoting again from Matthew Henry, he said,

> Rejoice because the honor and dignity, the pleasure and advantage, of suffering for Christ are much more considerable than the pain or shame of it. Not that we must take pride in our suffering, but we must take a pleasure in them.

Christ says in verse 11 that we will be blessed if we are reviled and persecuted on His account. And if we look at the parallel that He draws by inference in verse 10, where He says: "for righteousness sake," we can see that He, and He alone, is that righteousness that He speaks of. In both instances, the reward that He offers is the same, and we are to rejoice and be glad because great is our reward. It is nothing less than the kingdom of heaven.

We as finite and limited humans look at commands such as these, to be blessed and to rejoice and leap for joy when men hate us and can only wonder at what seems to be such a paradox between being hated and leaping for joy. All we can rely on is our unwavering faith that God's Word is true and the fact He has never broken a promise; the promise He gives us here is no exception. He is God, He is faithful in all things, and He will settle all accounts according to His will and His perfect justice.

Another commentator said that we currently hold the title or the deed to the reward that we will possess when we get to heaven. He goes on to say that our reward in heaven will be so great that it will transcend all the slings and arrows, and the pain and sorrow, that we have endured in God's service.[24]

---

[24] Regretfully, this is paraphrased from an unknown/unremembered source.

In talking about rewards, we sometimes have difficulty understanding the idea of our receiving rewards in heaven for what we endure for Christ. We see these endurances as some type of works, which in a sense they are. However, what we need to value is that our salvation, and the keys to the kingdom, are based upon the finished work of Christ. We get to heaven by faith alone, but the rewards we receive once we are there are based upon the works that we have done. The works don't get us there; they are just indicators of, or signs of, our faith in Christ alone. Those who are justified through Christ are called to live fruitful, godly lives that produce good works, and those works will receive heavenly rewards. Scripture tells us this, and although we don't deserve or merit any kind of a reward, we will receive it. One view is that when God distributes rewards in heaven, He will be crowning His own gifts, which means that God is the One who has gifted you to be able to do the work that you perform. It is only His grace that allows you to be able to perform these works, not through your own efforts and not without the Holy Spirits prompting and help.

These gifts, or crowns, will be those that we will cast at His feet and is similar to what we read in Revelation 4:10–11.

> The four and twenty elders fall down before him that sat on the throne, and worship him that liveth for ever and ever, and cast their crowns before the throne, saying, Thou art worthy, O Lord, to receive glory and honour and power: for thou hast created all things, and for thy pleasure they are and were created.

Verse 13

You are the salt of the earth, but if the salt has lost his flavor, it is good for nothing but road material.

Jesus tells His followers that they are the salt of the earth and sees His disciples as having value. Salt was a valuable commodity in ancient Israel, so much so that it was often used as currency. The word *salary* has its origins from it, with a good worker said to be worth his salt. God esteems the value of salt so much that in 2 Chronicles 13:5, we find that salt was used as a covenantal promise toward David and his descendants.

Eduard Schweizer tells us that a common expression in Israel at the time was to call the laws the "salt and the light" of the world, and that this verse may be an introduction to the Mosaic law that we will explore in more detail starting in verse 17.[25]

Salt was also used as a preservative, and those who are followers of Jesus, those who are not of this world, are preserving God's Word from the corruption of the world by faithfully keeping it as a practice of their daily lives, disseminating it to others through evangelism and the godly rearing of their children. In Ezekiel 16:4, we read that newborn babies were rubbed with salt, and further research shows that this practice was to signify that the child would be raised to have integrity and to always be truthful.

Christ's disciples are to be salt, and if they remain true to God's Word, their integrity would be preserved, but if they begin to mix God's message with some form of syncretic worship, polluting it with the impurities found in pagan ritual, they, and by association God's Word, would lose their value. They would become tasteless, without flavor, and to the unsaved and watching world, they would seem foolishness. We are to be vigilant in our efforts to preserve God's Word and to be the flavor that seasons and enhances, and by doing so, we can confidently say to the world, "O taste and see that the LORD is good: blessed is the man that trusteth in him" (Psalm 34:8).

Albert Barnes, an American theologian, wrote in his 1834 work *Notes on the Bible,*

> In eastern countries, however, the salt used was impure, or mingled with vegetable or earthy substances, so that it might lose the whole of its saltiness, and a considerable quantity of earthy matter remain. This was good for

---

[25] Eduard Schweizer, *The Good News according to Matthew* (Atlanta, GA, John Knox Press, 1975) 99.

nothing, except that it was used to place in paths, or walks, as we use gravel. This kind of salt is common still in that country. It is found in the earth in veins or layers, and when exposed to the sun and rain, loses its saltiness entirely.

Verse 13 tells us, "It is thenceforth good for nothing, but to be cast out, and to be trodden under foot of men."

VERSES 14–16

You are the light of the world, and you are to let your light shine before men, that they may see your good works and glorify your heavenly Father.

Genesis tells us that we are made in His image, in His likeness, and here in verse 14, when Jesus characterizes us as the light of the world, He further extends that likeness. In John 8:12, we read, "Again Jesus spoke to them, saying, 'I am the light of the world: he that followeth me shall not walk in darkness, but shall have the light of life.'" We who are His followers have the light of life, and through His church, His light shines brightly. We who have been saved out of the darkness are now living in the light of His truth. Not only that, but Jesus further proclaims that we are the light of the world. The Christian community must be "a city set upon a hill," and our illuminating light is a guiding light, and it is imperative that it shines forth brightly because in the Father of lights has no shadow (James 1:17). There is a purity in His light, and that same purity must be seen in us as living testimonies to the transforming power of the Holy Spirit so that others might be drawn to what they see, and what they should be seeing is Christ shining radiantly through our daily walk with Him. All that we do, say, or achieve is to be for His glory, and in our faithful witness, we and they who have eyes to see will glorify God.

VERSES 17–18

Jesus tells us that He didn't come to destroy the law but to fulfill it, as well as to fulfill the prophecies. He continues by telling us that until the earth and heaven pass away that not one scintilla of the law will pass away until all of the law has been fulfilled.

Jesus, in His incarnation, was the embodiment of the law. Each of God's commandments permeated every fiber of Christ's being such that He is the totality of the law and it is the essence of who He is and how He lived His life, always in perfect obedience to the Father's will.

When Jesus said that He had not come to abolish the law or the prophets, by implication He is telling them that He had the authority to do so but goes on to tell them that His divine purpose was to fulfill them. He neither abrogates any Old Testament laws nor gives any new laws; none of His teaching is contrary to Scripture. Jesus's purpose is to establish their true intent and to model them in the perfect obedience that is exemplified in how He lives His life; His actions are perfect because His very nature is perfection, and it is in this perfection He is able to fulfill the requirement for our atonement. What is manifestly different in the new covenant is that Jesus has come, and His perfect atonement has ended the sacrificial system and assuaged God's wrath, forever satisfying His holy justice.

For the Jews, the law was comprised of the Torah, the first five books of the Old Testament, and the prophets were comprised of the remaining books of the Old Testament. In all ways, Jesus fulfills the entire Old Testament. In His obedience, He fulfilled the law at every point, and we know that both the law and the prophets point to the coming of the Messiah. At His birth He fulfilled the revelation of that event.

As the Good Shepherd, Jesus redirected those who had gone astray by correcting them through authenticating the true interpretation of the laws that they had strayed from by their misguided use of tradition, especially those who had begun to supersede scripture itself. In verses 21–48, Jesus begins to set forth His divine understanding of the law over the misguided rationalizations of the scribes and the Pharisees, and He will clarify and present both the proper and the false interpretation and application of the Old Testament.

Jesus tells them, "Till heaven and earth pass, one jot or one tittle shall in no wise pass from the law, till all be fulfilled." The supreme significance of God's Word is to be revered in every aspect, which includes every jot and tittle. A jot is the smallest letter in the Hebrew alphabet, and a tittle is a small mark contained within a Hebrew letter, such as in English when we cross a T or put a tail on a Y.

John McArthur states,

> Here Christ emphasizes both the inspiration and the enduring authority of all scripture. He specifically affirms the utter inerrancy and absolute authority of the Old testament as the Word of God, down to the last jot or tittle.

The law in its entirety will not change until, in His timing, He creates a new heaven and a new earth. Until the end of the age, when all is fulfilled, God's law will remain as immutable as He is.

VERSES 19–20

He further teaches that if anyone relaxes the law, or teaches other men to do so, he or she will be called the least in the kingdom. On the other side of the coin, anyone who follows the law and teaches others to follow as well will be called great in heaven. He then hits the disciples with a stunning statement, that unless a person exceeds the righteousness of the scribes and Pharisees, they will never enter heaven.

God's commandments are to be obeyed as to their meaning and intent, just as Jesus exemplified them and taught them to us through His perfect interpretation of the Word. There are certain commandments that were fulfilled in His lifetime and therefore are no longer obligatory; for example, animal sacrifices are no longer required because of the atoning sacrifice in the finished work of Christ on the cross. Another example of a law no longer in effect is the dietary law of the Old Testament that was abrogated by Peter's vision, at which time he was told what God has called clean, let no man call unclean (Acts 10:15).

As disciples, or followers of Jesus, we are to not only keep the law, we are to teach the law to others. However, we are not to assume any righteousness or merit of our own just because we rigidly follow the law in some legalistic fashion. Galatians 2:21 clearly tells us, "for if righteousness come by the law, then Christ is dead in vain."

> However, the law stands as the perfect expression of God's ethical character and requirements. The law sends us to Jesus to be justified, because it shows us our inability to please God in ourselves. But after we come to Jesus, He sends us back to the law to learn the heart of God for our conduct and sanctification.[26]

Although they were often chastised by Christ for their traditions, which often usurped the authority of scripture, the scribes and the Pharisees were scrupulously invested in the study and living out of God's law. Orthodox Jews were the personification of righteousness, but Jesus requires us to do more and calls us to a more genuine and profoundly deeper holiness. The problem was theirs was an external righteousness, manifesting itself in an outward piety and a shallow conformity to the law without a proper inner attitude of the heart. That is why Jesus called them "whited sepulchers" or whitewashed tombs (Matthew 23:27) and told the people, "Whatsoever they bid you observe, that observe and do; but do not ye after their works: for they say, and do not" (Matthew 23:3). In their quest for a life of strict legalism and their focus on the letter of the law, they somehow missed the spirit and intent of the law.

In referring to a righteousness that exceeds that of the scribes and Pharisees, Jesus may be talking about what we call a "practical righteousness." This kind of righteousness is the general conformity to God's law that we work out in our sanctification. We can be called righteous in the sense that we bear the fruit of righteousness when we seek to love God, obey Him, and repent when we fall short. However, without an unequivocal assent to and faith in the sola "in Christ alone," all our practical righteousness is meaningless. The only righteousness that matters is that which belongs to

---

[26] From www.blueletterbible.org study notes on Matthew 5 by David Guzik.

Christ alone; it is His righteousness that God sees when He declares us as righteous. This is the gift of salvation that the incarnate Messiah went to the cross for, the one that we receive openhandedly without anything but our praise and worship to offer in return.

The only righteousness that has significance is a righteousness that is not our own. Paul, in speaking to self-righteousness, tells us in Philippians 3:7–9,

> But what things were gain to me, those I counted loss for Christ. Yea doubtless, and I count all things but loss for the excellency of the knowledge of Christ Jesus my Lord: for whom I have suffered the loss of all things, and do count them but dung, that I may win Christ, And be found in him, not having mine own righteousness, which is of the law, but that which is through the faith of Christ, the righteousness which is of God by faith.

This is a kingdom righteousness that can only be found in Christ as the Holy Spirit effects a change in our hearts and minds so that our motives and conduct are found to be within the will of God. And in this way, they will exceed the righteousness of the Pharisees.

VERSES 21–22

Jesus begins to talk about anger, pointing out that they had heard of old about the command not to kill and that those who do kill will fall into judgment. He now adds the teaching that just being angry with one's brother without cause shall also be in danger of the judgment. Furthermore, if in anger he calls his brother a fool, he is predisposed to the hell of fire.

Beginning with these verses, "Jesus draws a series of antitheses between what has been said and what He Himself is teaching."[27] John Calvin in his commentary said, "As the law had been corrupted by false expositions, and

---

[27] *Tabletalk Magazine* (Sanford, FL, Ligonier Ministries, Inc., February 27, 2008).

turned to a profane meaning, Christ vindicates it against such corruptions, and points out its true meaning."

On these matters, Jesus speaks with authority, and that

> authority does not lie in the newness of His instruction; what He says is not unknown in the Old Testament. Instead, His teaching is authoritative because He alone— not the scribes and Pharisees—determines the true meaning of the Law and the prophets. Jesus's authority reveals His deity; only the divine lawgiver Himself knows the full meaning of His own Law.[28]

Generally speaking Jesus's audience hadn't read scripture themselves, so Jesus states to them that they "have heard that 'you shall not murder.'" The scribes and the Pharisees had interpreted the scripture for them, and now Jesus, in the power of His authority, more fully developed the intent of the commandment against murder. Not only will whoever murders come under judgment, but so will everyone who is angry with his brother. In addition, whoever insults his brother will answer to the council, and whoever in an attitude of contempt says Raca (which means "You fool") or uses any other form of verbal abuse will be in danger of the fires of hell. Jesus showed that murder, anger, insults, and slanderous language all emanate from the heart and that God's moral law addresses not only the outward or final act of these sins but views them in their totality, from the beginning to the end, from their germination through to the fullness of the blooming of those actions that had been listed.

John Calvin also said,

> That they had changed the doctrine of the law into a political order and had made obedience to it to consist entirely in the performance of outward duties. Hence it came, that he who had not slain a man with his hand was pronounced to be free from the guilt of murder, and he

---

[28] *Tabletalk Magazine* (Sanford, FL, Ligonier Ministries, Inc., March 5, 2008).

who had not polluted his body by adultery was supposed to be pure and chaste before God.

However,

> murder begins with unjustifiable anger and hatred, and it includes insults, slander, and estrangement from people. This is the reason that Jesus said that no one escapes the weight of the law merely by refraining from actual murder.[29]

It should be noted that Jesus did not alter the laws that He was quoting; He was correcting the rabbinical understanding and what the people had "heard." "What Jesus was referencing was the oral tradition of the rabbis ('*halakha*'), and it is their superficial understanding of God's law that Jesus is criticizing."[30] There is no contradiction found in scripture, and as we learned in verse 17, Jesus said that He had not come to destroy the law but to fulfill it. And again in verse 20, He made it clear that God's laws were much stricter than the righteousness of the Pharisees because mere outward conformity to the details of the law, while important, is not enough. It is when inner purity and outward goodness concur, one's righteousness exceeds that of the scribes and Pharisees. As fallen creatures, we must recognize that we cannot achieve a righteousness of our own. We need to be reconciled to Christ in order to be accepted by God.

VERSES 23–26

Jesus goes on to highlight the importance of being reconciled to another and puts reconciliation above and before offering a gift at the altar. He talks about the vital need to come to terms with someone who has accused you as well. If you don't, you may wind up in prison.

---

[29] R. C. Sproul, *St. Andrew's Expositional Commentary on Matthew* (Wheaton, IL, Crossway, 2013), 108.

[30] R. C. Sproul, *St. Andrew's Expositional Commentary on Matthew* (Wheaton, IL, Crossway, 2013), 108.

Jesus has told us that love is one of the greatest commandments, and here we see that reconciliation with a brother is more important than performing a religious rite. Even if you have gone as far as to bring your gift to the altar and while performing your duty you remember that your brother has something against you because you have faulted him in some way, you are to leave your offering and immediately go and be reconciled. Only then can you come and finish giving your gift. If you omit this act of loving reconciliation, your offering will be corrupted, and it will be displeasing to God.

Jesus further teaches that we are to quickly come to terms with those who accuse us and not to ignore or let the unresolved issue fester to the point of no return. If you do let it go without taking some form of corrective action, you may be brought before the judge, found guilty, and put into prison until your penalty is paid in full. This is especially important when the issue is between two believers. In 1 Corinthians 6:1, Paul admonishes Christians to handle a grievance between one another and avoid appearing before an unrighteous judge and bringing shame upon the name of Christ in a public setting. If this is true on a strictly human level, how much more important is it for matters with eternal consequences. The devil is our accuser, and if we have put off asking for forgiveness or if we have never repented, we may find ourselves under God's judgment and wanting. Without Jesus having paid the price for our inequities, we will experience God's exercise of judgment without mercy and "shall be cast out into outer darkness: there shall be weeping and gnashing of teeth" (Matthew 8:12).

VERSES 27–30

He now begins to talk of lust and the commission of adultery, adding His teaching that lusting after a woman is the same as committing the act itself. He then teaches through hyperbole that for each member of the body that causes you to sin, you should engage in a form of self-mutilation, which was abhorrent to His Jewish listeners. It would be better to lose that member than to go to hell with your body intact.

As before, Jesus is moving His listeners from the rigid yet limited interpretation of what they had heard being taught to what God's intent of the law required. Adultery came with a death sentence as it not only violated another person but also broke the marriage covenant, which is reflective of the relationship between God and His people; we the church are the bride of Christ.

The teachers of His day rightfully taught that adultery was wrong, but they had narrowed the application to the act itself and not to the heart and mind that preceded the wrongful action. It is not that actual adultery and one's lustful thoughts are same thing. The physical act is far worse than the thought, but they are both sinful and prohibited by the full dimension of God's law and His command against adultery.

Christians may see a man or a woman and have a passing thought that they immediately choose to reject and not allow it to take their thoughts captive, and this type of response is an example of fleeing from temptation and trying to maintain the purity of one's heart. One commentator wrote of the difference between a casual look and one that was persistent, or a desire that was momentary or involuntary, versus one that was cherished, lingering, and with longing.

A right and more complete interpretation of scripture and God's commands requires us to remember that the Mosaic laws are implicit in nature, which means that whatever the law forbids, it also forbids the broader correlation of it within the laws' overall context. The other aspect of this implicitness is that whatever the law prohibits, it at the same time commands its opposite, and whatever the law commands, it also prohibits the opposite. *The Westminster Larger Catechism* may say it more clearly. "Where a duty is commanded, the contrary sin is forbidden; and where a sin is forbidden, the contrary duty is commanded."

Jesus's radical illustrations and figures of speech demonstrate the level of obedience and sacrifice that someone must be willing to make to preserve their eternal soul. Plucking out your eye or cutting off your hand has little effect on your heart and mind, the places from which sin emanates from. James 1:14–15 clearly tells us,

> But every man is tempted, when he is drawn away of his own lust, and enticed. Then when lust hath conceived, it bringeth forth sin: and sin, when it is finished, bringeth forth death.

Although speaking in hyperbole, Jesus is graphically reminding us that our eternal salvation should be of such value to us that we would be willing to take the necessary steps to ensure that it is obtained, just as we would to extend our life from the ravages of some type of disease that would require an amputation or some other invasive surgery to remain alive. These two parts of the body are representative of the various aspects of adultery, the hand being the physical act and the eye the lustful thoughts and fantasies that lead to it. This is how David was drawn into sin with Bathsheba after watching her from his balcony.

Jerome, an early church father, said, "What we conceive in the mind we might complete with an act." That is why we must flee from immorality, whether it be in thought or deed, and in these verses, Jesus is telling us that sin against God, and its deadly consequence, must be avoided no matter how drastic the cost.

VERSES 31–32

The teaching now concentrates on divorce and the only scriptural justification for it, along with the consequences of adultery that will ensue because of wrongful divorce.

In Matthew 19, we will find that Jesus teaches more about divorce, and I will more fully develop some of my research on the topic when we get to those passages. Within verses 31–32, we see that Jesus's focus was on the intent of the law, not the distorted tradition that had evolved around it.

Just as it is today, divorce was widely accepted in the first century, and the rabbinical tradition that was loosely based upon Moses's writ of divorce is here being rightfully challenged. Moses's writ of divorce was originally intended to uphold the sanctity of marriage and to protect women for being divorced for no reason.

Jesus always defaults to scripture. It alone dictates how we should handle our lives, not rabbinical traditions or misinterpretations that tickled the ears of many. Jesus defers to scripture as the solid ground for their discussion. It was something that the Pharisees should have had a deeply profound knowledge of. He asks them what Moses commanded of them. They responded that Moses permitted a man to write a certificate of divorce and to dismiss her. They were correct in saying that Moses allowed it, but he did not command it.

Jesus then tells them that the reason Moses granted the writing of the certificate of divorce was because of man's hardheartedness. It wasn't a command. It was a concession. Jesus emphasized that marriage is a permanent relationship between a man and a woman. Jesus further explained why the popular view of the day was wrong, and He demonstrated this by going back to God's act of creation. He reminds them of what Genesis 1:27 and 2:24 say. "So God created man in his own image, in the image of God created he him; male and female created he them" and "Therefore shall a man leave his father and his mother, and shall cleave unto his wife: and they shall be one flesh." Jesus continued to move toward the logical extension of God's creative design, and He would later say, "What therefore God hath joined together, let not man put asunder" (Matthew 19:6).

Jesus wasn't interested in the cultural understanding of the time that they were living in. He wasn't pressured by the social normative espoused by the religious leaders of the day. He went back to God's original intent for marriage and family. God's pattern or design for marriage hadn't changed. He is immutable, and there is an eternal perfection in His design.

When they are wed, a couple is not only joined together through a betrothal and a ceremony that consecrates the covenant of marriage; it goes much deeper than that. They are bonded together as one flesh: "flesh of my flesh, and bone of my bone." A man and a woman are joined together physically, emotionally, and spiritually; therefore, divorce is a radical surgery cleaving two out of the spiritually conjoined who are one.

The phrase "and whosoever shall marry her that is divorced committeth adultery" alludes to an illegitimate divorce, one which gives place to adultery because God doesn't acknowledge that type of divorce and sees a new relationship as being out of His will. It is possible for a person to have a divorce that is recognized by society but not by God. If that person goes on to marry someone else, God considers that relationship adultery because He sees them as still married to their original spouse.

VERSES 33–37

Continuing His using scriptural references dating back to the Old Testament prophets and writers, Jesus turns our attention to the use of oaths.

Once again, in their perversity, the scribes and the Pharisees had distorted God's prohibition of using His name in vain to allow every other name to be used in a false oath. John MacArthur tells us that "what Christ here forbids is the flippant, prophane, or careless use of oaths in everyday speech." In rebuttal of their misuse of God's law, Jesus gives as an example a short list of other things that you should not swear by, those which were used by some Jews to deceive their victims while hoping to avoid divine judgment by swearing their oath by another name, somehow forgetting that God is omnipresent. This type of thinking led them believe that they could make oaths in the name of anything other than God and that those oaths could be broken with impunity. Jesus points out the sinful ineffectiveness of these misguided tactics. By contrast, He says don't swear an oath at all. The use of them only underscores the weakness of your character and your word.

Instead of utilizing an oath to bolster what is said, you should let your integrity speak for itself and simply let your yes be yes and your no be no, with the truthfulness of your speech being in alignment with the legitimacy of what you are claiming. Jesus is not telling us that oaths are forbidden. after all, God made a covenantal oath when He swore by His own name before Abraham. Jesus spoke under oath when brought before Caiaphas and the counsel, and we see Paul making oaths throughout many of his epistles. Within the Westminster Confession of Faith, we find the following:

> The name of God only is that which men ought to swear, and therein it is to be used with all holy fear and reverences. Therefore, to swear vainly or rashly by that glorious and dreadful Name, or to swear at all by any other thing is sinful, and to be abhorred.

VERSES 38–42

The next topic Jesus wants us to take into consideration is that of retaliation and the misinterpretation of the phrase "an eye for an eye and a tooth for a tooth."

The whole idea behind "an eye for an eye" was to prevent and limit the retribution imposed by the civil authorities to a punishment that was equitable and fitting to the crime. It was to ensure equal justice under the law and not as a means for personal vengeance or retaliation. Over time, the original concept had been taken out of context and became a sanctioned obligation in personal relationships with its execution no longer enacted by the government but distorted into the practice of private revenge. In a paraphrase of the ESV Study Bible footnotes, we find that Jesus's meaning is that we should seek restitution in court and not seek individual or personal revenge. John Calvin points to Paul's letter to the Romans (12:19–21), where he enjoins Christians by telling them, "Dearly beloved, avenge not yourselves … Vengeance is mine; I will repay, saith the Lord … Be not overcome of evil, but overcome evil with good."

He goes on to tell us to turn the other cheek when someone slaps us on the right cheek. A careful consideration brings you to the conclusion that not only would this be an insult but could possibly be injurious due to the fact that most people are right-handed and to slap you on the right cheek would mean that they used their back hand to strike you. Christ is asking us to turn the other cheek, and this would put us in a vulnerable position, opening us up for further insult. Jesus modeled this teaching many times in scripture when He was insulted and spoken against, such as being called a glutton, a drunk, an illegitimate child, a blasphemer, a madman, and the many other verbal and physical atrocities that He endured.

Jesus uses another Mosaic law to make His point. Under the law, no one could take your cloak, and even if it was pledged as collateral, it must be returned at sunset so that they might have it for sleep. This outer garment was important to the health and well-being of a man, which further punctuates Jesus's teaching that if someone sues you for your tunic, which is a garment worn next to the skin, we are to let him have our cloak as well. The next example Jesus gives is that of the right of a Roman soldier to compel you to carry his load for no more than a mile. Jesus taught that if you are compelled to go one mile, out of godly love, take it to the second mile as well. In our love of God and our neighbor, we are to give more than we are required to.

In the spirit of Christian charity, we are to take a fresh look at those who beg, as well as those who would borrow from us. Some may look to 2 Thessalonians 3:10 and say, "For even when we were with you, this we commanded you, that if any would not work, neither should he eat." However, in a closer look at the context of 2 Thessalonians, we find that Paul is exhorting those who were idly standing around, not busy at work but busybodies and that they should do their own work and earn a living. In the case we are looking at, we are asked to sacrificially give to a person who cannot work for whatever reason and who are truly needy. We are to show them loving compassion, but there are limits and the requirement here does not include giving to those who would manipulate you. But it also doesn't exclude you from giving to them if you, by the leading of the Holy Spirit, turn your giving into a free act of love. God's wisdom and discernment are key in any decision.

Along this same vein, there are times when someone has an immediate and urgent need to borrow some money and, in your love for them, you feel moved to help them out. In this situation, the amount of the loan is only limited by the level of compassion you have for the person and how much you can sacrificially lend, while keeping in mind that you are to be a good steward with your personal finances.

On the other hand, there are those who are constantly coming to you with their needs but never do anything to better their situation and have never even attempted to pay you back. In a case like this, you should rely upon verse 42 and the following scripture from Psalms to help make your decision: "The wicked borroweth, and payeth not again: but the righteous sheweth mercy, and giveth" (37:21). It would be prudent to pray about these situations beforehand to establish a biblical position on lending. You probably have a good idea of those who are close enough to you to ask for a loan and what level of trustworthiness that they possess. Jesus is not demanding we give; He is looking into our hearts at our willingness to help and to give.

R. C. Sproul tells of an early Christian writing known as the *Teachings of the Twelve Apostles,* which contains the following aphorism: "Let your donation sweat in your hand." He says that the principle is to be wise in your giving. We are not to give to just anything. We must make sure that we give to worthwhile causes. He further states that such qualifications come from the overall teaching of scripture about almsgiving.

VERSES 43–47

Jesus now begins another seemingly radical teaching about our calling to love our enemies in addition to loving our neighbors. In these verses, He outlines how we are to go about following this command, while pointing out the common grace that God bestows upon all men.

Tradition wrongfully added "and hate your enemy" to Leviticus 19:18, and in these verses, Jesus gives the correct interpretation and says that we are to love and pray for those who persecute us. He also supplies a compelling reason, so that we may be sons of our Father in heaven. If we are to be His sons, we must follow His commands and to love our neighbors as ourselves. We who are His, saved by unmerited favor and grace, need to show the same love to others that God has shown to us. We are to remember that God loved us even when we were at enmity with Him.

He then teaches us about the common graces of God, such as the sun and the rain, that are bestowed upon all humanity, including the good and the evil and the just and the unjust. "God's common grace is just that—common.

Unlike the special, saving grace that God bestows on those whom He has chosen for salvation, common grace is indiscriminate. This grace is what leaves all people without an excuse."[31] These are examples of the benevolent and beneficent love that God has for His enemies, as well as to those He has called to be His own. He goes on to teach about love, and that if you only love those who love you, what have you gained? To his Jewish readers, Matthew's rendition of Jesus's teachings pulls no punches, telling them that both tax collectors and Gentiles love and greet their brothers. And then He asks them what more they were doing other than the same. He is wondering how Christian character, love, and fellowship could be exemplified if it didn't go beyond the confines our own clique and if it wasn't demonstrated in a greater measure than what the world had to offer. Jesus is the higher standard that we are to attain to so that the world will see His love reflected in our actions.

VERSE 48

We are now commanded to be perfect, even as our Father in heaven is perfect.

We are to be perfect and we are to be holy, just as our heavenly Father is. None of us are perfect, none of us are holy, but through the gift of regeneration, we have been indwelt with the Holy Spirit and are going through the process of sanctification. It is through this ongoing work that we become more Christlike and more holy as we move toward the perfection that is His alone. Our righteousness is not in following the law or any aberrant tradition. It is to be found in our relationship with Jesus Christ, it is His righteousness that we are cloaked in, and it is His perfection that has saved us from the wrath of God. All the laws and all the prophets find their perfect fulfillment in the perfection of God. They all point to Jesus, and He has fulfilled them to perfection on our behalf.

We are commanded to strive for holiness and perfection, and in obedience, we do so. On this side of heaven, we continue to work with the Holy Spirit toward the unattainable goal set before us, and while we do so, we praise God for His mercy and His grace.

---

[31] *Tabletalk Magazine* (Sanford, FL, Ligonier Ministries, Inc., March 6, 2017).

CHAPTER 6

GIVING, FASTING, LAYING UP TREASURE, BEING ANXIOUS

VERSES 1–4

Our instruction continues with the proper motive and attitude as we give to the needy. It is to be a private affair and not for show. If we make it a public display for our own edification, we will lose our heavenly reward. It is to be so private that the example given is that our left hand should not know what our right hand is doing. God will reward our secret endeavors to help by His openly rewarding us for our faithfulness.

What we do for others counts, not just for those who benefit from what we do but also for us as individuals on an eternal scale. What also matters is our motive behind our actions, the why behind what we do. If what we do is for public recognition so that others might extol our righteousness, our reward is already spent and there will be none from our Father in heaven. Jesus "applies this general principle to the three chief acts of Jewish piety; almsgiving, prayer, and fasting."[32] It is not that others will not recognize the fruit of what we do but that we are to be discreet and not making self-serving and overt displays of what we do. Our actions should be a natural

---

[32] *Tabletalk Magazine* (Sanford, FL, Ligonier Ministries, Inc., March 6, 2008).

extension of our Christian life, and nothing should be done for the sake of spectacle. Our motive should be purely for the glory of God with no thought or concern about what others might think about our personal and private piety. John Calvin's commentary said of this verse, "There is no room to doubt, that the design is, to correct the disease of ambition, when, in doing what is right, we seek glory from men."

In Numbers 10:10, we read about appointed feasts and the requirement to blow the trumpets over burnt offerings and the sacrifice of peace offerings, and perhaps Jesus was using this as an example of how doing so would draw attention to the giver. Another possibility was that

> whenever there was a great need in the community the priest would blow the shofar (a ram's horn trumpet), that was used to alert others of the need. Apparently this alert usually triggered an ostentatious display of men closing up shop and heading for the temple so that they might be seen as the first to respond to the call.[33]

The pretentiousness of this type of show of giving to receive praise from others is all the reward that these hypocrites will ever get. Jesus is admonishing His followers to give quietly and without fanfare, so much so that your right hand would not know what your left hand was doing. This is the private and secret piety that we looked at earlier. This is the type of giving that God will honor because our motives are pure, and in this, it glorifies Him. Charles Spurgeon wrote, "Let God be present, and you will have enough of an audience."

VERSES 5–6

Just as with our almsgiving, prayer is to be a private affair and not a public display of our self-perceived righteousness. Jesus says that those who flaunt their prayers to draw attention to themselves will have received their reward

---

[33] Paraphrased from *Tabletalk Magazine* (Sanford, FL, Ligonier Ministries, Inc., March 6, 2008).

from men, whereas those who pray in secret, with the right motive and intent, will receive God's heavenly reward.

Jesus begins to teach about prayer, the second of three important spiritual disciplines: giving, prayer, and fasting. He teaches His listeners that they should not pray like the hypocrites do. These men, like those in the earlier verses, were labeled hypocrites by Jesus. In the ancient Greek language, an actor in a play was a hypocrites or hypocrite. Actors were playing roles that weren't who they really were. By the first century, the word took on the meaning of those who began to roleplay in the real world, pretending to be or acting like someone they weren't. This perfectly described those with a false piety, those who were religious actors, roleplaying for the accolades of those who were watching them portray what was a false righteousness. Their motive was self-aggrandizement and had little to do with glorifying God.

> Jesus says they love to pray in the synagogue during a time set aside for public prayer and on the street corners at the set time for prayer (9 a.m., noon, and 3 p.m.). The later was not a normal practice, however if one strictly kept the prescribed times of prayer, they may have been tempted to just happen to be in the most public place at that very time of the day. We go back to the central concern of their motivation, who the glory was being sought for and was their intention for the prayer to be heard by God or to be seen by men.[34]

These hypocritical prayers are an offense to God. They lack the sincerity, reverence, and humility that ought to be exhibited in our heartfelt submission before our God and King.

Jesus says that they will have received their earthly reward but will have forfeited God the Father's heavenly reward that is reserved for those whose

---

[34] Paraphrased from several contributors within www.blueletterbible.org study notes on Matthew 6 by David Guzik and the footnotes in the ESV Study Bible (Wheaton, IL, Crossway, 2008).

focus is to exclusively seek God and by their secret prayers glorify and honor Him alone.

Charles H. Spurgeon said,

> Woe unto that man whose devotion is observed by everybody, and who never offers a secret supplication. Secret prayer is the secret of prayer, the soul of prayer, the seal of prayer, the strength of prayer. If you do not pray alone, you do not pray at all. I care not whether you pray in the street, or in the church, or in the barrack-room, or in the cathedral; but your heart must speak with God in secret, or you have not prayed.

VERSES 7–8

Our prayers are to be meaningful and not comprised of a useless repetition of words as we drone on without any significant purpose to our prayers. God knows our prayers and the intent behind them even before we make petition before Him.

When we pray, we are to pray with purpose, and it should be a prayer that glorifies God, even in our confessions and supplications. Our prayers should not be pointless repetitions, and as Ecclesiastes 5:2 teaches, "Be not rash with thy mouth and let not thine heart be hasty to utter anything before God: for God is in heaven, and thou upon earth: therefore let thy words be few." The pagans continually speak the name of their gods again and again, or they use the same words in superfluous repetition in the form of chant or mantra. This is the type of thoughtless and impassive babbling that Jesus is prohibiting. However, this admonition of Christ's by no means forbids earnest, persistent, and continuous prayer for our needs, or those of others.

We are to pray in all humility and not ramble on senselessly, especially in a corporate setting. Charles Spurgeon said that "Christians' prayers are measured by weight, and not by length. Many of the most prevailing prayers have been as short as they were strong."

In these verses, we are told that those who pontificate in prayer are misguided into believing that their many words will be more effectively heard by God, but Psalm 139:4 reminds us that our Father knows our needs before we even ask Him for anything. "For there is not a word in my tongue, but, lo, O Lord, thou knowest it altogether."

There is an approach to prayer called the ACTS method, which can be used as a guide. The letter A stands for adoration, and we should open our prayers by glorifying God as Lord over all. C stands for confession, and we are to confess our sins with true contrition. T is for thanksgiving where in gratitude we are to verbalize what we are grateful for in our lives. S is supplication, a time when we are to pray for our needs and those of others. As effective as this method can be, in the next few verses, Jesus will give us the perfect model to be used for our prayers.

Some in their confusion about the purpose of prayer ask why they should even pray if God already knows everything. They somehow feel that prayer is about informing God instead of it being a verbal reminder to ourselves of the misery and magnitude of the sin we have committed. It is a time for reflection on our thoughts and actions and in contrition to implore the Holy Spirit for His continued help because in our hearts and minds we know that we do not have the ability or strength to become more Christlike on our own. Prayer is an effective tool for change, and the most effective change is the one that takes place in our own lives.

VERSES 9–13

Jesus gives us an example of how we should pattern our own prayers.

> Our Father which art in heaven, Hallowed be thy name. Thy kingdom come, Thy will be done in earth, as it is in heaven. Give us this day our daily bread. And forgive us our debts, as we forgive our debtors. And lead us not into temptation but deliver us from evil: For thine is the kingdom, and the power, and the glory forever. Amen.

The prayer that Jesus models is brief and does not "not heap up empty phrases," yet its scope is comprehensive. There are six basic parts to this prayer. The first three are directed toward God, and the last three focus on our human needs.

We are to remember that this model is a guide for us to follow for our own prayers; Jesus said to pray using His example, and the key words are "after this manner." "The Lord's Prayer is an example of the kind of prayer that honors God, and its various elements show us what we should include in our prayers."[35] The Lord's Prayer was not given just as a series of verses to memorize and then, without further thought, to vainly repeat them while lacking a true understanding of their meaning or significance. Instead, "we are to take each element, or petition of the Lord's Prayer and apply it more directly to our own lives, for our own particular needs, sins, and the extension of His kingdom in and through our own family and friends."[36]

The Triune God consists of three persons: God the Father, God the Son, and God the Holy Spirit. Christians have the unique privilege, based upon the finished work of Christ, to have become coheirs with Christ and therefore be able to stand before our God and call Him Father. And when we pray to Him, although we have been granted the intimacy to call Him Father, we are always to remember that He is our God and is sovereign over the universe. We are to continually maintain a reverential and humble veneration for His absolute transcendence, holiness, and glory. We are blessed to be able to call Him Father.

In the utmost adoration of Him, we can begin our prayers by recognizing Him as our Father in heaven. One commentator sees this prayer as being meant to be prayed corporately as we are all within the family of God and come together as a body of believers to call upon His name (*our* Father), learn His will, and to offer thanks for His salvation.

---

[35] *Tabletalk Magazine* (Sanford, FL, Ligonier Ministries, Inc., October 30, 2018).
[36] Paraphrased from *Tabletalk Magazine* (Sanford, FL, Ligonier Ministries, Inc., March 11, 2008).

Jesus, when telling His disciples how to pray, says that God's name is hallowed, which has the meaning of being sacred, holy, and revered. This honors Him for who He is and how we view Him as the supreme object of our worship and in His being the only true God.

We are to pray that His kingdom advances, manifesting itself on earth as well as it is in heaven. Our prayer is that His kingdom will reign in the hearts and minds of believers, those who are the invisible church and that it will soon be expressed in its fulness. We are to pray that His revealed will is accomplished throughout the universe, which includes the fulfillment of His promise to end all our sorrows when Satan is finally cast into the lake of fire. Sin will be no more, and a natural obedience will have replaced our rebellious defiance as we glorify Him throughout eternity.

Our prayer shifts to one of supplication as we ask for His provision in our life. "Give us this day our daily bread." This is a prayer for the physical needs in life that sustain us, not for the things that we desire out of greed. In the wilderness, the Israelites were given bread daily; God perfectly rationed it to meet their needs, and it was without excess. All good gifts come from heaven above, and God is the provider of them all. In His providence, we get all that we need, both physically and spiritually. In the Old Testament, we find that Psalm 84:11 reminds us of this fact: "No good thing will He withhold from them that walk uprightly." And from the New Testament, we read, "God shall supply all your need according to his riches in glory by Christ Jesus" (Philippians 4:19).

We are to ask that our debt of sin be forgiven. Although Jesus paid for our sin finally and completely upon the cross, we are still to ask for forgiveness for the momentary sinfulness that we have slipped back into. This demonstrates true contrition and that we recognize the fallen nature that will be ours until we are glorified, and that sin is still a real part of our humanity and that we have an unyielding need for the continued support of the indwelling Holy Spirit as our advocate as He continues to work with us, moving us toward the holiness that God demands of us.

The next aspect of this prayer contains an aspiration, or a qualifier, within our petition for forgiveness. That phrase is worded "as we forgive our debtors." This can be interpreted in two ways. The first is that we have already forgiven them fully and have every expectation for our own forgiveness. However, from other verses in scripture, we can rightly read this as having the meaning that the level of forgiveness we are given is predicated upon the degree of forgiveness that we have given others. That is why I said that this was an aspiration and not a command. If it were a command, we could never measure up and would be doomed to eternal damnation. Once again, we need to praise God for His mercy and grace.

With our plea for God's forgiveness of our sins, His grace, and how it relates to our aspiration to forgive others in mind, we need to constantly question ourselves when we bring our gift to the altar. Does my brother have something against me? Have I forgiven? Or have I been forgiven for what that might be? Do I have an abundance of gratitude in my heart for the forgiveness that I have in Christ? And in the joy of that thankfulness, have I also forgiven those who have sinned against me?

Jesus concludes the Lord's Prayer with "and lead us not into temptation but deliver us from evil." Some manuscripts say: "but deliver us from the evil one."

James tells us that God does not tempt us to do evil (1:13). However, God does allow a form of the meaning of the word "temptation," and that is for us to be tested. Christian prayer should include a petition to be kept away or spared from temptation, and for the strength of the Holy Spirit to keep us from succumbing to the temptations that will inevitably come. We are to keep ourselves in check. We know what draws us away from God, what pushes our buttons, and we are to avoid putting ourselves in harm's way by steering clear of the dangers that we know can take control of us if we allow them to. If we have a weakness for alcohol, we should never go to a bar with our friends. If we are subject to pornography, we should ensure that our computers are not the tool we use to go down that road. Temptation should be avoided when at all possible. Charles Spurgeon says that 'lead us not into temptation' is shameful profanity when it comes from the lips of men who resort to places of amusement whose moral tone is bad.

Verses 14–15

Jesus now teaches us the benefit of our forgiveness and the severity of our not being forgiving.

Jesus has more to teach His disciples about forgiveness and emphasizes its importance as it relates to how God the Father has already forgiven us and how we should forgive others. Each of us as followers of Christ has experienced God's mercy and has been forgiven beyond what we can comprehend. Nor can we fathom the great cost that was required to effect that forgiveness. The longer that we are in Christ, the more we see the magnitude of our own sin as well as our need to forgive others. Jesus will teach more about forgiveness, but in these verses, His focus is on the imperative of forgiveness and the fact that it is not optional in that we have no valid rationale for not forgiving others. When we do so in obedience, our personal relationship grows more deeply toward God and the love that He displayed through Christ's sacrifice for our forgiveness.

The forgiveness spoken about here is not the forgiveness we receive at the point of our justification when we are born again. This is more of a daily cleansing to wash away the filth of sin in our lives as we seek new mercies for our transgressions. It is like the washing of Peter's feet and him not needing to wash his entire body. Or in Lamentations 3:22–23, where we read, "It is of the LORD's mercies that we are not consumed, because his compassions fail not. They are new every morning: great is thy faithfulness."

Verses 16–18

These verses are concerned with the dos and don'ts of fasting. We see once again the showmanship displayed by some versus the proper method of honoring God. There is the repeated promise of His faithfulness to reward us as opposed to an earthly reward that is received while trying to impress others through our hypocrisy.

Fasting can be viewed as the third prong in the trident of Jewish piety; one is praying, the second is giving, and here Jesus begins to teach about the third, fasting. Note that Jesus says "*when*" you fast, not "*if*" you fast, which makes it clear that Jesus had every expectation that His followers would fast.

During the Old Testament period, fasting was commonly practiced; however, there was only one fast that was commanded to be observed each year, and that was on the Day of Atonement.

Just as they had done with their giving and praying, the Pharisees made a show of their fasting by leaving their faces unwashed and sprinkled with ash so that it was evident to others that they were engaging in self-denial by abstaining from food. Because they actively sought the praise of men, Jesus again said that they had obtained their reward.

In contrast to the hypocritical display put on by the Pharisees, Jesus instructs His followers to wash their faces and anoint their heads so that their fasting would not be seen by their neighbors. God would see the honor they exhibited toward Him when they fasted in secret and He would reward them for it.

VERSES 19–21

We are told in these verses not to lay up our treasures on earth because they are all temporary, whereas those we build up for God's glory will be eternal. Jesus tells us that where our treasures are, so will be our hearts.

Jesus is teaching that earthly treasures are temporary at best and are subject to loss of value and theft, whereas heavenly treasure is secure in its permanence. Earthly goods and wealth are not intrinsically bad, but as a part of the created world, they have no lasting value. They are subject to decay and decomposition, whereas the treasures that we store up for ourselves in heaven are those that are everlasting and incorruptible. The material gifts that God has given us are best suited for sharing and for the promotion of God's purposes. This will honor and glorify Him now, and it will enrich the eternal treasures that will be ours, those that we can lay at His feet in further worship of Him. The rewards we will receive for the good works we do out of the thankfulness we have for the salvific gift that we have been given, the crowns that we will lay at His feet, are what Augustine categorized as God crowning His own gifts.

A Christian's heart should be focused on God and His glory. With this single-mindedness comes a right attitude about worldly wealth and how exceedingly incomparable it is to the riches we have in Christ Jesus.

Verses 22–24

The eye is the light of the body, and if healthy and wholesome, the body will be full of light. Conversely, if the eye is focused on worldly matters, the whole body will be full of darkness. Jesus continues his teaching on where our values lay by telling us that we cannot effectively serve two masters: God and money.

Jesus continues His teaching on how we deal with the treasures in our life and using the eye as a reflection of our inner life. At the time of Jesus's earthly ministry,

> Rabbis described those who love money more than God as those with bad eyes. A healthy eye would then refer to one who is generous with his resources and they would reflect the Lord's generosity and light.[37]

The concept of the eye being a lamp is that it can bring light into your life, and here Jesus is talking about the light of others' needs being met through generosity, and when we are openhanded with the material wealth that we possess, our bodies will be full of light. This state of being is one that has its focus on heavenly things: the kingdom of God, His will, and our loyalty to Him. But if our eye is bad no light can enter, and our bodies will be full of darkness. If our hearts are focused on earthly things, our selfish greed casts darkness over all that we think and do, and in that state

---

[37] Paraphrased from *Tabletalk Magazine* (Sanford, FL, Ligonier Ministries, Inc., March 12, 2008).

of being, the darkness within us is great because we are lacking the light of Christ within us.

The metaphor of light and darkness is replete throughout the New Testament and speaks of good and evil, right and wrong, and seeing with a new heart that proclaims Jesus as the Christ, or blindly remaining in the darkness and corruption of unbelief that is represented by a heart of stone.

To drive home His point that we must serve God alone, Jesus tells us that we cannot serve both God and money. A disciple of God cannot be divided. He will either serve God or chase after earthly treasures. Serve, as it is used here, has the meaning of being a slave, and a slave cannot serve more than one master. God must always be preeminent and never be presumed to be on an equal standing with anyone or anything. Their divided allegiance was a consistent problem with Israel in their syncretic worship, their mixing God's Word and sacraments with those of the pagans around them. In these verses, Jesus tells them that they can't worship God and money, and in some Bible versions, you will find the word "mammon" instead of "money." There are differing opinions on the exact translation of mammon, but clearly Jesus is referring to material goods or treasures, and He highlights that who or what you serve gets down to a matter of the heart. One you will devote yourself to, and the other you will spurn.

Because it is a matter of the heart, Jesus is not saying that those with wealth cannot be God's children. Scripture always interprets scripture, and because God and His characteristics are immutable, we can see that there are examples of men of wealth and power as being blessed and honored by God. One needs only to think of Abraham, Job, or Solomon to understand that the concern isn't with money, but that it is a matter of one's heart and where one's priorities lie.

VERSE 25

Life isn't about what we eat or drink, nor is it about the clothes that we wear, and we should not be overly anxious with these things.

In Philippians 4:6–7, we find a parallel to this admonition where we read,

> Be careful for nothing; but in everything by prayer and supplication with thanksgiving let your requests be made known unto God. And the peace of God, which passeth all understanding, shall keep your hearts and minds through Christ Jesus.

We are to be properly concerned about our and our family's well-being, but undue anxiety has no place in the Christian life. It must always be tempered by prayer and supplication. Our heavenly Father knows our needs, and the futility of worry will not change our circumstance. We are to be dependent upon God for the necessities in life, and if we have a need, we are to go to Him in prayer. He wants us to know that we can come to Him with every godly request. We must recognize that life is more than scratching out a meager existence, wearing the finest clothing, or any other worldly distress that plays out in our minds. We are to seek out His guidance and to live in obedience to His revealed will for our lives. We are to live at a point of balance between a natural and healthy concern over our lives and the overwhelming and tormenting pressure that is present in those who struggle through life without acknowledging God and His providential care for them.

Jesus rhetorically asks whether life is more than these concerns. This question should draw us back to "what man's chief aim or concern should be, and that is to glorify God and to enjoy Him forever."[38]

John Calvin has much to say about how we are to live in a material world without being ensnared by the worries and concerns that are a part of our fallenness. He gives us four principles as an aid to that endeavor. The first is to recognize that God is the source of every good gift and we are to give Him thanks for what He has provided. The second is to be content with and be good stewards of what He has already given. Thirdly, Calvin says we are to remember what our calling in life is to live in God's presence and for His glory. The fourth principle is to live calmly in God's world

---

[38] Paraphrase of the answer to the first question of the Westminster Confession of Faith's Shorter Catechism. www.apuritansmind.com/westminster-standards/shorter-catechism.

because you believe in God's gracious sovereignty and you know that He is your Father.[39]

He is our "Father who is in heaven and He will give good things to those who ask Him,"[40] so let us remain strong in our confidence that He is in control and not falter in our faith.

VERSES 26–30

Jesus points to creation, highlighting the birds of the air and the lilies of the field and just how much better we are than they. Our needless fretting and worries aren't going to change our situation. We are to have a greater faith than we do, for if God feeds the birds and clothes the fields of grass, how much more will He provide for us?

Matthew begins using God's creation as an example to the people of His provision and their needless anxiety in these matters. He isn't implying that the people remain idle or that they shouldn't exert themselves in God-glorifying labor to provide sustenance for their families, but that God will provide for them more abundantly than the birds of the air or the lilies of the field. He is telling the people that God's love and regard for them, those He made in His own image and empowered with dominion, is so much greater than any animal, flowering plant, or grass that if other means fail, His providence will remain sufficient. We are never to lose sight of God's undertaking in our lives. No amount of agonizing worry that stems from a lack of faith will change our material circumstance or add to the span of life, but by contrast, it can only have a negative effect on our health.

VERSES 31–34

We are to take no thought of these needs because our Father in heaven knows of our needs. We are first and foremost to seek after the kingdom of God and His righteousness, and if we do, these things will be added to

---

[39] John Calvin as quoted in Sinclair Ferguson, *Some Pastors and Teachers* (Carlisle PA, The Banner of Truth Trust, 2017).
[40] Paraphrase of the last portion of Matthew 7:11.

us. We are not to be anxious for tomorrow, because today's troubles are enough to deal with on their own.

With the peace in Christ that we possess when we live in faith, we have been freed from the type of anxiety that is common to the rest of the world. Those who don't know Christ are separated from His loving care and remain anxious about worldly trappings, whereas those who do know Christ can rely upon Him and therefore be able to primarily seek after His kingdom in the confidence of His promise that all else will be added. Christians are to set and maintain godly priorities, and in the establishment of them, the lesser matters of the world will fall to their rightful place at the bottom of our list of concerns. Christians are to live in the present moment with our eyes firmly fixed upon Jesus. We are not to beat ourselves up for any past sin that we have repented of and been forgiven, and we are not to be overly concerned about what tomorrow may bring. If we are in Christ, we live within the sphere of salvation and in faithful obedience have surrendered to His will for our lives while maintaining a joyous expectation for the hope that is set before us, an eternal life of glorifying Him.

CHAPTER 7

JUDGING, ASKING, GOLDEN RULE, I NEVER KNEW YOU

VERSES 1–2

We are not to judge others in the spirit of unforgiving condemnation, or others may judge us in the same manner.

Jesus shifts His focus to how we think about and treat others. He tells us that we should be careful in the way we judge others because often men judge from the standpoint of their own self-righteousness, feeling that they are superior to those that they deem to be lesser in some form or degree. This is a judgment of condemnation that often usurps God's prerogative to judge the motives of one's heart. Jesus further warns that we may very well be judged by others in the same harsh and unforgiving manner that we have judged. King David knew the capriciousness of men and how they might judge a man, and that is why he said to Gad his seer, "Let me fall now into the hand of the LORD; for very great are his mercies: but let me not fall into the hand of man" (1 Chronicles 21:13).

Jesus's warning on the way in which we judge others was not a command against our using a godly judgment to rightly assess or discern the fruit, or lack of it, in the lives of others and ourselves. We are called to love our brothers and sisters in Christ, but that is not a call for an unconditional approval of how they live their lives. If we are forbidden to use godly judgment, how can we quietly go to our brother and tell him his fault (Matthew 18:15)?

One commentator pointed out that during Jesus's lifetime, some rabbis taught that God had two measures that He used to judge people. One was a measure of justice, and the other a measure of mercy. They maintained that whichever measure that you want God to judge you by, you should use that same measure with others. No one wants God's justice because His holiness cannot allow for our provoking sin to endure without the punishment that it deserves, but we all want the unmerited mercy He grants us through the propitiation that is ours due to our being reconciled by finished work of Christ.

VERSES 3–5

In our rush to judgment, we often look to the minor faults of others while ignoring the grievous sin in our own lives, and Jesus uses the analogy of a speck in someone else's eye versus the log or plank in our own eye.

In these verses, Jesus may have used hyperbole based upon His experience as a carpenter when He contrasted a speck or splinter in someone else's eye to a log lodged in one's own eye.

A man's heart is deceitfully wicked and can blind him from his own sin, yet he still manages to somehow direct his focus on and then magnify the sins of others. Jesus continues to teach on the inappropriateness of pointing an intolerant and judgmental finger toward a brother in Christ, especially when you are so anxious to see his minor fault while hypocritically not taking note of the faults that are so prevalent in your own person. This type of dissention in the church can cause a disunity that has the potential to destroy fellowship within the body. All sin is an affront to God, but if the speck in the eye of your brother is just a speck, then the Christian love that brings back a wanderer should cover a multitude of sins (James 5:20), if the log in our own eye hasn't blinded us to this truth.

In 2 Samuel 12, we read about King David's anger that grew in intensity as he responded to Nathan's tale about the rich man who had many flocks but took the only lamb from a poor man to prepare a meal for his guest. This is the story of David, Bathsheba, and the murder of Uriah, which tragically exemplifies the hypocrisy that brings a heavy judgment to bear upon another while all along your sin is far greater.

We are to help our brothers with the speck in their eye, but only after we are sure that we can see clearly to remove it and that our vision is not obscured by our own self-indulgence toward the magnitude of our own sin.

VERSE 6

Jesus commands us not to deal with these two types of spiritually unclean people, which He characterizes as dogs and swine and who are therefore unworthy of God's holiness and the gift of His precious Word.

Those who claim that we are not to judge others will have a hard time coming to grips with this command of our Lord. If we don't fairly judge others with godly discernment as evidenced by the fruit of their works, then how are we to determine who the dogs and swine are, those that we are to withhold God's good and precious things from? These will be those who have hardened their hearts and are hostile toward the kingdom of God, Jesus's ministry, and the work of the Holy Spirit within us.

Dogs were denoted as unclean animals and scavengers by the Jewish community, and they used this terminology for all those who were enemies of Israel's covenant community. Likewise, under the Old Testament law, pigs were designated as ceremoniously unclean. They too are scavengers and would trample into the filth under their feet the pearl of great price which is symbolic of someone dishonoring the value of the message of the kingdom of God. Christians are to use discernment in the judging of such men and at the appropriate time discontinue in proclaiming God's truth to those who are adamantly opposed to, mock, and reject it. Christians are to "shake off the dust under your feet for a testimony against them" (Mark 6:11).

Charles Spurgeon's commentary tells us,

> When men are evidently unable to perceive the purity of
> a great truth, do not set it before them. They are like mere
> dogs, and if you set holy things before them, they will be
> provoked to "turn again and rend you": holy things are
> not for the profane. "Without are dogs": they must not be
> allowed to enter the holy place. When you are in the midst
> of the vicious, who are like "swine," do not bring forth the
> precious mysteries of the faith, for they will despise them,
> and "trample them under their feet" in the mire.

VERSES 7–8

We are to be in constant prayer as we seek God's will for our lives, asking
Him for guidance through the work of the Holy Spirit. We are to ardently
seek answers to our questions about how to walk in the spirit, knocking
on every access of opportunity so that He opens the door of our salvation
through regeneration.

While reading these verses, we must remember Christ's admonition to us.
"But seek ye first the kingdom of God, and his righteousness; and all these
things shall be added unto you" (Matthew 6:33). This prerequisite is not
to be overlooked, and the motive behind all prayer is to be in alignment
with this verse and its being consistently front and center in our prayer life.

In these verses, we find the use of a literary device known as synthetic
parallelism,

> which presents statements that build one upon the other,
> and in this case, it is *ask, seek, and find.* Each portion of
> the verse basically expresses the same truth, that God gives
> to those who ask, the restatement and repetition form a

parallel structure that alerts us that Jesus is placing a heavy stress on this truth.[41]

There is a progressiveness in the type and fervency of our prayers, as well as the resultant reward obtained in the continued escalation of our pursuit of a personal relationship with Christ. If the motives of our hearts are pure and if it is in God's will, we will get what we ask for. If we diligently seek Him with all truth and spirit, we will find that He is within us and will provide what is best for our every need. If we faithfully knock with humble expectation, we will gain entrance to His promised kingdom even as we remain within the realm of our worldly existence.

God hears our every prayer, and our prolonged and faithful persistence is a tribute to the honor and praiseworthiness that we have for Him, even as we continue to be found under tribulation. Answers to our ardent prayers will be given, and in the truthfulness of our seeking, we will find that as we display our steadfastness while standing before heaven's gate, we will be rewarded by its being opened to us. God's promises are sure, and James 5:16 reminds us that the effective prayer of a righteous person has great power as it is working, but this also requires that our prayers have a legitimate need before they are advanced. There should be no room in our prayer life for selfishness. God knows our needs and we are to search His Word for His decreed will for our lives and pray that the Holy Spirit will intervene and pierce our hearts with the truth of what God would have for us.

VERSES 9–11

Jesus asks us to look into our wicked hearts and compare our good and loving giving toward the needs of our own sons set against both the incomparable common and special graces bestowed upon those who ask of our heavenly Father.

---

[41] Paraphrased from *Tabletalk Magazine* (Sanford, FL, Ligonier Ministries, Inc., September 28, 2000).

Jesus is speaking to the hearts of those who are fathers, men who are lost and evil by their very nature but would still be inclined to give every good gift that he could to his children. These men, who have been convicted by the Holy Spirit, are disciples of Christ, and know their own corruption and depravity, also know that the love they have for their children is such that they would always choose what is best for them.

Jesus's point is that in the perfection that characterizes God, He would do much more and better things for them, even though at the time they may not see or understand that through His goodness and mercy God may very well have spared them from their own selfish desires. This fact presses the necessity to openly declare that our prayers do not assure us that we will get everything we ask for, but only those things that we need, but we often lack the wisdom to distinguish between the two. James 4:3 reminds us, "Ye ask, and receive not, because ye ask amiss, that ye may consume it upon your lusts." John Calvin says,

> It is the duty of the children of God, when they engage in prayer, to strip themselves of earthly affections, and to rise to meditation on the spiritual life. In this way, they will set little value on food and clothing, as compared to the earnest and pledge of their adoption, and when God has given so valuable a treasure, he will not refuse smaller favors.

VERSE 12

Jesus now speaks of the Golden Rule, that whatever we wish would be done for us, that we do likewise to others. He further tells us that this rule comprises the law and the prophets.

In the last several verses, Jesus had focused our attention on the goodness of God and now transitions His listeners to an imperative that outwardly seems somewhat unassuming. In his commentary, John Calvin tells us that Jesus gave these words to His disciples as an exhortation to be just, and that this verse is a simple definition of what justice looks like.

We know how we like to be treated by others, to be made to feel special and to delight in the kindness that we have received, and that is what Jesus wants from us in our relationship with others; and this is especially true when it comes to our dealings with other brothers and sisters in Christ. In this positive command, we find within its simplicity a summary of all that is found in the law and the prophets. The seemingly straightforwardness of the Golden Rule allows us to understand the humility that we are to bear in our association with others, but the paradox we find ourselves in is that it is nearly impossible to fulfill this essential mandate with any consistency.

This is not a passive command by any means. What Jesus said was "do also to them." This is an active directive, a call to service. We are to do, and this is a functional, working action that is to be part of our daily lives if we are to have any hope or wish of being treated in a like manner.

> If we want others to love us, we must first love them. If we want to be prosperous, we must first share what we have. The Golden Rule makes it known that the citizens of God's kingdom are to put others first, endeavoring to love them first as Christ first loved us. (1 John 4:7, 19)[42]

VERSES 13–14

We are told that in our journey through life, we are to take the narrow path, the one least traveled by the world. It is a harder path, and few are its travelers, but those who do travel along it will find that it leads to eternal life. Whereas the world generally follows the easy path but eventually finds that it becomes the road to perdition.

The narrow gate that leads to eternal life is one that is least entered, and the path that it opens before us is less frequently traveled upon because it is replete with difficulty and persecution. Nonetheless, it is the only way that will ultimately take us beyond heaven's gate and into the throne room of God. Interestingly, "the term Christian was first used in derision toward

---

[42] Paraphrased from *Tabletalk Magazine* (Sanford, FL, Ligonier Ministries, Inc., March 18, 2008).

those of Jesus's followers in the first century. Prior to that they were known as "people of the way" (Acts 9:2), because Jesus often used the metaphor of a road being traveled upon to refer to the Christian way of life."[43]

This command to enter through the narrow gate is being given by Christ to His followers. On our own, we cannot choose the narrow gate. We only take this path by the grace of God's redemptive work in our lives, which brings us to salvation through faith in Christ. Those who remain unrepentant and dead in their sin will ultimately chose what they desire most at the time of their choice, and being dead in their sin, that will never be a choice that turns away from the way of the flesh.

Jesus points out that there is another gate, one that is necessarily wide because those who enter through it are many. This is the gate that is entered by those seeking an easy journey through this life, an illusional shortcut that seemingly promises all that this world has to offer, but in the end, one will discover that it is found to be the road to perdition and eternal separation from God.

VERSES 15–20

We are to be cautious of false teachers who seamlessly blend into our churches, but they are inwardly filled with heresies. If we maintain a scriptural perspective, we will recognize them by the fruit of their actions. Every good tree bears good fruit, but a corrupt tree brings forth evil fruit. John the Baptist proclaimed that the axe was already at the root of bad trees bearing bad fruit and that it will be chopped down and cast into the fire. We are to be a discerning people and emulate the Bereans.

Jesus commands His followers to pursue the path that lies beyond the narrow gate, and now He warns against the false prophets who would try to persuade and guide them onto the path that leads to destruction. The false prophets among them might appear to be genuine in their intent, but here they are described as ravenous wolves in sheep's clothing. Some are so

---

[43] Paraphrased from R. C. Sproul, *St. Andrew's Expositional Commentary on Matthew* (Wheaton, IL, Crossway, 2013), 200–201.

well practiced in deception that they become self-delusional and begin to deny the falsity in their character and become true believers, not in Jesus but in their own hype.

In order that we might not be swayed by their false doctrine and their silver tongues, we are to be wisely discerning and to observe various aspects of their lives. We need to question how well their walk-through life stacks up to scriptural mandates and if they reflect the consistency found in a kingdom centered life. We are to determine if they are living a life marked by righteousness, humility, and an abiding faithfulness to God's Word. We are to be good Bereans and pay close attention to the content of their teachings to determine if they are comprised of a man-centered or self-serving message or if their message can be substantiated by scripture. John Calvin commented, "All doctrines must be brought to the Word of God as the standard, and that, in judging of false prophets, the rule of faith holds the chief place."

These are the fruits by which we recognize them. Jesus tells us that a healthy tree bears good fruit, and conversely, a diseased tree bears bad fruit and should be cut down and thrown into the fire. For a second time within these few verses, Jesus emphasizes that we will recognize them by their fruit.

Before we move on, we need to look at what is explicit within these verses, although it is not specifically stated. We ought to conduct a self-examination to ascertain what type of fruit that we bear or whether we are bearing any fruit at all. Elsewhere in scripture, we read about barren trees or vines and that they are to be cut off and thrown into the fire. We also read in Revelation 3 where Jesus proclaims that the works of the church in Laodicea were neither hot nor cold, and because of this, He would spit them out of His mouth. Charles Spurgeon said, "It is not merely the wicked, the bearer of poison berries, that will be cut down; but the neutral, the man who bears no fruit of positive virtue must also be cast into the fire."

VERSES 21–23

We are not only to be discerning about what we are being taught by others but also what we have assimilated into our own lives. We need to question ourselves and our motives as compared to God's Word and whether or not we are living in conformance and obedience to what scripture has taught us. Jesus gives us warning that not everyone who professes Him as Lord will enter the kingdom of heaven—only those who are living within the will of His heavenly Father. Many will assume because of their false profession of faith that they are children of God, but Jesus will tell them, "Depart from Me. I never knew you."

Just as with other weighty matters, the right motive and the purity of our hearts are needed to persuasively confess that Jesus is our Lord. You can mouth the words and they can be heard audibly by those within the church, but if Jesus isn't the Lord of your life, no self-admission, no matter how sincere it sounds, will make it so. There are some members of the visible church, and only God knows them, who are not a part of the true church, which is often referred to as the invisible church. These people are in fact outside of the faith and they are those who Jesus says will not enter the kingdom of heaven. They may do many great and admirable works, but the reason behind them may be tainted by pride in their own magnanimity, or a false sense of duty behind the civic good that they perform. There is any number of other misguided purposes, and they may also hold to an errant theology which can give a false sense of assurance, such as a works righteousness or the Universalist's belief that all will be saved. God demands perfection, and we all fall short of His holy standard and can only be saved by grace alone. If a repentant heart that gives all glory to God isn't the supreme driving force behind our thoughts and actions, then all our works are meaningless. This is the poverty of spirit we read of in Matthew 5:3, which involves abandoning any effort to earn the Creator's favor and casting ourselves by faith wholly upon His grace as we have nothing to offer Him but contrition for our sin.

On that day, the Day of Judgment, they will see that without the gift of abiding faith that God instills within them, the works they bring before their Judge, Christ Jesus, are as if they were nothing. The object of their affection was not focused on Christ, and therefore they have not lived their lives in obedience to the will of God, and without a true fellowship with Jesus, there is no basis for their salvation. These are not people who have lost their salvation, and with Jesus's proclamation that He never knew them, we can plainly see that they were never saved to begin with. Adam Clarke's commentary on these verses states,

> You held the truth in unrighteousness, while you preached my pure and holy doctrine; and for the sake of my own truth, and through my love to the souls of men, I blessed your preaching; but yourselves I could never esteem, because you were destitute of the spirit of my Gospel, unholy in your hearts, and unrighteous in your conduct.[44]

In *Tabletalk Magazine's* March 2008 issue, we find the following words of encouragement to reflect upon regarding our own assurance:

> God knows we will never be perfect in this life, but He does expect us to grow in faith and increasingly conform to Christ by loving our fellow Christians, understanding true doctrine, and following His precepts (1 John 3:23–24). Those whose lives increasingly reflect such things can be sure that they do not profess Jesus falsely. Let today's passage prompt you to take a "spiritual inventory." Where have you seen growth? Where do you need to be more obedient?

VERSES 24–27

As a follow-up to what He taught about false profession of faith, Jesus gives an example of two men who have built their houses on two different

---

[44] Adam Clarke (1760 or 1762–1832) was a British Methodist theologian and biblical scholar. He is chiefly remembered for writing a commentary on the Bible that took him forty years to complete and was a primary Methodist theological resource for two centuries. www.studylight.org/commentaries/acc.html.

foundations. The first builds it on a strong foundation of rock, such as the foundation of His church in the prophets and apostles, where He is depicted as the Cornerstone that holds it all together. The house built on rock will withstand the storms of life. Whereas the foolish man built his house on the shifting sands of false doctrine, which will not withstand the storms of life. Its collapse will not only be forthcoming, but it will be a great fall indeed.

James tells us that we are to be doers of the Word; merely hearing the Word is no assurance of salvation. Jesus's example is likened to what we read in Proverbs 10:25, where it is written, "As the whirlwind passeth, so is the wicked no more: but the righteous is an everlasting foundation." What Jesus adds is the blueprint for a strong foundation, one that is built on the apostles and the prophets, one that has Christ as the Cornerstone of our faith (Ephesians 2:20). Psalm 127:1 tells us, "Except the LORD build the house, they labour in vain ..." For the elect, God has set the foundation, and in gratitude, we must be doers of the Word, building upon God's Word for our strength in times of trouble when the storms of life seem to be relentless. He is our refuge and our shelter. Christ's sacrifice has made our way blameless. Let us rejoice in Him and live in thankful obedience for what He has accomplished on our behalf. When the rain of divine judgment subsides, the house that God built, and in which the Holy Spirit dwells, will remain standing upon the finished work of Christ.

The unwise are those who feign Christianity through a form of religious deception by building their lives on the sinking sand of cultural norms or the shifting winds of false doctrine that continually tickles the ears of those who follow a god of their own making while they distort or ignore the immutable truth of God's Word.

VERSES 28–29

Jesus concluded this teaching, and the people were astonished at His doctrinal messages because He taught them with authority, an authority lacking in the teachings of their scribes.

After a reading of a biblical passage from a scroll, most of the teachings heard in the synagogue from their teachers were merely quotes that were attributed to other rabbis, but when Jesus spoke, it was with words of authority based upon the power of scripture. Jesus did not teach tradition or opinion but taught with the authority and the majesty of truth.

One commentator remarked that the teachers and scribes taught by an authority other than their own, the authority of tradition, but Jesus spoke with an authority that was derived from the Word of God.

John 1:14 tells us that "the Word was made flesh and dwelt among us (and we beheld his glory, the glory as of the only begotten of the Father) full of grace and truth." He spoke with the authority of divine authorship because God's Word was and is Jesus's Word. He needed no one to interpret for Him, and as He taught, He clarified and corrected, as well as rightfully consigned tradition, that often usurped the authority of the Word, to a subordinate position to it. Jesus astonished His listeners through the power and authority that are inherent in the unchanging truth that is found in God's Word.

CHAPTER 8

Leper, Centurion, Storm, Casts Out Demons

Verses 1–2

In these verses, Jesus comes down from the mountain, and we find that He is being followed by a great crowd. As He came down, a leper approached Him and knelt before Him, saying to Him that if He was willing Jesus could cleanse him from his disease.

Matthew had recently mentioned how the crowds were astonished at Jesus's teachings, and here he writes about the great multitudes that followed Him down from the mountain and elsewhere when the crowds pressed in on Jesus so much so that He had to get into a boat and have it pushed a little way from the shoreline so that He would be able to continue His teaching without being swarmed by those who wanted to get close to Him. Jesus's teachings drew large crowds, but His miracles did so as well. He had demonstrated His authority through His teachings and now would continue to reveal that He was Messiah through the many miracles that He would accomplish alongside His teaching ministry.

We find that a leper came and worshipped Him. Leprosy was a terrible disease, not only in its progressively debilitating effects upon one's body but by being ostracized by all others, including family and friends. A leper had to keep six feet away from others, but if there was wind blowing toward another person, they had to keep 150 feet away. We have some idea of the disease, but a brief review of how it ravages the body of one who contracts it we will begin to see the compassion that Jesus shows to this man. Here I quote from William Barclay, who wrote,

> Leprosy might begin with the loss of all sensation in some part of the body; the nerve trunks are affected; the muscles waste away; the tendons contract until the hands are like claws. There follows ulceration of the hands and feet. Then comes the progressive loss of fingers and toes, until in the end a whole hand or a whole foot may drop off. The duration of that kind of leprosy is anything from twenty to thirty years. It is a kind of terrible progressive death in which a man dies by inches.[45]

This leper came to Christ with no pretensions that Jesus would come near him, let alone heal him. This man had no doubt that Jesus could heal him, and this is evident by his stating, "Lord, if you will, you can make me clean." The leper came possessing the faith that Jesus was Lord, and that if it was within Jesus's will then the man would be cleansed. It should be noted that not only did the man have faith, he brought that faith to bear when he knelt before Jesus and called Him Lord. The word *Lord* was used to translate the Hebrew word Yahweh, and those who Matthew was writing to would be familiar with the Jewish context of that word. The leper had acknowledged the deity of Christ before he even stated that Christ could make him clean, and this cleansing went beyond the disease of leprosy that this man was suffering from.

---

[45] William Barclay (1907–1978) was a Scottish scholar and theologian who taught at the University of Glasgow for twenty-eight years. I do not ascribe too much of what I have read of his theology, but this description was a concise overview of leprosy. https://www.studylight.org/commentaries/dsb/matthew-8.html.

VERSES 3–4

Jesus told the man that He was willing, reached out and touched him, and by the power of His Word, Jesus healed him. We aren't told how long this man had been suffering from this disease or been without human contact, but another's touch, let alone that the touch was that of the Messiah's, must have been incredibly poignant. To heal him did not require Jesus to touch the leper, but the man longed for and needed the intimacy of the physical contact that Christ so compassionately bestowed upon him, a touch that was a tangible expression of Christ's infinite grace and goodness.

Jesus directs him to tell no one and sent the man to the priest, instructing him to take a gift for the ceremonial sacrifice, give testimony, and to be declared clean just as Moses commanded. This man was a new creation, healed physically and cleansed spiritually. Although miracles attest to the authenticity of Christ's message, Jesus did not want them to overshadow His message. His ministry, and the reason that He had come, was to proclaim the arrival of the kingdom of God.

VERSES 5–6

Jesus entered Capernaum and a centurion came pleading to him, saying: "Lord, my servant is at home suffering terribly with an unbearable paralysis."

Jesus entered Capernaum, the town out of which He based His Galilean ministry, and where He lived (Matthew 4:13). When He had arrived, a centurion, an officer in the Roman army, and therefore most likely a Gentile, humbly came to Jesus on behalf of his servant. It seems that his servant was suffering horribly from some sort of paralysis and was lying in the home of the centurion. The centurion humbly came so that Jesus might help his servant. Under Roman law, he would have had every right just to kill his servant if he wasn't able to work any longer, but out of the compassion and kindness that stems from the common grace that God alone bestows, he pled for the well-being of his servant. Luke's parallel account of this incident cites that the centurion had sent the elders of the Jews as emissaries with his plea as he counted himself unworthy to make this request in person. Luke's account also tells us that these emissaries relayed the love of this centurion for the Jewish nation, and that he had built their synagogue.

VERSES 7–9

Jesus tells the centurion that He will go with him to his house, but the centurion responds that he is not worthy of having Jesus enter his home, further stating that if Jesus merely says the word that the healing will happen. He tells Jesus that he recognizes His sovereign authority because he himself was both under authority and had men under him, all of whom followed orders.

Without the hesitation borne out of Jewish custom that might keep others from going with a Gentile to his home, Jesus tells the centurion that He will come and heal the servant. The centurion's reply to Jesus showed a level of sensitivity because of his knowledge of this custom and his knowing that most Jews believed that a Gentile's home was not worthy of them. The centurion knew of Jesus and that He was a Rabbi with great authority and told the Lord that he and his home were not worthy of Christ coming under his roof. He relays to Jesus that he himself was a man both under authority and with authority. He continues to explain that with authority there is an inherent acknowledgment that orders given will be followed. Then, in a remarkable testimony to his faith, the centurion says that he knows without a doubt that Jesus by a mere expression of His will needs to "but speak the word only, and my servant shall be healed." As Calvin tells us, the centurion may not have understood that Jesus was the Christ, and therefore God manifested in the flesh, but it was unmistakable that he was thoroughly convinced and that he clearly recognized that the power of God was evident within Jesus. The centurion knew that "he who, by the mere expression of his will, restores health to men, must possess supreme authority."

VERSES 10–13

When Jesus heard the centurion's response, He proclaimed to those around Him that He had not found such great faith as this in all Israel. He then speaks of the great many Gentiles who will come and will sit down with Abraham, Isaac, and Jacob in the kingdom of heaven, but that the children of the kingdom, the Israelites, would be cast out into outer darkness where there shall be weeping and gnashing of teeth. Jesus, turning back to the centurion, told him to go. Because he believed that his servant would be healed, it came to pass that very hour.

Jesus admired and commended the understanding that the centurion had for Jesus's spiritual authority, so much so that He proclaimed that nowhere had He seen the great faith that the centurion possessed in His ability to restore someone to health by merely declaring that the healing would take place.

The faith that was presently displayed by this Gentile gave cause for Jesus to announce that there would be Gentiles from all parts of the world who would be found in the kingdom of heaven. With the fact of their salvation assured, they too would have a cherished fellowship with the Jewish patriarchs. And at the same time, Jesus reminds them that it takes more than being a son of Abraham to be welcomed into the kingdom of God. The term "sons of the kingdom" was a Semitic term for the nation of Israel, but Jesus points out that their racial identity was not a free ticket to heaven. Without a contrite heart and a right relationship with Christ, they would be cast into hell, where they will experience an eternity of suffering and agony in the absence of God.

Jesus concludes His remarks to the centurion by telling him, "Go thy way; and as thou hast believed." The strength of this man's faith, by the grace and power of God, was the catalyst for his servant's healing, and scripture tells us that the servant was healed at that very moment.

VERSES 14–15

Jesus arrived at Peter's house and saw that Peter's mother-in-law was sick with a fever. He touched her with a healing hand, she got up, and she tended to their needs.

Jesus often demonstrates His compassion on those in the crowds that swarm Him and who need a healing touch. When He goes into the quiet and familiar setting of Peter's home, He sees that Peter's mother-in-law is lying down and is feverish. Within the context of this setting, and based upon Christ's relationship with Peter, we can be confident that Jesus knew this woman well because of the many times that He had been in their home. According to tradition, it was improper to touch a fever-ridden individual, and Jesus once again quietly ignores the cultural norm. We can almost imagine the sweetness in Jesus's gentle and healing touch upon her hand and then envision her, in the completeness of her restoration, quickly rising to serve the Lord as she was accustomed to do. It is with this same compassion that our Savior touches our hearts, and we too should respond with an earnest resolve to action that is befitting our gratitude for the spiritual healing He has bestowed upon us.

VERSES 16–17

That evening, Jesus was still compassionately working as He cast out demons and healed all who came to Him. This was in fulfillment of Isaiah's prophecy that Jesus would take our infirmities and bare our sicknesses.

Jesus's reputation as a great healer proceeded Him wherever He went. There was such an immense need that Jesus was called upon from early morning and on into the evening. Mark 1:29–31 contains the parallel verses of Jesus's healing of Peter's mother-in-law, and in an earlier verse in Mark 1, we read that this took place on the Sabbath. Going back to Matthew 8:16, we read the words "that evening" the people brought to Him those who needed healing. The people brought them in the evening because it marked the end of the Sabbath and they had waited until sundown in fear of the Pharisees and their position that healing on the Sabbath would break God's law.

We are not told why there were so many cases of demonic possession in Jesus's time, but Adam Clarke[46] opined that the nation of Israel had advanced to the very height of sinfulness. Josephus, the ancient Jewish historian, said of Israel that there was not a nation under heaven more wicked than they were. And because they were strongly addicted to *magic*, they invited evil spirits to be familiar with them.

No matter the reason for so many to be afflicted, Jesus with a word cast the spirits out. In addition, all the sick who were brought to Jesus were healed.

Matthew tells us that these healings were done to fulfill Isaiah's prophecy that He would take away our infirmities and bear our sickness (Isaiah 53:4–5). Jesus released those who in their suffering came to Him, and they found healing from both the bondage and consequences that sin has on a fallen world.

VERSES 18–20

Great multitudes continued to press in on Him, and He told the disciples that they were going to depart to the other side. At that time, a scribe came and said: "Master, I will follow you wherever you go", and Jesus replied that "foxes have holes, and birds have nests, but the Son of man had nowhere to lay his head".

Jesus's fame continued to grow, and throngs of people seemed to beset Him everywhere He went. Jesus commands that the disciples take Hm to the eastern side of the Sea of Galilee. Matthew is silent on His reasoning, but many commentators have stated that He was seeking a quiet place to rest. As they were readying the boat to depart, a teacher and interpreter of the law came forward. Calling Him teacher, the scribe told Him that he would follow Jesus wherever He went. The fact that generally most Pharisees and scribes were adamantly opposed to Jesus makes this public

---

[46] Adam Clarke (1760 or 1762–1832) was a British Methodist theologian and biblical scholar. He is chiefly remembered for writing a commentary on the Bible that took him forty years to complete and was a primary Methodist theological resource for two centuries. https://www.studylight.org/commentaries/acc.html.

profession on the part of this man an extraordinary profession of faith and dedication. Jesus didn't outright refuse this scholar's attempt to follow Him but told him of the stark reality of what it was like to be a disciple and to follow Him. Jesus was an itinerant preacher who moved about, always traveling from one place to another and without a permanent place of His own to rest. Although He was the Son of Man, Jesus lived a life of faith, trusting in the guidance of the Holy Spirit and relying on the provision of His heavenly Father to meet His and His followers needs. It was a simple life, a life marked by sufficiency, but it was by no means a life of ease and comfort that a scribe might have been accustomed to. Jesus wanted this man to count the cost of such a decision as this and was asking him if he could deny himself and to daily take up his cross.

VERSES 21–22

Another disciple requests that Jesus let him go and bury his father, at which Jesus said follow me and "let the dead bury their dead".

A casual reading of this disciple's request makes it appear on the surface that this man wanted to perform a burial ceremony for his deceased father. Providing a burial for one's parent would fulfill the obligation to honor one's departed family member. However, what we find is that this phrase was a common figure of speech which had the meaning of "Let me wait until I receive my inheritance,"[47] which has a much different connotation as his father may have lived for many more years before he passed away.

Jesus then tells him to let the secular world which was comprised of the spiritually dead bury the dead. The overarching demand upon disciples of Christ is to put Him foremost in our lives and that any allegiance that would lessen that commitment needs to be set aside. Jesus makes this same demand in Luke 14:26, where He said, "If any man come to me, and hate not his father, and mother, and wife, and children, and brethren, and sisters, yea, and his own life also, he cannot be my disciple." Obviously, Jesus is not advocating that anyone hate their family as such. What He is

---

[47] John MacArthur, *The MacArthur Bible Commentary* (Nashville, TN: Thomas Nelson Inc, 2005), 1136.

stating is being said through the literary devise of hyperbole in order to make His point with a critical emphasis on our devotion and the supremely sovereign standing that He should have in our lives.

John Calvin comments,

> Children should discharge their duty to their parents in such a manner that, whenever God calls them to another employment, they should lay this aside, and assign the first place to the command of God. Whatever duties we owe to men must give way, when God enjoins upon us what is immediately due to Himself.

VERSES 23–25

They got into the boat, and as they were crossing over, a great storm swept over the sea and the wind and the waves threatened to capsize them while Jesus slept. These seasoned men were so afraid that they woke Jesus from His rest as they cried out for Him to save them from perishing.

The Sea of Galilee is known for the sudden and furiously violent storms. John MacArthur points out the facts that the Sea of Galilee is 690 feet below sea level and that just to the north Mount Hermon rises to an altitude of 9,200 feet. From May through October, strong winds sweep down and through the narrow surrounding gorges and into the valley surrounding Galilee, which causes these sudden and vicious storms. The severity of the storm in this passage of scripture becomes more evident when you consider that most of the occupants of this boat were seasoned fishermen, yet they were terrified of the raging tempest they found themselves in. The ferocity of the wind upon the waves was such that they were crashing over the sides of the boat, threatening to sink it as it began filling with water at a faster rate than it could be bailed out. In fear of their lives, His disciples came and woke Him up, crying out, "Lord, save us: we perish."

Scripture tells us that in the fatigue of His humanity, Jesus was asleep. Leviticus 26:6 tells us that a sound sleep ("and ye shall lie down, and none shall make you afraid …") is a gift from God. Jesus could sleep through this torrent in the loving trust of His heavenly Father, knowing that all had not yet been fulfilled.

VERSES 26–27

Jesus asked why they were afraid and told them that they were men of little faith. He got up from where He slept and admonished the wind and the sea, and immediately there was a great calm. His disciples were in awe and wondered at how even the wind and the sea obeyed Him!

Fear and the deficiency of a convicting faith combine to create the substance of unbelief. This is the reason why, upon being awakened, Jesus spoke these words about their being afraid and having little faith. Jesus often told them to fear not, and when we trust in God, there is no room for fear in our hearts.

Jesus arose from His position in the boat and rebuked the winds and the sea, and although scripture is silent on the cause of the squall, there are many commentators who believe that there was a demonic element to the ferocity of the storm and that Jesus's rebuke was directed as much toward the satanic attack as it was for the physical elements of the storm itself. It should be enough that we clearly see the deity of Christ as He sovereignly controls the forces of nature. Through the power of His word of rebuke, the winds and the waves immediately obey His command and a great calm supervenes.

Matthew tells us that the men marveled, saying, "What manner of man is this, that even the winds and the sea obey him!" The only answer is to look to the deity of Christ as only God can sovereignly control the winds and the waves. We can look to Psalm 89:8–9 and Psalm 107:23–30 as proof texts to this fact.

Psalm 89:8–9 says,

> O LORD God of hosts, who is a strong LORD like unto thee? or to thy faithfulness round about thee? Thou rulest the raging of the sea: when the waves thereof arise, thou stillest them.

Psalm 107:23–30 says,

> They that go down to the sea in ships, that do business in great waters; These see the works of the LORD, and his wonders in the deep. For he commandeth, and raiseth the stormy wind, which lifteth up the waves thereof. They mount up to the heaven, they go down again to the depths: their soul is melted because of trouble. They reel to and fro, and stagger like a drunken man, and are at their wit's end. Then they cry unto the LORD in their trouble, and he bringeth them out of their distresses. He maketh the storm a calm, so that the waves thereof are still. Then are they glad because they be quiet; so he bringeth them unto their desired haven.

Jesus, without doubt, is God incarnate, and the disciples' fear and reverence for Christ increased.

VERSES 28–29

When they arrived on the other side, they were in the country of the Gergesenes. Two men possessed with devils came out of the tombs. They were so fierce that no one dared to pass by them. They cried out to Jesus and asked Him what they had to do with Him, calling Him "Jesus, thou Son of God". They were concerned with being dealt with before their allotted time.

By the miracle of Christ, they had just weathered a storm, the magnitude of which many onboard had never experienced, and Jesus and His followers arrived on the other side. The terminology used here by the wording "other side" is a way of referring to the movement to or from an area that is considered Jewish territory or to or from a territory that would be considered Gentile. The country of Gadarenes refers to the town of Gadara, which is located about six miles southeast of Galilee, and it also includes the surrounding region.

Here they meet two demon-possessed men who are described as exceedingly fierce. In Matthew's account of the incident, he mentions two men, whereas the other gospel accounts only mention one man. There can be reasonable explanations for what may appear as a discrepancy. One reason may stem from the fact that Mark and Luke were closely associated with the apostles, with Mark's gospel being called an autobiography of Peter, and Luke's writings were to ensure that the record was true and faithful. So he wrote,

> As many have taken in hand to set forth in order a declaration of those things which are most surely believed among us, Even as they delivered them unto us, which from the beginning were eyewitnesses, and ministers of the word. It seemed good to me also, having had perfect understanding of all things from the very first. (Luke 1:1–3)

If two are mentioned in Matthew, then the other accounts are also correct in saying they met one because if there are two, then there must logically be at least one. R. C. Sproul says, "Actually there is no contradiction at all. If there were two men there, there was surely one." The ferocity of the one mentioned in Mark 5 and Luke 8 may have been so great that his presence overshadowed the other man in the eyes of those present. He was called Legion as he was possessed by many demons and a Roman legion was comprised of about five thousand men in several units of infantry. Scripture is silent on why the number of possessed men seems dissimilar, so we should not speculate too much on the differences. What we do know is that these men lived in the tombs and were therefore unclean and that the other gospels tell us that they were so powerful that they could not be bound. They were fiercely demonic, and no one could even pass that way. What we also know is that they recognized Jesus as the Son of God and used this title when, in their fear of His sovereignty, they questioned their potential torment and what they perceived as the timing of their fate. The Greek for "time" in this context was derived from *kairos* and refers to a special moment that takes place in time that defines the meaning and significance of that time, and in this instance, it has eschatological significance. They were aware that they would be judged at the divinely appointed time at the end of the age and that their fate was the eternal torment of hell.

VERSES 30–34

At some distance, there was a herd of pigs feeding. So the demons implored that if He were to cast them out, let it be into the pigs. And he said to them, "Go" and they went into the herd of swine. At this, the whole herd ran intensely down a steep bank and into the sea, where they drowned. Those who cared for the herd fled to the city and told everything and emphasized what had become of the possessed men. The whole city came out to meet Jesus, and when they saw Him, they begged Him to leave their region.

This was a large herd of pigs, with Mark's gospel numbering them at two thousand. Pigs were deemed as unclean to the Jews. No old covenant Israelite would ever be so closely associated with these animals, and because this was primarily a Gentile area, this herd more than likely was owned by a Gentile. The demons didn't care who owned them; all they knew was that they were about to be cast out of these men and begged Jesus to send them into the pigs rather than into the abyss. With the single word *go,* Jesus cast them out of the men and into the pigs, wherein "the whole herd of swine ran violently down a steep place into the sea and perished in the waters."

John Calvin said that one reason that the demons asked to be cast into the pigs was to incite the people who made their living off the pigs to curse God for the loss of their livelihood. Some today may pick up on that theme and wonder at the cruelty of God to take away their livelihood, but what they don't see is that they, and the men of the city, counted the value of the pigs over the value of the eternal souls of the two men who were cleansed of these demons and the control that they formerly had over their lives.

The entire city rushed to the scene and saw the formerly possessed men in their right minds, as well as the devastation of their loss. Instead of rejoicing over the miracle of these men's salvation, in their incomprehension and perhaps fear, they begged Jesus to leave their region.

CHAPTER 9

HEALINGS, MATTHEW CALLED, RESTORED LIFE

VERSES 1–2

Jesus got back into the boat and crossed over to his own city. When He arrived, they brought to him a paralytic man lying on a bed. Jesus, in seeing and acknowledging their faith, said to the paralytic, Son, be of good cheer your sins have been forgiven.

Jesus returned to Capernaum, the home base for His ministry in Galilee. The next event to take place is explained in greater detail in the accounts as provided in Mark 2 and Luke 5. The friends of this man went up on the flat roof of the house and literally tore a hole in it so that they could lower this man and his bed through the hole and into the presence of Jesus. The man and his friends each possessed the convicting faith that he would be healed from his paralysis and would walk out of this home on his own two feet. What Jesus does next would cause no little controversy among those who heard what He spoke to the man, and I am sure that it generated some level of disappointment on the man's part as well. After seeing their faith, Jesus did heal the man, but it was a spiritual healing that was spoken into him and not the physical healing that he and his friends had hoped for.

Forgiveness of sin, or spiritual healing, is the prerogative of God alone, and this was not lost on the scribes who were present to hear Jesus's words. As for the man, the forgiveness of his sins should have been enough as it was the greater healing of the two, and this is the reason that Jesus told him to "take heart." The belief of those who practiced the Jewish faith was that any physical malady was related to the sin of a person, their parents, or someone else important in their lives. This traditional belief is what was behind His disciples asking Him whose sin caused the blindness in a man He had healed: his own or that of his parents. The ESV Study Bible Commentary reminds us, "Although individual sin is not always the direct cause of a person's disease or illness (John 9:2–3), ultimately all corruption and death result from the entrance of sin into the world."

VERSES 3–5

Certain of the scribes who were present said within themselves, "this man is blasphemous". Jesus knew their thoughts and asked why they thought evil of Him in their hearts. He then asked them if it was is easier to say a person's sins were forgiven or to say get up and walk.

The scribes who took umbrage to Jesus telling the man that his sins were forgiven did so within themselves. Perhaps they kept silent because they had seen or heard about how Jesus responded to those who questioned the authority of the actions that He undertook or how He quoted scripture to validate His teachings and they feared being the focus of His upbraiding. They weren't getting off by being silent as Jesus knew their thoughts pertaining to what they perceived as blasphemy. This knowledge of what they held in their hearts should have been another validation of who Jesus was. First Corinthians 2:11 tells us, "For what man knoweth the things of a man, save the spirit of man which is in him?"

Jesus questions the evil intent held in their hearts and poses a question that was sure to concentrate their attention on what was coming next. He asks which is easier: to merely say to someone that your sins are forgiven, which none of them could verify if it were so, or for Him to say, "Rise and walk," which would result in a miraculous change in the man's physical condition, one that would have an immediate and observable outcome. And it would be something that only the power of God could accomplish.

The scribes were right in that only God can forgive sin, and Mark and Luke attribute to them as having said, "Who can forgive sins but God alone"? However, what they were mistaken about was Jesus's identity and only attributed to Him what they saw as His human nature, while not yet recognizing His deity as "God manifest in the flesh" (1 Timothy 3:16). Jesus knew that the forgiveness of sins was harder as it required the greatest sacrifice ever made, but for these carnal men, the physical healing of the paralytic would be an outward sign, and it appeared to them to be the harder of the two.

VERSES 6–8

In a demonstration of His sovereign authority and so that they might know that He, the Son of Man, possessed the power on earth to forgive sins, He told the paralytic to get up and take his bed and go home. Jesus didn't wait for an answer to His question about which statement would be the easier to make. There were many times when Jesus posed questions to the scribes and Pharisees, who seemed to be present whenever He was teaching, and they often refused to give Him an answer.

Just prior to the healing, Jesus told them that the miracle that He was going to perform was for their own edification, so that they may know that the Son of Man has the authority to forgive sins. When the crowd saw what happened, they were in awe, and they glorified God for having given such power to men.

As we see so many times when people find themselves in the presence of God, they are struck by astonishment and they were afraid, and in that fear, they glorified God. What they missed is the fact that they were standing in the presence of deity. I say this because it was stated that "they glorified God, which had given such power unto men." They were right to glorify God, but they had also overlooked that although Jesus was a man, He was also fully God and the authority of the Father was already an authority that was ascribed to the deity of Christ. This healing was an outward sign that was given and was explicit evidence of the authority that Jesus had to both heal and to forgive, a prerogative that is God's alone.

VERSE 9

After Jesus left from there, he saw a man by the name of Matthew sitting at the tax booth and said to him, Follow me. And Matthew got up and followed Him.

Matthew abruptly transitions from this miracle and the crowd's astonishment with a simple and straightforward phrase: "as Jesus passed forth from thence …" We are left up in the air as to what transpired between when He spoke a word of healing and His leaving the incident behind Him while He continued about His Father's work by calling to Him another disciple. Was it a casual walk back toward His home, or was He being continually pressed by the crowd?

This choice of Jesus's next disciple would cause even more consternation among the scribes who followed His every move, as well as within the whole Jewish community. Jesus called out to this man and said follow me, at which point Matthew, a tax collector, got up and followed. Tax collectors were odious men to the Jews. They were traitors to their own countrymen because they both worked for and under the authority of Rome. These men paid a set fee to the Roman government for the franchise of collecting the taxes that were imposed upon the citizens. They in turn, under the power and force of the Roman soldiers, collected a much higher amount than the people were obligated to pay, and whatever they collected, over and above what the people owed, went directly to them as profit. Among other things, in the estimation of the Jewish community, tax collectors were less than dogs. They weren't allowed to be a judge or a witness in court, and as traitors and extortionists, they were excommunicated from the synagogue and shunned by their Jewish compatriots.

Matthew didn't hesitate in making his decision to follow Jesus, not only for that moment but for all time. This calling was not just an external call but an inward and effectual call that changed Matthew's life forever. John Calvin said that "Matthew was not only a witness and preacher but was also a proof and illustration of the grace exhibited in Christ."

VERSES 10–13

After this, Jesus reclined at a table and many other tax collectors and sinners came and sat with Him and his disciples. Of course, when the Pharisees saw it, they questioned His disciples as to why their Master ate with this type of people. Jesus heard them and responded by saying that those who were well didn't need a physician, only those that were sick. He further instructs them to go and learn what the following phrase meant: "I will have mercy, and not sacrifice: for I did not come to call the righteous, but to call sinners to repentance".

Matthew had left everything to follow Jesus, and now the fellowship of a shared meal gave Jesus another opportunity to teach the gospel message. Matthew's former means of employment had limited the class or type of people that would attend one of his dinner parties. The Pharisees, in their continual pursuit of finding something to condemn Jesus about, were there too. On this occasion, their complaint was centered on the fact that the invited guests were tax collectors and sinners. The Pharisees were again questioning Jesus's motive for being there, and with recrimination in their voices, they specifically asked His disciples why Jesus was eating with "these kinds of people?" Some were guilty of publicly known sin, and others were recognized as being less rigid in following the law as the Pharisees interpreted it. Matthew himself was probably highly scorned by the Pharisees and by Orthodox Jews overall. Matthew's name was Levi, making it likely that he was a Levite (Luke 5:27–28). This fact made his collusion with Rome even more heinous because God had set the Levites apart for Himself, not in service to the pagans (Numbers 8:5–22).[48]

It is not certain where this banquet took place, but many believe that it was held in a private hall and that there were many guests in attendance. The Pharisees positioned themselves close enough to hear what Jesus had to say and close enough to be heard, and Jesus replied to their criticism directly. He told them, "They that be whole need not a physician, but they that are sick." Jesus then gave them something to ponder by saying, "But go ye

[48] Paraphrased from *Tabletalk Magazine* (Sanford, FL, Ligonier Ministries, Inc., April 10, 2008).

and learn what that meaneth, I will have mercy, and not sacrifice." Jesus directed their thoughts to several verses in Hosea (4:1; 5:6; 6:6). In Hosea's day, the people had given up any truly intimate knowledge of God. They were still bringing empty sacrifices to the altar, but they were derelict when it came to mercy. Their hearts had become hardened to the truth of God's Word and they placed an emphasis on God's ceremonial requirements over and above moral standards. The Pharisees, despite outward appearances and ritual, had also forsaken God's truth and had molded their religious practices around their traditions, which often usurped God's authority. They had become scornfully self-righteous and harshly judgmental while their blindness to their own spiritual poverty and sickness continued to remain an impediment to their own salvation.

Jesus ended by reproof, saying that He had come not to call the righteous but sinners. If the Pharisees had set aside their pride, they would have admitted to their own sin and realized that Jesus had come offering His own righteousness to save all those that the Father had given Him.

VERSES 14–15

The disciples of John came to Jesus and asked why both they and the Pharisees often fast, but His disciples do not fast. Jesus replied to them with a question. He asked them whether the guests of a wedding mourn as long as the bridegroom was with them? He then tells them that the days will come, when the bridegroom shall be taken from them, and that at that time they will fast.

Although he lived in the New Testament era, John the Baptist is considered the last of the Old Testament prophets. John's message was centrally focused on repentance and the practice of fasting and is strongly linked with the type of repentance found throughout the Old Testament (Nehemiah 9:1–3; Jonah 3:5–9). John was an ascetic, one who practiced self-denial, which included periods of fasting. For this reason, it was appropriate for those who were John's disciples to follow his examples.

Jesus had responded to the question of why His disciples didn't fast, not with condemnation to those who did fast but with another analogy. This analogy not only addressed the question but implicitly highlighted His deity. Christians are known as the bride of Christ, and in this instance, Jesus uses a wedding as an example. "Christ is figured as the bridegroom, and the friends and guests at a wedding (His disciples), in accordance to rabbinical tradition, did not have to observe the law during a wedding feast."[49] Luke 18:12 tells us that the Pharisees in their piety fasted twice each week, but this tradition was set aside during the joy of the weeklong celebration, an event that superseded religious rituals.[50] For now, Christ's disciples should rejoice in His company. Once He is taken away, they would return to prayer and fasting as they sought the presence of God. The day will come for fasting when He is "taken away," and these words are a reference to His arrest, crucifixion, and ascension. But while He, the Son of God, was with them, fasting was unnecessary.

VERSES 16–17

He continues by telling them that no man uses a piece of new cloth to patch an old garment, for when the garment is washed, that patch will shrink, and the tear will become even worse. Using another example, He explains that if men put new wine into old wineskins, they burst, the wine will run out, and the wineskins will be ruined. Instead, if men put new wine into new wineskins, both are preserved.

Jesus had come with a new perspective on their view of the Old Testament teachings; it was a new perspective to those who heard Him, but it was also a right understanding of those teachings. He hadn't come to destroy the law but in its fulfillment. With His coming, much of the old ritual and tradition could be set aside.

> Sometimes, the need for reform is so great that the fresh
> work of God cannot be contained in old or expected

---

[49] Paraphrased from www.blueletterbible.org study notes on Matthew 9 by David Guzik.

[50] I have used words like *tradition* and *ritual* here because the Old Testament only prescribed one fast. It was observed on the Day of Atonement (Leviticus 16:29, 31). The Pharisees' semiweekly ritual was way over the top in its practice.

forms. If they were to receive Him, they would have to adjust their expectations[51]

The Pharisees themselves needed to be made new, to be born again. Their old structure could not bear the new form or structure of the new covenant in Christ, which was already tearing at the fabric of their traditions.

He, and His teachings, were like a new garment, and it was time for renewal; it was the advent of the new covenant. The old garment of ritual and tradition was worn thin and torn. Patching it with new cloth would only make it worse and trying to patch it with the old cloth of more ritual and tradition would leave you with the same old garment. People needed to have a new robe, to be clothed in the righteousness of Christ.

The same can be said of the example of the old and new wineskins. Jesus brings a new era with new ways, proclaiming that He is the Way, the Truth, and the Life. In the strength and perseverance that we have in Christ, we are likened to the strength of the new wineskins. As the wine ferments and expands, we too expand in our knowledge and faith in Christ Jesus. We need the message of the new covenant teachings, and John MacArthur states that these two parables

> illustrate that His new and internal gospel of repentance from and forgiveness of sin could not be connected to or contained in the old and external traditions of self-righteousness and ritual.

VERSES 18–19

While Jesus was still speaking, a certain ruler knelt down and worshipped Him, saying, "My daughter has just died, but if you come and touch your hand upon her she will live." Jesus and His disciples got up and followed him.

---

[51] *Tabletalk Magazine* (Sanford, FL, Ligonier Ministries, Inc., February 4, 2016).

The ESV and NIV Bibles say that this ruler came and knelt before Jesus, and the KJV and the 1599 Geneva Bible say that he worshipped Him. Both show a high level of reverence for Jesus. In fact, it could be argued that kneeling is a form of worship, especially when the Greek translates it as both "kneeling" and "worship" (Strong's G4352). This ruler's daughter had died, and *Vine's Expository Dictionary of New Testament Words* defines "ruler" as a chief ruler of the people, such as a member of the Sanhedrin or a magistrate within the synagogue. R. C. Sproul's commentary says that Jairus was one of those who were the most resistant and hostile toward Jesus, and still he went to Christ. Some say that he had been transformed by the power of the Holy Spirit and proclaimed that if Jesus came and laid His hand on her that his daughter would live. Christ alone is to be worshipped, and with some level of faith, Jairus knew that Jesus could bring his daughter back to life.

Matthew tells us that Jesus rose and, along with His disciples, followed the man, but before He got to Jairus's home, He was delayed by the desperate act of another person.

VERSES 20–22

A woman who for twelve years suffered from an issue of blood came up behind Jesus and touched the hem of His garment. Her thinking was that if she could only touch His garment, she would be healed. Jesus turned around, and when He saw her, He told her to be comforted and that her faith had made her whole. And the woman was healed from that hour.

As Jesus is making His way through the crowd, a woman suffering from a consistent hemorrhage that had plagued and weakened her for twelve years worked her way through the throng. Although ceremonially unclean, she had resolved to get close enough to touch the hem of Jesus's garment. Her faith in His power to heal, although it was probably mixed with some superstition, was such that she knew through the prompting of the Holy Spirit that if she was able to get near enough, she would be made well. The healing grace was not in the touching of His garment but was found in Christ Himself, He alone should be the focus of our faith.

Matthew, as is his habit, and with a sense of urgency, gives us the barest of essentials surrounding each event that he writes about. The other gospels mention Jesus questioning who touched Him, with the disciples passing it off as the normal bustle and jostling of the crowd's clamoring to get close to Him. Jesus tells them that He has felt power of God being drawn from Himself. In this account, He turns and sees the woman and in compassion says to her, "Daughter, be of good comfort; thy faith hath made thee whole," and in that instant, she was healed.

"Your faith" is a phrase that Jesus often uses in the miraculous healings that He performs. Jesus tells her that it was her faith that healed her, the implication being that it was not accomplished through the touching of His robe. Faith is not the power behind the miracles, but it is the divinely appointed means for physical healing and spiritual salvation, and through it, those who look to Jesus as the object of their faith will receive the blessings of His kingdom.

Later in Matthew 17, we will read more of the role of faith when it comes to healing. His disciples had attempted to heal a demon-possessed boy without success. When Jesus rebuked the demon, it came out and the boy was healed. When they were alone, the disciples questioned why they could not cast out the demon. Jesus pointed to their lack of faith and told them if they had faith like a grain of mustard seed, nothing would be impossible for them.

VERSES 23–26

When Jesus arrived at the ruler's house, He saw the musicians and the people making a noise. He said to them that they should go away because the girl was not dead but only asleep. And they laughed at Him, but when the people went outside, He went in and took her by the hand, and the girl stood up. And His fame and the news of this event spread everywhere.

Jesus had arrived at Jairus's home to find the professional mourners were already at their task. Even the process of grieving for the dead had fallen under specific requirements, and those included hiring a minimum of two flute players and at least one mourning woman. As He approached them, He told them to go away because the girl was not dead but asleep. When they heard Jesus's statement, the façade of weeping quickly turned to ridicule as they began to deride Jesus and to laugh at such an assertion. Despite His reputation and the stories of the miracles that He had performed, the God-Man's deity remained veiled to many and they could not reconcile themselves to the fact that He and no other held the keys to everlasting life and death, including the final death of hell itself. Once the unbelieving crowd, those who lacked faith, had been sent outside, Jesus went in and gently took the girl by the hand, and at His command, she arose. The unimaginable result of His act of compassion and grace immediately silenced the astonished mockers, and the testimony of this miraculous event, like so many others, rapidly spread throughout the entire district.

VERSES 27–31

Jesus left Jairus's home and two blind men cried out to Him, asking for mercy. As they cried out, they didn't use Jesus's name. They used His messianic title, the Son of David, a title in recognition of His deity.

They cried out for His mercy and for the compassion that they had been hearing about when His miracles were being proclaimed by the masses. These men humbly begged for mercy without any hint of the arrogance of one who feels that they are entitled as sons of Abraham, or some other trivial reason often given in support of a fraudulent claim or right to merit.

As they followed Him, Jesus didn't stop along the way but continued until He got to the house where He was staying, and the blind men came to Him. Jesus set the stage for what was to happen. It was a quiet, unassuming, and private setting that was out of the public's eye.

Jesus then speaks to them and asks if they believe that He can heal them, and it was really a question of their faith. Their answer was simple and straightforward. They said, "Yes, Lord." It should be noted that Jesus asks if they believe that He can heal them. It wasn't a question of their faith being the instrument of their healing, but it was their faith in Him as Christ that was the prerequisite to their healing. It is only His divine prerogative that initiates and completes their physical and spiritual healing.

Upon their affirmation of belief, Jesus touched their eyes and said, "According to your faith be it unto you." Their eyes were immediately opened, and once again, Jesus warns those who were healed not to tell anyone, and in disobedience they went away from Him and once more His fame was spread through all the district. Although they glorified His name, they did so in disobedience. Jesus's intent was not to have these miracles be the reason for the crowds to come to Him. His main mission was to preach about the kingdom of God through the gospel message. The miracles were secondary to that mission, and they were meant only as a testimony to His power and authority.

VERSES 32–34

As they were leaving, others brought before Him a man who was mute and possessed with a devil. And when Jesus cast the devil out, the man was able to speak, and the multitudes marveled and commented that this had never been seen in all of Israel. Then in the hardness of their hearts, the Pharisees said that Jesus cast out demons by the power of the prince of the demons.

A man who was demon possessed and mute was thought to be beyond help. The Jewish understanding of the ability to exorcise a demon was to first compel the demon to tell what his name was. They somehow got the idea that they could use the demon's name as some sort of means to exorcise him, with one commentator suggesting that the demon's name was some type of handle by which the demon could be removed. If the possessed person was also mute, there would be no way to find out the demon's name; therefore, they would be unable to free the man from his possession.

That is why when Jesus cast out the demon and the man spoke, the crowds marveled and said, "It was never so seen in Israel." The healing that they witnessed was undeniable; therefore, their antagonistic attitude toward Jesus and the power of God that they had repeatedly seen in His works was inexcusable. This inexcusability extends to their lack of recognition in the scriptural fulfillment of Isaiah 35, where the prophet foretells that the tongues of the mute would be loosened in the messianic age.

In their blindness, the Pharisees saw this as a subtle undermining and a demonstration of the weakness in yet another of their long-held traditions. Instead of seeing Jesus's total power over the demonic realm, in their shallowness, they saw this as a threat to their own power and authority and immediately attributed this work of Jesus to Satan by saying, "He casteth out devils through the prince of the devils." In their zeal to discredit Jesus and His work, they come perilously close to uttering, if not having uttered, the unpardonable sin of blaspheming the Holy Spirit.

VERSES 35–38

Despite the Pharisees' unbridled wickedness toward Him, Jesus continues His ministry of teaching and preaching in the synagogues in cities and villages throughout the region. He also continued His healing ministry through the types of miracles that He had performed in Capernaum. He persisted in both ministries because the plight of the people was great, and He was moved with compassion. William Barclay (1907–1978), a former Professor of divinity and biblical criticism at the University of Glasgow, said that the Greek translated as "moved with compassion" "is the strongest word for pity in the Greek language … it describes the compassion which moves a man to the deepest depths of his being."

Jesus saw that the people, apart from God, were without a shepherd and were scattered and weary, and this is even more concerning because the people did have scribes, priests, and Pharisees. In this one statement, Jesus discounts these spiritual leaders from having any true value because they had failed to carry out their responsibilities to nurture and care for the people's spiritual needs.

Their lackluster performance of duty and Jesus's rebuke are a reoccurrence of what we read in Ezekiel 34:1–10.

> And the word of the LORD came unto me, saying, Son of man, prophesy against the shepherds of Israel, prophesy, and say unto them, Thus saith the Lord GOD unto the shepherds; Woe be to the shepherds of Israel that do feed themselves! should not the shepherds feed the flocks?

Ye eat the fat, and ye clothe you with the wool, ye kill them that are fed: but ye feed not the flock. The diseased have ye not strengthened, neither have ye healed that which was sick, neither have ye bound up that which was broken, neither have ye brought again that which was driven away, neither have ye sought that which was lost; but with force and with cruelty have ye ruled them. And they were scattered, because there is no shepherd: and they became meat to all the beasts of the field, when they were scattered. My sheep wandered through all the mountains, and upon every high hill: yea, my flock was scattered upon all the face of the earth, and none did search or seek after them. Therefore, ye shepherds, hear the word of the Lord; As I live, saith the Lord God, surely because my flock became a prey, and my flock became meat to every beast of the field, because there was no shepherd, neither did my shepherds search for my flock, but the shepherds fed themselves, and fed not my flock; Therefore, O ye shepherds, hear the word of the Lord; Thus saith the Lord God; Behold, I am against the shepherds; and I will require my flock at their hand, and cause them to cease from feeding the flock; neither shall the shepherds feed themselves anymore; for I will deliver my flock from their mouth, that they may not be meat for them.

Jesus saw a plentiful spiritual crop but a lack of laborers. He commands that we pray that the Lord of the harvest sends laborers to reap the bountiful yield. There was, and still is, a great need for laborers to be engaged in kingdom work because the harvest is still ripe as there are many who are ready to hear the good news of His gospel message and be gathered into His kingdom. As kingdom laborers, we must work to our utmost while we prayerfully ask God to bring in the harvest of those who are sovereignly His elect, because He alone gives and then brings in the increase.

CHAPTER 10

TWELVE APOSTLES, PERSECUTION, REWARDS

VERSES 1–4

Jesus had just told His followers to pray that God the Father would send laborers to bring in the harvest, and He Himself was about to take direct steps to bring this exhortation into practical action. Out of the many disciples that followed Jesus, He now calls a select few men who have little in common with one another, and even some who may have been at odds with one another if it were not for the stabilizing force of reconciliation that could only come about by the power of Christ Jesus. This is a diverse group of men from various backgrounds, vocations, and political affiliations.

These men for the most part were simple and uneducated, with little understanding or training in religious matters, but they were called by God to serve His purpose in their lives, as well as in ours. Paul wrote about God's providence in 1 Corinthians 1:26–29.

> For ye see your calling, brethren, how that not many wise men after the flesh, not many mighty, not many noble, are called: But God hath chosen the foolish things of the

world to confound the wise; and God hath chosen the weak things of the world to confound the things which are mighty; And base things of the world, and things which are despised, hath God chosen, yea, and things which are not, to bring to nought things that are: That no flesh should glory in his presence.

Jesus didn't just call these men; He took them under His wing and trained them for three years as they followed His footsteps and listened to His teachings. Not only did He train them, but He delegated them with authority and equipped them with the power that they would need to cast out demons in His name as well as to heal every disease and affliction. Christ's work, and what they were about to do in His name, would be a sign to all who had eyes to see and would substantiate Jesus's messianic and sovereign authority over both the physical and the spiritual realms. Irenaeus, one of the earliest church followers, said that anyone who rejected the apostles also rejected Christ because Jesus had delegated them with the authority that the Father had given to Him. Therefore, not only did they reject Christ, but ultimately they rejected God the Father as well.

Matthew concludes these verses by naming twelve apostles, the men Jesus had singled out from the other disciples and called to be His emissaries with all the power and authority to carry out what He had been doing and had now commissioned them to do. Interestingly, this is the only time that Matthew uses the title of apostle when referring to himself and the others. The title of "apostle refers to qualified representatives who are sent on a mission, whereas a disciple is a student that is being taught by another."[52]

Scripture says little about most of these men, but what we do know helps explain Matthew's ordering of their names. Peter is listed first because he is the most prominent of the twelve, the first to declare Jesus as the Christ, the first to preach the gospel after Pentecost, and the first apostle to see Gentiles converted. Peter, Andrew, James, and John are often listed together as they had become Jesus's inner circle of disciples and they are

---

[52] John MacArthur, *The MacArthur Bible Commentary* (Nashville, TN: Thomas Nelson Inc, 2005), 1140.

the most familiar to most Christians. Judas with his betrayal of the Lord earns him the last place in any listing of the apostle's names.

Verses 5–6

Jesus sent forth the twelve and commanded them not to go to the Gentiles or into any city of the Samaritans. Their assignment was to go to the lost sheep of the house of Israel.

This initial sending out of the apostles specifically tells them not to preach to the Gentiles, and we know that these original instructions were in line with all that Jesus Himself did whenever He entered a town or village with a synagogue. He first went to the Jews, the covenant people. It was the lost sheep of the nation of Israel who were the focus of His initial ministry. We should remember that in chapter 8:10 Jesus commended the faith of the centurion and said that it was greater than anyone's in Israel and that many would come from the east and the west and recline at the table of Abraham, Isaac, and Jacob. We further know that the command of Christ not to go the Gentiles is no longer in force, because after His resurrection, our Savior instructs His followers to preach the gospel to all nations (Matthew 28:18–20), with another example being Peter's vision before being summoned to Cornelius's house and while Peter preaches to them the Holy Spirit falls upon the Gentiles (Acts 10). Nonetheless, in these verses, we see the faithfulness of God's promise throughout redemptive history, and as Paul puts it in Romans 1:16, "to the Jew first, and also to the Greek." And in Romans 15:8–9, we read, "Now I say that Jesus Christ was a minister of the circumcision for the truth of God, to confirm the promises made unto the fathers: And that the Gentiles might glorify God for his mercy …"

Although Jesus restricted the initial missionary efforts of the apostles, this shouldn't be seen a prohibition against the Gentiles or Samaritans to receive the gospel message but a prioritizing of the gospel being preached first and foremost to the Jews, God's covenantal people, the lost sheep of the house of Israel.

VERSES 7–8

The apostles were to preach to those that they were sent to, and the message that they were to proclaim was that the kingdom of heaven was at hand. While they preached they were to heal the sick, cleanse the lepers, raise the dead, and to cast out devils as signs of the authority given to them.

These twelve men, the apostles of Christ, were commanded to meet the physical and spiritual needs of the lost. They were to proclaim, as Jesus had, that the kingdom of heaven was at hand. Only Matthew uses the expression "the kingdom of heaven," whereas the remaining gospels use the expression "the kingdom of God." After the preaching of this message, there would surely be questions about just what they meant. In their answer, it is more than likely that the apostles would reiterate Jesus's teachings that He had given during the Sermon on the Mount because in that message, He taught what life in the kingdom of heaven should be like.

The apostles were admonished to heal, to cleanse, to raise the dead, and to cast out demons. In the strength of their faith, they were to carry out the same extraordinary feats that Jesus had been accomplishing in His ministry. These miraculous activities were to be undertaken in the name of Jesus, in whose authority the power to do so was vested. These were to be signs that the kingdom was at hand, signs which assuredly pointed to the deity of Christ.

VERSES 8–15

Jesus now reminds His disciples that they have been given the gift of salvation and a place in the kingdom through His teachings, and they had received the grace of this gift at no monetary cost. Because of this, they too should preach God's Word to others without any thought of accepting any wage for their godly ministry. He continues by telling them that they are not to take a lot of supplies with them or to obtain and carry an extra amount of money or clothing beyond what they currently possessed was adequate for this mission. They were to fully expect God to provide for their needs as the laborer deserves his food, and there is the sense that these disciples were not only to preach and pray for those that they were ministering too but to work alongside them as they worked in the fields, shared meals, or in whatever occupation that they were involved. When they entered a town or village, they were to seek lodging and give their greetings to those who responded favorably to the gospel message, and it is they who would be worthy to have the apostles' peace bestowed upon them. Their command to remain in the lodging they were provided also speaks of the short duration of their stay in one place so as not to be a burden to their hosts.

On the contrary, if they came upon those who would not positively respond to the Lord's teachings, they were to shake the dust off their feet as they departed. This was in keeping with the Jewish tradition that when leaving a Gentile area, and in an expression of contempt, they were to shake off the dust from their feet. For Christ's missionaries, it would be a sign of judgment against those who refused to hear the gospel message. Their refusal would have been a rejection of the apostles, a rejection of the Word of God, and a rejection of Christ Himself. The weightiness of this judgment against their hardened hearts is highlighted by Jesus saying that it would "be more tolerable for the land of Sodom and Gomorrah in the day of judgment, than for that city."

VERSES 16–18

Jesus continues to prepare His disciples for their missionary journey by telling them that He is sending them out into a hostile environment, as sheep in the middle of wolves, those who were the false prophets who continued to persecute Christ's church. He has no delusions about how they will be treated, and for this reason, He wants them to be as wise serpents, which portends a level of shrewdness and cunning, and this level of awareness would help them to avoid situations that would unduly put them in harm's way. He also tells them to be as harmless as doves, which is representative of a simple innocence and a spirit of guilelessness which would prevent them from being overcome by the temptation to retaliate for any wrongdoing that might befall them. We too are to exemplify a demeanor of combined wisdom and innocence, and Augustine is quoted as saying, "Innocent as doves that we may not harm anyone; cautious as snakes that we may be careful of letting anyone harm us."[53]

Jesus warns them that the persecution that they will face would go beyond a mere rejection of their message and warns them to be aware of the potential of being brought into the civil courts on trumped up charges, or even into the synagogues, which were not only a place of worship but also a place of discipline where floggings could occur. He prophetically spoke of the likelihood that they would be dragged before various political authorities for His sake and be required to testify before them as well as to the Gentiles, a prophecy that would come to pass as we can see from Acts 4:1–22, Acts 12:1–4, and again in Acts 14:5.

VERSES 19–20

When they are brought before the courts, they are not to be concerned about what they will say, for it will be given to them at the appropriate time. It will not be them who speaks, but it will be the Spirit of the Father that speaks through them.

Jesus further punctuates the reality of their impending persecution by saying, "When they deliver you over ..." and continues by instructing the apostles not to worry about how they will respond to those they are brought before. He doesn't give them a list of what to say but tells them that their response to their persecutors will be given to them in the hour of their need. As always, they were not to be anxious as they faced their own human weaknesses, but they were to prayerfully put their faith and trust in Him. Jesus further comforts them by saying a prepared response wasn't needed because they would not be speaking but the Spirit of God would be speaking through them.

VERSES 21–23

When this occurs,

---

[53] *The Works of Saint Augustine: A Translation for the 21st Century* (Hyde Park, NY, New City Press, 2018) volume 3.

brothers will deliver up their brother to death, and the father his child, and the children shall rise up against their parents and have them put to death. And you shall be hated of all men for my name's sake but he that endures to the end shall be saved. When they persecute you in this city, flee to another, for truthfully I tell you, you will not have covered the towns of Israel, until the Son of Man comes.

Today we often hear it exclaimed that when you are at a family gathering, you shouldn't talk about politics or religion because they are topics that can sever family relationships. Jesus knew how volatile religious beliefs were. In fact, we have already read where His own family came to get Him and said that He was out of His mind. During the time of this teaching, religion and politics were very much entwined, which is why He continued to tell those He had healed not to proclaim their healing lest the government come down upon Him because of their fear of a political insurrection. He was hated and reviled by the religious establishment who often appealed to the government and the Roman army to intervene on their behalf. This same level of vitriol would be extended to His followers as well, and there would be persecution.

He tells His apostles, and us, that we will be hated for His name's sake, and it seems today that you can publicly speak of Buddha, Mohammed, Vishnu, or any name other than Jesus. We in America suffer through a covert or indirect manner by subtly being ostracized, passed over for job promotions, and other mild forms of persecution, but we have no idea what it is like for Christians around the world who are being beaten, tortured, and murdered for their faith.

Jesus tells His apostles that if they face persecution in one town to flee to another, they are not to become martyrs. It is for them to escape to another place and to continue to preach His Word.

Jesus also says that they would not go through all the towns of Israel before the Son of Man comes. This is one of those passages that nonbelievers and skeptics point to after a cursory reading of the text to say that the prophecy Jesus proclaimed here was wrong. Many scholars believe that the concept that Jesus was conveying in these verses was the fulfillment of the Day of Judgment that He was talking about earlier in Matthew 10:15. This judgment against Israel was the coming destruction of the temple by the Roman army in AD 70. Others believe that He was talking about His crucifixion and resurrection, still others the sending of the Holy Spirit at Pentecost. Christians know that God's Word is true, and we also know that the mind of God is not ours. Because of the limitations of our finite minds, there have been and will be things that we cannot explain.

There are many commentators who believe that verse 23 is to be understood as a reference to the widespread persecution that occurred prior to the destruction of the Jewish temple in AD 70. This would be another example of a near-term fulfillment of prophecy that foreshadows the final judgment that will come at the end of the age to all who reject Christ.

John MacArthur's commentary states,

> These verses clearly have an eschatological significance that goes beyond the disciples' immediate mission. The persecution that He describes seems to belong to the tribulation period that precedes Christ's Second Coming, alluded to in verse 23.

We will take a deeper look at this when we get to Matthew 24 and the Olivet Discourse, where Jesus says much more about this subject. For now, it is important to note that here again Jesus gives us the assurance that with God's saving grace, those who persevere to the end, through the trials and tribulations that come their way, will be saved.

VERSES 24–25

> The disciple is not above his master, nor the servant above his lord. It is enough for a disciple to become like his teacher, and the servant like his lord. If they have called

the master of the house Beelzebub, how much more will they call those of his household?

A disciple of Christ is one who has died to himself and has dedicated his life to Christ Jesus, no longer belonging to one's self but wholly dedicated to Christ and His teachings. We are to be imitators of Christ in all of our being, and by the grace of God, we have been predestined "to be conformed to the image of his Son, that he might be the firstborn among many brethren" (Romans 8:29).

Jesus is the suffering servant prophesized in Isaiah 53, and we as His servants will be persecuted and maligned for His glory. If they called Christ Beelzebub,[54] how much more will we as His servants be falsely accused and denigrated if we are viewed as servants of the lord of the dunghill?

In John 15:20, Jesus had told them, "Remember the word that I said unto you, The servant is not greater than his lord. If they have persecuted me, they will also persecute you …" First Peter 4:12–13 further tells us,

> Beloved, think it not strange concerning the fiery trial which is to try you, as though some strange thing happened unto you: But rejoice, inasmuch as ye are partakers of Christ's sufferings; that, when his glory shall be revealed, ye may be glad also with exceeding joy.

John Calvin more bluntly said it like this: "Be bold and courageous, that [we] may be always ready for martyrdom."

---

[54] R. C. Sproul, *St. Andrew's Expositional Commentary on Matthew* (Wheaton, IL, Crossway, 2013), and John Calvin's commentaries (https://www.studylight.org/commentaries/cal.html) said that one translation for Beelzebub, the Philistine god worshipped in Ekron, was "Lord of the Flies," and another was "Lord of the Dung Heap." These terms were often used by Jews who applied them to Satan as an insult.

Dennis Cornish

VERSES 26–33 (HCSB)

> Therefore, don't be afraid of them, since there is nothing covered that won't be uncovered and nothing hidden that won't be made known. What I tell you in the dark, speak in the light. What you hear in a whisper, proclaim on the housetops. Don't fear those who kill the body but are not able to kill the soul; rather, fear Him who is able to destroy both soul and body in hell. Aren't two sparrows sold for a penny? Yet not one of them falls to the ground without your Father's consent. But even the hairs of your head have all been counted. So don't be afraid, therefore; you are worth more than many sparrows. Therefore, everyone who will acknowledge Me before men, I will also acknowledge him before My Father in heaven. But whoever denies Me before men, I will also deny him before My Father in heaven.

Jesus in His humanity was of aware of the nature of fear that the apostles might be struggling with as they prepared to be sent out to preach the gospel. In these verses, He continues to give them the encouragement that they need to follow through with His commands.

Those who would persecute the apostles are not to be feared as fear is a tactic of Satan to keep us from boldly speaking His truth. None of the evil works of those who would persecute them would be hidden or not known to Him who sees and judges all, and there will be a day of reckoning when every act of the wicked will be revealed.

Jesus taught His disciples both publicly and in private. In Christ's day, most of the houses had flat roofs and served as patios of sorts, and they were often used proclaim the latest news. This is the meaning of Jesus's instructions to announce the good news of the gospel on the housetops. What has been revealed to them in secret is what they must now proclaim to everyone they are sent to preach to. Not everyone who hears the message that they preach will understand or accept it, but it is imperative that God's Word be openly preached.

God plainly tells them that in awe and reverence, it is He who is to be feared. And we should remember that Psalm 111:10 teaches, "The fear of the LORD is the beginning of wisdom …" He alone can destroy both the body and the soul, and those who would persecute you can only harm the body. Although we walk through the valley of the shadow of death, we should fear no evil, and we are never to deny our Lord. "Though we may face opposition and persecution now, we know that in the end all will be set right, and the servants of Christ will be vindicated."[55] We are to lean on His strength as we proclaim His glory. Jesus goes on to say that they should not fear because God cares for every sparrow and that not one falls without His knowledge. Because we are made in His image and have been adopted as coheirs with Christ, we are much more valuable to Him than the sparrows. He even knows the number of hairs on our head; therefore, we should not fear but have every confidence that He is watching over us and reigns fully over even the most minute detail. He is sovereign, and His divine providence is at work in even the most insignificant events within the universe.

Having just told His apostles that any fear they have should be a fear of God, the One who is sovereign over all, and just before they set out on their mission, He continues to encourage them by telling them that everyone who acknowledges Him before men, those who testify to His gospel message and deity, He in turn would testify and acknowledge before His Father in heaven. Conversely, those who deny Him before men, He will deny before His Father.

John Calvin tells us that,

> confession of Christ, though it is regarded by the greater part of men as a trifling matter, is here represented to be a main part of divine worship, and a distinguished exercise of godliness.

---

[55] *Tabletalk Magazine* (Sanford, FL, Ligonier Ministries, Inc., April 29, 2008).

On the other hand, the ungodly, those who would deny Christ, are faced with the eternal consequence of their refusal to acknowledge Jesus as their Lord and Savior. They will suffer a far worse fate than the persecution they attempted to avoid through their denial.

In his commentary, John MacArthur clarifies this denial by saying,

> This describes a soul-damning denial of Christ—not the sort of temporary wavering Peter was guilty of—but the sin of those who through fear, shame, neglect, delay, or love of this world reject all evidence and revelation and decline to confess Christ as Savior and King, until it is too late.

The apostles can take courage and have faith in Jesus's words, not only for themselves but for those who positively responded to the message that they would be preaching. Jesus's promise doesn't end with those He was speaking to. They are extended to His faithful followers throughout the history of the world. Therefore, we too are to proclaim Jesus through our open profession of faith and in how we live it out in our daily lives.

Charles Spurgeon made the following comment on these verses:

> What Christ is to you on earth, that you will be to Christ in heaven. I shall repeat that truth. Whatever Jesus Christ is to you on earth, you will be to him in the day of judgment. If he be dear and precious to you, you will be precious and dear to him. If you thought everything of him, he will think everything of you.

VERSES 34–39 (NIV)

> "Do not suppose that I have come to bring peace to the earth. I did not come to bring peace, but a sword. For I have come to turn a man against his father, a daughter against her mother, a daughter-in-law against her mother-in-law—a man's enemies will be the members of his own

household. Anyone who loves their father or mother more than me is not worthy of me; anyone who loves their son or daughter more than me is not worthy of me. Whoever does not take up their cross and follow me is not worthy of me. Whoever finds their life will lose it, and whoever loses their life for my sake will find it."

The message of Jesus—as reflected in the Sermon on the Mount—is indeed a message of peace. Yet since it calls the individual to a radical commitment to Jesus Himself, it is a message of peace that *divides* between those who choose it and those who reject it. The division between these two choices explains how Jesus did not come to bring peace but a sword.[56]

Jesus uses the metaphor of a sword to highlight the inevitable separation between those who believe and those who do not. Quoting from the Old Testament (Micah 7:6), Jesus makes plain that the potential for division is so deep that it even crosses over and severs family ties, setting them at odds with one another as one accepts Jesus and another one rejects Him. Each of us will stand before our Creator as individuals to answer for the way that we have conducted our lives. Our individual destiny is in God's providence and goes beyond familial ties that will no longer be binding from an eternal perspective. Our Creator predestined each individual, either as one of the elect or for reprobation, and our allegiance and first love should be to our heavenly Father, who first loved us. Jesus clearly states that our worthiness depends upon our absolute and unconditional love for Him above all else.

Jesus goes on to tell them that in obedience they must take up their cross and follow Him. This image of their taking up their own cross must have been horrifying as the cross meant certain death. That was the point. Jesus demands that we die to ourselves as we embrace God's will, but at the same time, He promises each of us as believers a resurrected life. His words of reassurance were that "he that loseth his life for my sake shall find it." The

---

[56] www.blueletterbible.org study notes on Matthew 10 by David Guzik.

disciples must be unwavering in their commitment and unwavering in their message to those they would be preaching to.

VERSES 40–42

The apostles go out with the full authority of Jesus, and anyone who receives them, receives Christ and by extension receives God the Father, the One who sent Jesus to humble Himself as a man. We are to receive both a prophet and a righteous person because in their obedience they are representative of Christ, and our reception of them is in the sincere hospitality we show them, even to the seemingly insignificant offering of a cold cup of water.

Hebrews 13:2 tells us, "Be not forgetful to entertain strangers: for thereby some have entertained angels unawares." In context, Hebrews is talking about the continuation of brotherly love. That is why it is included here, as when we show this brotherly love through our hospitality, and within the essence of purity, Jesus tells us that the spiritual reward for our actions will not be lost.

CHAPTER 11

JOHN THE BAPTIST, WOES TO UNREPENTANT CITIES, REST

VERSES 1–3

After He commanded the twelve, He parted ways with them and went into the cities of Galilee to continue His mission of teaching and preaching while they were free to go elsewhere to complete the commission that He had given them.

Here we are told that while he was imprisoned, John heard about all the miraculous deeds that Jesus was performing and sent some of his disciples to ask if Jesus was the one who was to come or whether they should look for another. There are differing opinions on the reasons for John's questions. It is to be remembered that John had proclaimed that Jesus was the Lamb of God and the Savior of the world and he had said,

> I am not the Christ, but that I am sent before him. He that hath the bride is the bridegroom: but the friend of the bridegroom, which standeth and heareth him, rejoiceth

greatly because of the bridegroom's voice: this my joy therefore is fulfilled. He must increase, but I must decrease (John 3:28–30).

John clearly recognized Jesus as the Messiah, and it is for these reasons it is believed that John's sending of his disciples was a way of focusing their attention and devotions on Jesus and away from himself as his time was quickly fading.

There are others who contend that John's trial and long imprisonment in the dungeons of Herod Antipas had weakened him to the point of confusion regarding the distinction between the prophet promised to Moses in Deuteronomy 18:15 and the Messiah. This confusion would have been heightened when viewed in conjunction with the prevailing Jewish expectation of a coming Messiah who would use His power to overthrow the tyranny of the Roman empire and establish the kingdom of God in its place. This vision of the Messiah's coming would have included bringing blessings to those who in repentance followed the Christ, while bringing crushing display of judgment against those who did not. John had proclaimed of Christ, "Whose winnowing fan is in his hand, and he will thoroughly purge his floor, and gather his wheat into the barn; but he will burn up the chaff with unquenchable fire" (Matthew 3:12). Although his proclamation points to an eschatological fulfillment, this future implication, along with John's continued incarceration, didn't seem to fit his current concept or expectations for Jesus's ministry.

VERSES 4–6

Jesus with grace and compassion sends John's disciples back with the blessed assurance of the good news of the gospel that is being preached along with eyewitness accounts of the signs and wonders that are performed, demonstrating the fulfillment of Isaiah 35:5–6 as a witness to His deity. These words of encouragement would bolster John's faith during his time of persecution.

It is notable that Jesus did not include verse 35:4 when He quoted Isaiah, a verse which predicts the vengeance of God. There will be a final Day of Judgment and vengeance will come, but for now Jesus's power was not to be wielded against a form of worldly government but to highlight the kingdom of God that was with them in the very present moment as it was being made manifest in God's unfolding plan for His earthly ministry. Jesus concludes His message for John with the words "Blessed is he, whosoever shall not be offended in me." Jesus bestowed a blessing on all who believed in Him and the mission that the Father had sent Him on. He knew that there were expectations of Him by the masses that were not being met, but He was obedient to God the Father's plans for His incarnation and ultimately the eternal salvation of those who believed.

Charles Spurgeon's comment was this:

> Blessed is he who can be left in prison, can be silenced in his testimony, can seem to be deserted of his Lord, and yet can shut out every doubt. John speedily regained this blessedness, and fully recovered his serenity.

VERSES 7–15

As the apostles were heading out on their way to their mission fields, Jesus addressed the crowd and inquired of them about John the Baptist and their expectations of him. He questioned their motive for going out into the wilderness to see him. Why did they go, and what did they go to see? Were they looking for a doctrine that swayed like a reed growing alongside the Jordan River, a doctrine that moved back and forth to maintain relevance to some societal condition based upon the whims of men? No, they were looking for a faithful preacher and a true prophet of God.

He then told them that John was indeed a prophet but that he was more than a prophet in that John had the distinction of being the herald of the Messiah who was now among them. Jesus tells them that it was John who was spoken of in Isaiah 40:3 and Malachi 3:1 as the messenger sent out before Christ to prepare the way for Him. Jesus then says that of all those who have been born of women, which was a Jewish idiom for an ordinary birth, there has not risen one greater than John the Baptist. This must have captivated the attention of those in the crowd who saw Abraham as their spiritual father, not to mention the other great prophets, such as Isaac, Jacob, Joseph, David, Isaiah, and a host of other Old Testament prophets who were highly revered.

Jesus goes on to tell them that although this is true, he who is least in the kingdom of heaven, having been born of the spirit and regenerated, is greater than John. Jesus says this because John was the last of the Old Testament prophets and had not been born again under the new covenant because he had lived and died prior to the fulfillment of Jesus's own mission, which led Him to the cross, the resurrection, and His ascension.

John Calvin says the new covenant minister's preaching is greater than John the Baptist's because

> it holds out Christ as having rendered complete and eternal satisfaction by his one sacrifice, as the conqueror of death and the Lord of life, and because it withdraws the veil, and elevates believers to the heavenly sanctuary.

Jesus then speaks of the spiritual warfare that surrounds His earthly ministry and describes it as a time of increasingly intense violence, which included all types of wickedness along with demonic forces and possessions. He follows this with a statement about the kingdom of heaven, "and the violent take it by force", which many see as including the religious establishment of Israel and those such as Herod who had arrested and eventually executed John the Baptist.

The same intensity brought against the kingdom of heaven must be met and exceeded by those who would see the kingdom of heaven eminently glorified in the name of Jesus. There were, and still need to be, men and women who will stand in the gap, even to the point of martyrdom, for the sake of the gospel truth. With complete dependence upon the boundless strength of Christ, His followers must persevere in a concerted effort to fight for the kingdom under His banner until He, in the fullness of time, finally throws Satan into the lake of fire. To God alone goes the victory.

Jesus tells of all the prophets of the law who prophesized of the coming Messiah before John, who came to herald the fulfillment of their prophecies. One such prophecy was that before the advent of the Messiah, Elijah would come and restore all things. And in this verse, Jesus says, "And if ye will receive it, this is Elias, which was for to come." John had come in the spirit and the power of Elijah, just as the angel of the Lord had told Zechariah in Luke 1. Jesus will teach more on this in Matthew 17, but before leaving this subject, He proclaims, "He that hath ears to hear, let him hear." These words signified the importance of what Jesus was saying and the elect, those graced with spiritual discernment, would come to an understanding of what He was saying.

VERSES 16–19

Jesus rhetorically asks how He should compare this generation, and the generation that Jesus speaks of is those who comprise the crowds and the religious leaders who have rejected both John and Christ's teachings. They are the children who stubbornly default to their own way of thinking about and interpreting scripture. They have rejected Jesus and John because what they preach does not conform to tradition. Some had criticized John for his indicting message of repentance, his appearance, and his ascetic lifestyle, while others condemned Jesus for His loving association with those on the outer fringe of society, sinners in need of a Savior, as well as His refusal to fast in a way that was acceptable to them, all the while calling Him a drunkard and a glutton. Their hearts were hardened to God's Word, and they were never satisfied with one condition or the other. They were always ready to criticize and find fault, never taking a high view of or being at peace with either Jesus's or John's methods or their message.

John MacArthur's commentary explains it this way:

> Christ used strong derision to rebuke the Pharisees. He suggested they were behaving childishly, determined not to be pleased, whether invited to "dance" (a reference to Christ's joyous style of ministry, eating and drinking with sinners), or urged to "weep" (a reference to John the

Baptist's call to repentance and more austere manner of ministry).

Jesus tells them that wisdom is justified by its children. It is through their wise actions (his children) that they are justified. The outcome of one's actions, their consequence, if you will, demonstrates the thoughtfulness of that course of action. The holiness that was clearly seen in Jesus's and John's lives and their teachings were manifest evidence of their abundantly righteous wisdom.

VERSES 20–24

Jesus then began to denounce the cities where most of his mighty works were done, because they continued in their unrepentance. He pronounced a woe on both Chorazin and Bethsaida! He proclaimed that if the mighty works that they had witnessed had been done in Tyre and Sidon, those cities would have repented long ago in sackcloth and ashes. He tells them that on the Day of Judgment, it will be more tolerable for Tyre and Sidon than for them. And Capernaum, which had been highly exalted, will be brought down to hell because had the mighty works performed in Capernaum been done in Sodom, it would have remained until this day. "But I say that on the Day of Judgment, it will be more tolerable for the land of Sodom than for you."

Luke 12:48 tells us that "whomsoever much is given, of him shall be much required." The Galilean towns who had witnessed Jesus's miracles and heard Him preach had received a much fuller revelation of the Messiah than had the Old Testament cities Jesus had named and therefore were more culpable in their unrepentant sin. Matthew Henry said, "The stronger inducements we have to repent, the more heinous is the unrepentance and the severer will the reckoning be."[57]

In these passages, Jesus begins to rebuke and to denounce those cities in which most of His miracles had been performed. These miracles were not done because those who benefited from them were entitled to receive them.

---

[57] *Tabletalk Magazine* (Sanford, FL, Ligonier Ministries, Inc., May 6, 2008).

They were done out of God's grace, mercy, and compassion, as well as for a greater reason, as a sign of the Christ being in their presence. These cities had seen the light and glory of God's mercy and love firsthand through the works of Jesus, yet as a whole, they remained indifferent to the gospel message and unrepentant. To those who had ears, this was a wakeup call as Jesus points to specific cities that had been destroyed when God's wrath had fallen, yet in the final Day of Judgment, those cities would fare better than the cities Jesus was now rebuking. Jesus declares that Sodom's punishment will be more tolerable than those that these cities can expect, and this is indicative of various levels or degrees of punishment being meted out to the reprobate who suffer eternal punishment in hell.

An interesting aside is that two of the cities mentioned, Chorazin and Bethsaida, are rarely mentioned in the Bible at all. Chorazin is mentioned twice in the New Testament, once in this verse and again in a parallel verse in Luke 10:13. Bethsaida is mentioned several times as the city of Philip, Andrew, and Peter; again where Jesus healed a blind man; and finally as a destination on the other side of the Sea of Galilee at the time when the apostles encountered a violent storm and Jesus came to them walking on the water.

Apart from the blind man being healed outside the village of Bethsaida, there is no mention of the miracles that He performed in these two cities, miracles which He describes as "the miracles that were done in you." Yet Jesus declares that there were mighty works performed in those cities. This is a proof text of what was written in John 21:25, where we read,

> And there are also many other things which Jesus did, the which, if they should be written every one, I suppose that even the world itself could not contain the books that should be written. Amen.

VERSES 25–27

Jesus now thanks His Father in heaven that He has kept the mission and message of the kingdom of heaven from those who are unrepentant and who would seem wise in the eyes of men, but in His sovereignty, He has revealed them to those who are His children, those who the world would see as unlikely candidates for God's wisdom. In 1 Corinthians 1:27, we are told that "God hath chosen the foolish things of the world to confound the wise; and God hath chosen the weak things of the world to confound the things which are mighty." Jesus tells us that it is but by the grace and good pleasure of God that He has revealed to His followers the things of God, the truth of His earthly ministry, and His being Messiah.

Jesus goes on to say that no one truly knows God the Father, except He Himself and to an infinitesimal degree those He has chosen to reveal God's will to. God the Father and God the Son are of the same essence, and in that, they are wholly unified in their omniscience. We, however, can only know God through what He has revealed in scripture and through our knowledge of Christ and what He has revealed to us through our relationship with Him. It is only by way of Christ that those who are called can come to know our Father in heaven. Upon Christ's ascension to the right hand of God's throne, God has delegated to Him all power and authority over heaven and on earth. Jesus reigns supreme, and divine will is His to execute and to judge. Therefore, it is only through the imputed righteousness of Christ and His advocacy that we can be declared righteous in God's eyes.

VERSES 28–30

This is a personal invitation from God to come to Him. It is an invitation to those who feel the burden of life pressing in on them and recognize that nothing that they, or anyone else, can do to alleviate their situation. One commentator viewed labor as the burdens we place upon ourselves whereas *heavy laden* implies the burdens others put upon us. In both cases, we feel the weight of these burdens squarely upon our shoulders with no way of relief to be found. On our own, the weight is unbearable, but Jesus promises to that He will bear it with us, making it easy and light. The Greek word used for "easy" *(chrestos)* in the context of His yoke has the meaning of being well fit or suited for the burden, and because of this making it manageable, and it is the very point that Jesus makes when He promises that He will give us rest.

The Reformation Study Bible says that a yoke symbolizes submission and slavery and that Jewish sources spoke of the yoke of the law and of wisdom. And although the law was a good gift from God to His people, the scribes and the spiritual depravity of sinful humanity turned the law into an unbearable burden. Whereas following Jesus is a demanding discipleship, it is made easy by His gentle nature and the fact the He has fulfilled the laws righteous demands perfectly, therefore easing the burden of His followers.

> The ancient Jews commonly used the idea of yoke to express someone's obligation to God. There was the yoke of the kingdom, the yoke of the law, the yoke of the command, the yoke of repentance, the yoke of faith, and the general yoke of God. In this context, it is easy to see Jesus simplifying [*it all*] and saying, "Forget about all those other yokes. Take My yoke upon you and learn from Me."[58]

To take His yoke upon ourselves, we must also give ourselves to Him, become His disciples, repent of our sin, and release our burdens to Him. Jesus tells us of His servant's heart and that He is the only one who is able and willing to carry our burden upon His own shoulders in just the same way that He has taken our sin upon Himself as our Savior when He died upon the cross so that we might have everlasting life. This is the rest for our souls that He speaks of.

> John Calvin writes that Christ does not elect us and redeem us that we may sin freely. Instead, Christians are "raised up by his grace, [that] they may also take his yoke upon them, and that, being free in spirit, they may restrain the licentiousness of their flesh." We put on the light and easy yoke of Jesus's commandments when we trust Him, and we move from being slaves to sin to being slaves of Christ.[59]

---

[58] Adam Clarke as cited from www.blueletterbible.org study notes on Matthew 11 by David Guzik.
[59] *Tabletalk Magazine* (Sanford, FL, Ligonier Ministries, Inc., May 7, 2008).

CHAPTER 12

LORD OF THE SABBATH, BLASPHEMY, JESUS'S FAMILY

VERSES 1–2

It was the Sabbath day. Jesus and His disciples were passing through a grain field, and His disciples were hungry. They began to pluck the heads of grain and to eat. The Pharisees saw it and said to Him that His disciples were doing what was unlawful on the Sabbath.

The various fields of crops surrounding the cities often had paths and roads that ran through them, and there was an expectation that those who traveled those paths would glean from those fields. This was done without guilt or any thought of it being theft as the farmers, in obedience to scripture (Leviticus 19:9; Deuteronomy 23:25), left produce or grain for the explicit purpose of helping to feed travelers and the poor.

The Pharisees were not concerned with what Jesus's disciples were doing but that they were doing it on the Sabbath. Jesus had just taught about the burdens laid upon the people's shoulders by tradition, and now we see some of those traditions being played out as the Pharisees became incensed about Christ's disciples having broken the laws that they had imposed, laws which had become so subtly ingrained into the daily life of Jewish society that many actually usurped scripture. In the text we are looking at, the Pharisees viewed what the disciples were doing as breaking several of the laws on their self-ascribed "thou shalt not" lists. "The Pharisees saw them as being guilty of reaping, threshing, winnowing, and preparing food on the Sabbath."[60] What they didn't see was the need for hungry men to nourish themselves as they traveled to their destination.

In John MacArthur's commentary, he states,

> Actually no law prohibited the plucking of grain in order to eat on the Sabbath. The law permitted a person to glean handfuls of grain from a neighbor's field to satisfy his immediate hunger (Deuteronomy 23:25). It prohibited only labor for the sake of profit. Thus, a farmer could not harvest for profit on the Sabbath, but an individual could glean enough grain to eat.

The Reformation Study Bible footnotes echo MacArthur's comments and further state that the Pharisees' objections are based upon oral tradition that misinterprets, obscures, and counters the true purpose of God's law as found in scripture.

Another interesting aspect is how the Pharisees would view what they were doing in consideration of their own law about travel on the Sabbath. We are not told of the exact distance of these fields from Jerusalem, but Jewish law only allowed them to travel the distance of a "Sabbath's journey," which equated to the distance between the Mount of Olives and Jerusalem, which was about five furlongs or 0.625 miles. It may well be likely that going out to observe Jesus and His disciples and then returning to the temple would have been in excess of a lawful distance. Charles Spurgeon further comments on the Pharisees' own guilt when he said,

---

[60] Paraphrased from www.blueletterbible.org study notes on Matthew 12 by David Guzik.

The Pharisees here seem hard at work supervising and accusing the disciples. This was a greater violation of the Sabbath. Did they not break the Sabbath by setting a watch over them?

VERSES 3–8

Jesus points them back to when David went into the tabernacle and ate of the twelve loaves that were consecrated each Sabbath, bread that was only to be eaten by the priests (Leviticus 24:5–9). He and his men were weakened from hunger and desperately in need of sustenance, so they ate the showbread yet were not condemned in scripture. Charles Spurgeon tell us,

> To have eaten the holy bread out of profanity, or bravado, or levity, might have involved the offender in the judgment of death; but to do so in urgent need was not blameworthy in the case of David.

Jesus further points to the law and that although the priests profane the letter of the law each Sabbath as they carry out the temple duties while they work at the slaughter and presentation of the animal sacrifices, they are found guiltless based upon allowances in the law. Jesus is reminding them that the intent of Sabbath was to bring rest and well-being. It was never meant to become a yoke of bondage. In Luke 6:9, Jesus reiterates this often repeated theme on what one can rightfully do on the Sabbath when He questions, "I will ask you one thing; Is it lawful on the sabbath days to do good, or to do evil? to save life, or to destroy it?" John MacArthur had this to say,

> The Sabbath laws forbade labor for profit, frivolous diversions, and things extraneous to worship. Activity per se was not unlawful. Good works were especially appropriate on the Sabbath—particularly deeds of charity, mercy, and worship. Works necessary for the preservation of life were also permitted. To corrupt the Sabbath to forbid such works was a perversion of God's design.

Jesus then quotes from Hosea 6:6 to emphasize to them the greater good of mercy over the ceremonial regulation of sacrifice and the knowledge of God over burnt offerings. He was putting an order and a priority to the values and traditions that they held so tenaciously to. "In Christ we know that mercy and justice, biblically defined, must guide how we apply the letter of the Law."[61] As a result of their lack of a full understanding of the scriptures and their subsequent denial of Jesus as Messiah, they unknowingly condemn themselves.

In declaring that something greater than the temple was present, Jesus clearly points to His deity. It has been said that at the time of this incident, the ark of the covenant was not present in the temple. If it had been there, it would have been viewed as a sign of God's presence, yet in their blindness, they didn't see the supremacy of God the Son, the Son of Man, who stood before them as the rightful Lord of the Sabbath. Jesus is Immanuel, "God with us," and He is greater than the temple that had been built as God's dwelling place. Jesus being the living Temple and the very presence of God among them was the reason that John wrote that "the Word was made flesh, and dwelt among us, and we beheld his glory ..." (John 1:14).

VERSES 9–14

Matthew has begun to relay the increasingly hostile environment that surrounded both Him and His disciples. Despite the opposition that He faced, Jesus continued to faithfully attend synagogue, and in this passage, He was again asked probing questions. These questions were not being asked to further their knowledge of God and His will; they were asking questions geared toward their being able to further accuse Him.

Jesus often heals those who come to Him on the Sabbath, and on this day, there was a man present with a withered hand. Those in the synagogue disingenuously asked Him if it is lawful to heal on the Sabbath. They were acutely aware of Jesus's healing ministry, as well as His compassion toward those who needed that healing.

---

[61] *Tabletalk Magazine* (Sanford, FL, Ligonier Ministries, Inc., May 8, 2008).

The Pharisees remained deeply entrenched in tradition, and although there is no Old Testament text that prohibits healing on the Sabbath, they looked to the legalistic prohibitions found in the Mishnah[62] and were under the opinion that their Sabbath law could only be broken in extreme cases of life and death. They viewed this man's condition as one that could be healed on any other day but the Sabbath. Paraphrasing the Reformation Study Bible's footnotes, when rules designed to cover every possible instance of work (in this case a healing) are exalted above God's gracious intent, the Sabbath is changed from a delight into a burden.

Jesus's reply begins with a rhetorical question about their flocks, and particularly if one of their sheep fell into a pit on the Sabbath. He asks if there were a man among them who would not rescue that sheep from the pit, even on the Sabbath. Jesus goes on to point out the greater value of a man over a sheep and with authority affirms that "it is lawful to do well on the sabbath days." After having declared it was lawful to heal on the Sabbath, Jesus directed His attention to the man and commanded him to stretch out his hand. Prior to Jesus's command, this action was an impossibility for this man, but not only did Jesus command the man, He also, through divine directive, gave the man the ability to obey.

Luke 6:11 tells us that the Pharisees "were filled with madness," their hearts remained hardened against the Christ, and they, in their own grievous sinfulness, left the synagogue with murderous intent and began to plot against Jesus.

VERSES 15–21

Jesus, in His awareness of their plan, withdrew from that area, not out of fear of reprisal but for the same reason that He continually told those that He healed not to tell everyone about their healing. He withdrew out of His respect for the fulness of the Father's timing in all that must transpire before the completion of His earthly ministry. His requiring their

---

[62] The Mishnah is an authoritative collection of exegetical material embodying the oral tradition of Jewish law and forming the first part of the Talmud. The Talmud is a body of Jewish civil and ceremonial law and legend.

silence and their suppression of their joy and amazement at these healings came about because as His ministry grew, so did the crowds, and in these verses, we are told that great multitudes followed Him wherever He went. Scripture also tells us that He healed them all. We are not told how many, but we can infer from the large throngs of people and their desire for healing for themselves or others that there were many persons who benefited from His healing ministry. As was His habit, He admonished those He healed not to tell others about it, and this admonishment had a twofold purpose; the first that His healing ministry might not eclipse His teaching ministry; the second, as mentioned above, was that He didn't want to generate a notoriety that went beyond what was prudent so that the Roman army might not see Him as a threat because of His great number of followers and the fact that He was known as the King of the Jews.

In His quoting Isaiah 42:1–5, Jesus again points to His true essence as the second person of the Triune Godhead. God the Father commands that we focus our attention on Him, the suffering servant He has anointed with the Holy Spirit, the One in whom He is well pleased. "Jesus would not be a servant in the ordinary meaning of the word, but He would be by way of eminence as the One to whom God has committed the charge and office of redeeming His church."[63] This prophetic passage definitively shows that the Messiah would not be the political leader and military strategist that the Jewish rabbis had expected. On the contrary, He would be gentle and meek as He declared God's message of righteousness, even to the Gentiles.

Scripture follows with a list of Christ's characteristics in terms that we may not be familiar with and the use of language and examples that we are unaccustomed to. However, they can be easily summed up by saying that Jesus compassionately cares for those who have been abused and trodden underfoot. He is faithful and will not give up on us because of the failures of our weakness. He has a plan for us, plans for welfare and not for evil, to give us a future and a hope (Jerimiah 29:11).

---

[63] Paraphrased from John Calvin's Commentary https://www.studylight.org/commentaries/cal.html.

Isaiah 42:2 (HCSB) says, "He will not cry out or shout or make His voice heard in the streets," which is representative of the fact that Jesus would speak with authority and would be guided by the empowerment of the Holy Spirit. He would not be leading any type of revolt, nor would He force Himself into an earthly position of power. He Himself said that His kingdom was not of this world. This is not to say that Jesus would never raise His voice, especially in defense of a true interpretation of scripture, but it does speak to the way He communicated with those who followed Him, with love and compassion for their plight.

The next characteristic is that of gentleness, where His care of a bruised reed was such that it would not be broken. A reed is a fragile plant, yet if Jesus finds that one of His followers is bruised, He will handle that person with a gentleness and caring that will not break him physically or spiritually but strengthen him through the power of the indwelling Spirit of God.

The smoking flax that He will not quench refers to the flax used as a wick in an oil lamp. If it is smoldering and not burning to produce light, He will not extinguish it but nurture it by fanning it into flame again. Some of us are no longer on fire for the Lord, but He is nurturing us through the process of sanctification, fanning our waning embers until we too ignite to the point that we radiate the light of Christ to those around us, drawing them to His glory.

He finally alludes to His ministry to the Gentiles, many who, to the consternation of the Jewish religious elite, had already come to faith in Him and those who would come to a saving faith after being ministered to by both Peter and Paul.

VERSES 22–24

They brought before Jesus a man possessed with a devil, and who was both blind and dumb, and Jesus healed him. All the people were amazed and questioned among themselves, "Is not this the son of David?" But when the Pharisees heard this, they attributed this miracle not to God's glory.

They said that Jesus cast out demons by the power of Beelzebub, the prince of the devils.

Jesus, in casting out the demon who possessed this man, and by restoring his sight and speech, once again demonstrated His power and authority. These miraculous works were further confirmation of His deity, and this was not lost upon the people. In their amazement of what had just transpired, they questioned among themselves, "Is not this the son of David?" Many, if not most, of the Jewish community, especially their leadership, had every expectation that the Son of David would be a warrior who would come to rescue them from Roman tyranny and not a gentle healer. Yet what they had just witnessed was reflective of the mighty arm of their heavenly Father, and this caused them to question their perception of He who had come. And it began to edge some of them closer to the truth of who Jesus was. Even Nicodemus, one of the Pharisees, on one occasion came to Jesus and said, "Rabbi, we know that thou art a teacher come from God: for no man can do these miracles that thou doest, except God be with him" (John 3:2). Although this is not an outright affirmation of Jesus's deity, it is acknowledgment that the Pharisees knew that Jesus was not of Beelzebub.

The Pharisees could not deny the reality that the demon had been cast out of the possessed man and that he was no longer blind or mute. In the perverseness of their hatred of Jesus and His threat to their traditions and their authority, most of the Pharisees did not see Jesus as the fulfillment of prophecy. Instead of confirmation of His Messiahship through the signs and wonders, they contributed what had happened to sorcery. They further claimed that it was only through Beelzebub that Jesus was able to cast out demons. In a few more verses, Jesus responds to this charge and will teach the crowd that blaspheming the Holy Spirit will not be forgiven. However, in their unquenchable malice and their zealous efforts to destroy Jesus, they attributed to Him a crime that was deemed a capital offense punishable by stoning.

VERSES 25–29

Jesus knew their thoughts, and this knowing can be attributed to His divinity, but it can also be a knowing that was derived from the Spirit of God. We know that after Jesus's baptism He was filled with the Holy Spirit, and in that filling, Jesus would be able to discern and to declare knowledge that could only be revealed supernaturally (1 Corinthians 12:8). In either case, Jesus's knowledge of their thoughts was divinely initiated, and He said to them,

> Every kingdom divided against itself is brought to desolation; and every city or house divided against itself shall not stand: And if Satan cast out Satan, he is divided against himself; how shall then his kingdom stand? (Matthew 12:25)

Jesus demonstrated how illogical the Pharisees' claim was and that what they said about Him made absolutely no sense. Jesus was pointing out that there would be no beneficial advantage for Satan in Christ having cast out this demon. Charles Spurgeon said, "Envy causes persons often to condemn in one, what they approve in another."

He goes on to say if they presumed that the Pharisees' claim was true, then by what means do the Jewish exorcists use to cast out demons? The Jewish historian Josephus, in his writings *(Jewish Antiquities)*, tells of various rituals that were used to cast out demons, but the ESV Study Bible notes say that it is unclear as to how successful they were.

Jesus continues to refute the Pharisees' statement and further stated, "But if I cast out devils by the Spirit of God, then the kingdom of God is come unto you" (Matthew 12:28). And in response to this verse, Spurgeon further says, "Though our Lord had power all his own, he honored the Spirit of God, and worked by his energy, and mentioned the fact that he did so."

Jesus continues to show the foolishness of the Pharisees' claim by using the analogy of binding a strong man before being able to steal anything from his house. Satan is the strong man, and his house is representative of the world, and within Jewish apocalyptic literature the binding of Satan is a symbol of the Messianic age.[64] Satan and his demons are no match against Jesus's power and authority. Jesus, by the power of His Word, has bound Satan and robbed him by plundering Satan's goods. And in this situation, it was the rescue and healing of the very soul of this demon-possessed and physically impaired man.

VERSES 30–32

In no uncertain terms, Jesus draws a line in the sand; you are either with Him or you are against Him. There is no middle ground; there is no neutrality. Being with Him constitutes much more than a passive awareness of Him. You must actively be about your Father's business; if you aren't gathering God's people, you are scattering them. It is through your obedience to the new commandment that you love one another just as He has loved you. You can find the strength to uncompromisingly witness with your own testimony to those who need Christ. Because He loved us so much that He gave His life for our sin, can we not give of our time and money so that we might gather others to Christ?

He again speaks of sin and of blasphemy, telling us that every instance of it, except for blasphemy against the Holy Spirit, can be forgiven. He goes on to say that even blasphemy against Him, the Son of Man, will be forgiven when the Spirit grants repentance, but if it is uttered against the Holy Spirit, it will never be forgiven.

Because this provokes a serious question about eternal security, there has always been a grave concern that has been voiced by many Christians that they may have committed such a blasphemy, but we must remember that God in His preserving grace will restrain His elect from ever committing such a sin. If there are Christians who are fearful that they may have committed this sin, it is probably a good indication that they haven't. Those

---

[64] A portion of this sentence is paraphrased from the footnotes found in *The Reformation Study Bible* (Sanford, FL, Reformation Trust, 2018) 1692.

who would actually commit such a sin would possess a hardened heart and would think nothing of any type of sin let alone feel any remorse for it.

True blasphemy against the Holy Spirit is more than just the formalization and the speaking of words. It is a settled disposition in one's life that through the hardness of one's own heart one continues to reject the truth despite one's personal awareness of the faithful testimony of the Holy Spirit regarding Jesus and His ministry. It comprises a total denial of the truth that the Holy Spirit proclaims that Jesus is our Lord and Master, the second person of the Trinity, and the propitiation for the elect. *The Westminster Dictionary of Theological Terms* defines sin against the Holy Spirit, also called the unforgiveable sin, as having been understood as the ultimate rejection of the truth of salvation that the Spirit conveys.

In the verses just prior to this section, the Pharisees attribute to Satan what has been accomplished by the power of God, and they did this through flagrant, willful, and persistent rejection of God and His commandments. R. C. Sproul in his commentary tells us that the Pharisees

> had no excuse for missing the appearance of the Son of God. The scriptures plainly taught about what the Messiah would do, and there was Jesus performing miracle after miracle right in front of their eyes. How could they miss it? They did not want God in their thinking. Their minds were blinded by their bias against Jesus, and so they lost themselves in willful ignorance.

Taking in the whole counsel of God, we must also consider what the author of Hebrews had to say when he wrote,

> If we deliberately keep on sinning after we have received the knowledge of the truth, no sacrifice for sins is left, but only a fearful expectation of judgment and of raging fire that will consume the enemies of God. Anyone who rejected the law of Moses died without mercy on the testimony of two or three witnesses. How much more severely do you think someone deserves to be punished

who has trampled the Son of God underfoot, who has treated as an unholy thing the blood of the covenant that sanctified them, and who has insulted the Spirit of grace? (Hebrews 10:26–29 NIV)

Yet by God's mercy and grace, we know that Jesus prayed from the cross, "Father, forgive them, for they know not what they do" (Luke 23:34). When we read of Jesus's compassion for those who had crucified Him, we can only wonder and say amen to what Paul wrote in Romans 11:33. "O the depth of the riches both of the wisdom and knowledge of God! how unsearchable are his judgments, and his ways past finding out!"

VERSES 33–37

Jesus begins to speak about good and corrupt trees and that each will produce the type of fruit that is marked by the type of tree it is—good from good and corrupt from corrupt. He calls the Pharisees a brood of vipers and says that they, being evil, cannot speak of good things. This is because the pattern of our speech is a matter of what lies within our hearts, and what is spoken of idly will be accounted for on the Day of Judgment.

Jesus had moved seamlessly from His warning about the unforgivable sin to a warning about speaking careless words. The Pharisees, in the pride of their arrogance, may have thought that all that they spoke was both true and harmless rather than the woeful evidence of their own spiritual state.

The words that came out of the Pharisees' mouths were disingenuous and were derived from the bad fruit that was produced by the evil root that grew in their hearts. Without a new heart, slanderous malcontent and blasphemous words would continue to flow from their mouths in opposition to the person and work of Christ. Jesus calls them a brood of vipers and tells them that they cannot speak of good because they themselves are evil. Out of the abundance of the good or the bad treasure that is stored in one's heart, there is an outpouring of a like treasure. Out of the healthy heart comes good, and out of a diseased and sinful heart comes evil. John MacArthur's commentary says that "God judges a person by his words, because they reveal the state of his heart."

Scripture tells us that at the coming judgment, in the last days, every idle word will be accounted for. The Greek for the term "idle word" has the meaning of a word that does not minister grace, instruction, or edification to those who hear it. It is not a good word but a word that is trivial. The good words toward Christ will be judged as righteous, and those whose speech is meaningless or evil will be condemned for the sin that is evidenced by their words by which they are storing up wrath for themselves on the day of wrath when God's righteous judgment will be revealed (paraphrase of Romans 2:5).

James 3:6 reminds us,

> And the tongue is a fire, a world of iniquity so is the tongue among our members, that it defileth the whole body, and setteth on fire the course of nature; and it is set on fire of hell.

In Romans 10:8–9, Paul teaches us,

> The word is nigh thee, even in thy mouth, and in thy heart: that is, the word of faith, which we preach; That if thou shalt confess with thy mouth the Lord Jesus, and shalt believe in thine heart that God hath raised him from the dead, thou shalt be saved.

What these verses highlight is that saving faith constitutes a profession of faith as well as the use of words that emanate out of the good treasure of our hearts and reveal our affection for Christ as well as our love for the things of God. We must continue to guard against the idea that anything we do or say is a work of our own that merits God's mercy, and we are to remain humble in the knowledge that we are only saved by His grace.

There is no middle ground. You are either standing solidly with Jesus or you are against Him. And in Revelation, He tells the church in Laodicea,

> I know thy works, that thou art neither cold nor hot: I would thou wert cold or hot. So then because thou art

lukewarm, and neither cold nor hot, I will spue thee out of my mouth. (3:15–16)

There can be no pretentiousness to righteousness and empty professions will avail nothing so long as a person is double minded, because they must be either good or bad.[65]

VERSES 38–42

Jesus had just cast out a demon from a man, restored his sight, and given him back his ability to speak, and still some of them say that they wanted to see a sign from Him. What were they thinking? How could they witness all the blessings that Jesus had bestowed upon this man and still ask Him for a sign? Jesus and His miraculous works were God's validating sign, but they continued to close their eyes to them. This makes it patently obvious that these men are doing nothing but baiting Jesus. They had seen signs and miracles enough to know in their hearts who Jesus was. It wasn't about what they might see, it was more of a heart issue. No matter what happened in the realm of the miraculous, they would remain blind to the reality of Jesus being Messiah. In their malice, they were looking for something more to criticize Him for.

Jesus condemns them for their spiritually adulterous unbelief and their unfaithfulness to God as they perpetually sought signs. He is emphatic that the only sign they will see was one reminiscent of Jonah telling them that the Son of Man, by contemporary Jewish reckoning, will have been three days and three nights in the heart of the earth and will be resurrected from the dead. In addition, He states that the men of pagan Nineveh who had repented after Jonah's preaching will rise in judgment against this current generation of unbelieving and cynical Jews because Jesus and His kingdom, being greater than Jonah and his message, had arrived. Further, He told them that the queen of the south would testify against this generation at the final judgment because she had traveled from the ends of the earth to see the wisdom of Solomon, yet Jesus, being wisdom

---

[65] Paraphrased from John Calvin's Commentary https://www.studylight.org/commentaries/cal.html.

incarnate and therefore greater than Solomon, stood before their spiritually blind eyes.

> In stating that something greater than both the Ninevites' repentance and King Solomon is present in Israel. Jesus teaches us an important point about Himself (Christology). Jonah and Solomon represent the offices of prophet and king, respectively, and that which is greater is, of course, Christ Jesus and His coming. In short, Jesus is better than all the prophets and kings who came before Him. He is also greater than the priesthood because He is greater than the temple which represents the priestly office. Jesus, then, is clearly presenting Himself as the consummate prophet, priest, and king, a teaching found elsewhere in the New Testament. Knowing the greatness of Christ's threefold office as our prophet, priest, and king helps us to interpret today's passage. The magnificence of Jesus means that there can be no neutral ground once you have seen the working of His power. Either you are for Jesus or you are against Him.[66]

VERSES 43–45

The ongoing discussion and dispute over Jesus having rid a man from demonic possession leads Jesus to use an analogy of an unclean spirit who had gone out of a person to demonstrate the dangerous condition that is created when there is a spiritual vacuum. In this vacuous state, and devoid of the indwelling of God's Spirit, a man subjects himself to even greater evils. In His example, Jesus tells of an unclean spirit who returns to the man after having left him and found him empty because the man had not invited the Holy Spirit to come into his heart. The unclean spirit then summoned seven more to abide with him. In the Jewish tradition, the number seven is the number of completion and one commentator felt that these seven additional unclean spirits signified the thorough fullness

---

[66] *Tabletalk Magazine* (Sanford, FL, Ligonier Ministries, Inc., May 19, 2008).

of demon possession and that now the person's state was worse than it was before. John Calvin says,

> We know that the punishment which is here threatened is addressed to none but those who despise the grace of God, and who, by extinguishing the light of faith, and banishing the desire of godliness, become profane.

This analogy was a means that Jesus used to explain the serious condition of men who have completely rejected Him in the manner that the religious leaders of Israel had. The Reformation Study Bible says,

> Unless God's Spirit takes up residence, a person purged by self-denial becomes vulnerable to re-infestation by graver evils such as pride, hypocrisy, and contempt for others.

John MacArthur puts it this way: "Reform apart from regeneration is never effective and eventually reverts to pre-reformed behavior." And finally, R. C. Sproul's commentary says that this was a stern warning and a forceful call to repentance, and that the Pharisees needed a reformation from above, a conversion, and a new birth.

> Christ is emphasizing once again the necessity of whole-hearted commitment to Himself. It is not enough to experience the good things of the kingdom; repentance and obedience must follow. Life-transforming discipleship must fill the void left by sin and evil. Otherwise, it would be better not to be freed from such slavery at all.[67]

VERSES 46–50

While Jesus was teaching the people, His mother and brothers had come and were outside wanting to speak with Him. Someone in the crowd let Jesus know that they were there.

---

[67] *Tabletalk Magazine* (Sanford, FL, Ligonier Ministries, Inc., May 19, 2008).

Charles Spurgeon states,

> The members of his family had come to take him because they thought him beside himself. No doubt the Pharisees had so represented his ministry to his relatives that they thought they had better restrain him.

And this interpretation can be supported by Mark 3:21, where scripture tells us, "When his friends heard of it, they went out to lay hold on him: for they said, He is beside himself."

Jesus asks, "Who is my mother? And who are my brethren?" He then signifies with an outstretched hand "and said, Behold my mother and my brethren! For whosoever shall do the will of my Father which is in heaven, the same is my brother, and sister, and mother." The disciples, in their obedience, are in sharp contrast to the evil and adulterous generation that Jesus spoke against earlier. We too are His brothers and sisters in Christ and, by the grace of God, in our obedience to our heavenly Father and His precepts, we are coheirs in His kingdom. No matter how important they are to us, or how much we love and cherish our familial relationships, our commitment to Jesus and the supremacy of His ministry must be preeminent.

CHAPTER 13

PARABLES, SOWER, WEEDS, TREASURE, PEARL

VERSES 1–9

On the same day, Jesus went out from the house and sat by the sea as the crowds gathered around Him and sitting was the normal position from which a rabbi taught. It is interesting that Matthew used the plural form of the word *crowd,* which implies that a greater number of people had come than what would ordinarily be considered a crowd. Other Bible versions use the term great *multitudes* to convey the size of the crowd. The pressing number was so large that Jesus got into a boat to sit down while the crowd stood on the beach. A couple of things were in play here. Jesus was able to put some space between Himself and the throng; He was just out of reach of anyone who would want to reach out and touch Him in hopes of drawing out His healing power; and He could take advantage of the natural acoustics that the setting provided.

> Local tradition locates the place of this teaching at what has been named "The Cove of the Parable," a natural horseshoe-shaped amphitheater whose environmental acoustics could have carried Jesus's voice over three

hundred feet from the boat to a crowd of hundreds on the shore.[68]

As was His custom, He began teaching them by use of a parable. A parable is an analogy often in the form of a story based upon common experiences. It is told with the purpose of teaching a greater truth, either moral or spiritual, in a manner that would easily be remembered by those who heard it.

This parable was one clearly related to by the crowd as the examples given were based upon what was a common agrarian event, the sowing of seed, which was done before the seed was plowed into the soil. The practice of sowing was done by hand, with the sower walking through the field scattering seed in front of him using a practiced and methodical swing of his arm from side to side as he dispersed the seed onto the ground. As you recall from our discussion about the Pharisees who were chastising Jesus's disciples for eating grain as they traveled through a field, it was common to have paths going right through a field, and in this case, some of the seed that was being scattered fell along the hardened path and the birds swooped in and ate them where they fell. Jesus goes on to describe the various conditions of the soil. There was rocky ground and ground that had thistles and thorns, conditions that resulted in a lack of harvest. He then tells of the seed that fell on good soil and produced an abundance of grain. The typical yield ranged from fivefold to fifteenfold. A return of a hundredfold would have been extraordinary, and we see in Genesis 26:12 that Isaac had the Lord's blessing of just such a harvest.

For many in the crowd, this was nothing new, and they wondered at the purpose of His teaching. Jesus knew how they would respond, and that is why He concluded the parable with the words "who hath ears to hear, let him hear." This phrase was intended for those in the crowd who were spiritually inclined to hearing the truth behind what was being said, not a general call for those who were present to pay close attention. Without ears to hear, no amount of attentive listening would make what was being said any more perceptible and the teaching behind the parable would

---

[68] ESV Study Bible footnotes (Wheaton, IL, Crossway, 2008) 1847.

remain hidden. John MacArthur says that Jesus's veiling the truth from unbelievers is both an act of judgment and an act of mercy: judgment because it kept them in the darkness that they loved and mercy because they had already rejected the light, so any exposure to more truth would only increase their condemnation.

VERSES 10–17

The disciples question Jesus about His teaching technic, and they ask Him why He speaks to the people in parables. We know from scripture that the disciples sometimes question the meaning of Jesus's parables, and if they, in their close relationship with Him, have a hard time deciphering the truth that He is teaching, it is understandable that they ask Jesus why He doesn't teach the crowds in a more straightforward manner.

Jesus tells them that they have been given hearts that have been prepared to hear the truth, but others have not received the blessing of this gracious gift from the Father. It is a gift that He has bestowed upon those that He sovereignly has called as His elect. Those with unreceptive hearts cannot hear the clarity of the truth, further denying what they do hear, and in their rejection, they become even more hardened. It is for this reason that for their sake, Jesus speaks in parables.

He tells His disciples that whoever has spiritual discernment will gain even more awareness and a deeper comprehension of the truth of the kingdom of heaven through listening to the parables. But it remains that the reprobate, those who are not open to the truth, will become more confused and will not come to any understanding. John Calvin says,

> Still it remains a fixed principle, that the word of God is not obscure, except so far as the world darkens it by its own blindness. And yet the Lord conceals its mysteries, so that the perception of them may not reach the reprobate.

To further explain His reasoning for teaching in parables, Jesus quotes the prophet Isaiah and shows that His teaching fulfills this prophecy and at the same time mercifully protects the impenitent from further condemnation.

His parables, like Isaiah's prophetic messages, were instruments of God's judgment implemented to hide the truth from a faithless people.

Jesus continues to instruct His disciples by telling them that they are blessed with a clarity of spiritual discernment in their seeing and hearing the truth of what was being taught, as well as their being guided by the Holy Spirit with the willingness and ability to positively respond. These, along with the fulfillment of the Messiah's incarnation, are all things that the prophets of old and many righteous people had longed for in their own lives. First Peter 1:10–11 (NIV) speaks to this truth where it is written,

> Concerning this salvation, the prophets, who spoke of the grace that was to come to you, searched intently and with the greatest care, trying to find out the time and circumstances to which the Spirit of Christ in them was pointing when he predicted the sufferings of the Messiah and the glories that would follow.

VERSES 18–23

Jesus explains the parable of the sower in a straightforward manner without any ambiguity of what He has taught, which is nothing less than the gospel of the kingdom of God. The seed of God's Word is eternally good, and the quality of His Word is unchanging and never diminished throughout all time. The power and efficacy of God's Word equally rests within the seed that is sown on each of the types of soil; it is the quality and condition of the soil of a man's heart that varies significantly, ranging from that which is fully barren to that which is richly fertile.

The seed that has been sown and fallen onto the beaten path represents those who do not hear the Word of God with any understanding. The seed hasn't had any opportunity to germinate because Satan has snatched it away before there was any possibility of it being perceived as truth.

The seed that fell upon the stony soil is likened to those who hear the Word and are immediately on fire for God. Their profession of faith and enthusiasm for the Word, although superficial, is emotionally all-consuming and therefore short-lived because when trials come as a result of their alleged faith in the Word, they are lacking the depth of knowledge and the root of wisdom that are required for perseverance and so fall away.

Those seeds that fall among the thorns represent those who begin to thrive under God's Word, but their spiritual growth begins to become stunted and then is stopped altogether by everything else that is happening in their lives. Their climb up the ladder of success along with dreams of a bright future of financial reward, their hobbies, their children's sports teams, nights out with friends, and the anxiety caused by the cares of the world in conjunction with all the false promises and deceitfulness of all who cater to their whims and desires, each of which contributes to and inevitably chokes out God's Word, and their spiritual life withers away.

And finally, the seed that falls on the good soil. These are the regenerate who hear the Word in faith and by God's grace understand it. In theological terms, what we are seeing from Christ's example of the good soil is the order of salvation, or the *ordo salutis*, and this is outlined very neatly by Paul in the Golden Chain, which we find in Romans 8:29–30. Those of the good soil, in their obedience to His Word, grow, mature, and bear much fruit by the testimony seen in the way that they live life and in their witnessing of God's Word to others. This type of soil is always fruitful, with some yields being more fruitful than others, but the importance lies not in the quantity but in the fact that these soils always result in the presence of fruit.

In our passage, Jesus teaches of the differing yields that come from good soil. Some of the higher yields of fruitfulness from this type of soil derive from it having been prepared and cultivated for a time such as this. Some have not only heard the Word but have received it with a nurtured and fertile heart; therefore, it has produced an even more bountiful crop. As teachers and preachers, they come alongside God's Word and continue the process of sowing it to an even larger number of people within the congregations of their churches as well as in the homes of their brothers and sisters in Christ.

VERSES 24–30

Jesus continues in His use of seed in this parable. The sower plants good seed, but the enemy, who is Satan and his followers, go to the field and plant bad seed throughout the field. The bad seed is representative of any form of corruption that is sown into the church. When the bad seed germinates, and during the initial growth, it has the same appearance as that of the good seed that was sown to produce wheat. This represents the difference between believers and unbelievers throughout the world. Within the body of Christ, we know that there is a difference between the invisible church, who are God's people, and the visible church, which is comprised of both God's people and those who are not. In the parable of sowing good seed for a wheat crop, bad seed is sown in with it. This bad seed may have been darnel, which is a poisonous plant related to wheat, and they are virtually indistinguishable from one another until the head is formed. In the church, both the invisible and the visible church members initially look identical, carry the same Bibles, and for the most part sound a lot alike when they speak of God's Word. As the invisible church becomes more comfortable with all the members of the church, they may miss the subtle comments or remarks that the false teachers make that sound scriptural, but upon closer scrutiny they may be found to be a vastly different interpretation to what the Bible teaches. These new teachings, whether subtle or overt, are poisonous to the church and can easily distort the truth to the point of heresy.

John Calvin offers his view of these passages.

> In my opinion, the design of the parable is simply this: So long as the pilgrimage of the Church in this world continues, bad men and hypocrites will mingle in it with those who are good and upright, that the children of God may be armed with patience and, in the midst of offenses which are fitted to disturb them, may preserve unbroken steadfastness of faith.

The wheat and the tares are left until they ripen into fullness, at which time they are easily identified as to which is the good crop and which is the bad crop. In the same way, believers and unbelievers remain in the world and in our churches until the fullness of time and the Day of Judgment is at hand. It is then that the sheep will be separated from the goats. It is only then that the righteous will no longer have to live alongside unrighteousness.

VERSES 31–32

Jesus begins to compare the kingdom of heaven as being like a grain of a mustard seed in that when it is first planted, it is one of the smallest or least of seeds. However, when it becomes grown, it is one of the greatest among garden herbs, so much so it becomes treelike and the birds of the air can come and nest within its branches.

There are a couple of divergent views of these two verses. The first seems to be the majority opinion, which believes that this is a description of the growth and eventual dominance of the church. Adam Clarke is a good example of the majority opinion on the meaning of this parable and the one following:

> Both these parables are *prophetic*, and were intended to show, principally, how, from very small beginnings, the Gospel of Christ should pervade all the nations of the world and fill them with righteousness and true holiness.[69]

The nesting of birds for those of this opinion represents the supernatural size of the "tree" as allowing for divine blessing for all of God's creatures who take refuge there and cite verses such as Psalm 91:1, where we read, "He that dwelleth in the secret place of the most High shall abide under the shadow of the Almighty."

Those of the minority opinion see the growth of the mustard plant as having become abnormally large, and they focus on the nesting of birds within its branches and subsequently point out that in other parables

---

[69] www.blueletterbible.org study notes on Matthew 13 by David Guzik.

birds were emissaries of Satan. These birds were sometimes viewed as being "elements of corruption that take refuge in the very shadow of Christianity."[70]

Other counterpoints to this minority opinion come from both the Reformation Study Bible footnotes and John MacArthur's commentary. They each cite Ezekiel 17:22–23, which also references birds nesting in the shade of a tree that God has planted. MacArthur states that the verses in Matthew undoubtably refer to several Old Testament passages, including Ezekiel, that prophesized the inclusion of Gentiles into the kingdom. The Reformation Study Bible states, "The birds represent the Gentile nations taking refuge in the Messiah and enjoying the blessings of the covenant."

VERSE 33

Jesus taught using parables so that His examples would be engagingly familiar to His listeners. He had just spoken of an agricultural phenomenon in the extraordinary growth of the mustard seed, and the men of the field would readily grasp the concept. He now moves to the use of leaven in the baking of bread. He tells of a woman who uses enough leaven for three measures of flour. That would equate to about fifty pounds, and that the amount of bread would be enough to feed around one hundred people. For one woman to start out small and then to enlarge her efforts to make that much bread by herself would be on par with the amazing growth of the mustard seed.

John Chrysostom[71] comments, "The leaven, though it is buried, is not destroyed. Little by little it transmutes the whole lump into its own condition. This happens with the gospel" with slow growth at first. It penetrates and transforms society. The leaven in this parable is symbolic of the truth of the scripture we hold in our hearts and in our relationship with others; the gospel message spreads throughout the world. It has been

---

[70] G. Campbell Morgan, https://www.studylight.org/commentaries/gcm/matthew-13.html.

[71] John Chrysostom was an early church father and archbishop of Constantinople in AD 397.

hidden from the eyes of unbelievers, but it was working to change the world.

VERSES 34–35

Whenever He was teaching the crowds, Jesus spoke in parables. This too was in fulfillment of words spoken by the prophet who had said, "I will open my mouth in parables; I will utter things which have been kept secret from the foundation of the world." (See Psalm 78:2.)

As opposition to Christ's teaching increased, it became His practice to publicly teach by using parables. Jesus has already told us that He spoke in parables so that those with hardened hearts would not perceive what He was teaching and become even more hardened by their unbelief, which would add to their condemnation. Even so, Jesus's parables reveal truths that might have otherwise been hidden. He now points to His speaking in parables as the fulfillment of prophecy and quotes Psalm 78:2. This whole psalm is a parallel and a foreshadow of Israel's unbelieving pattern that is now being repeated by their faithless unresponsiveness to Jesus's ministry.

VERSES 36–43

Jesus left the crowd, and some versions say that He sent them away and then entered the house. His disciples gathered to Him and were looking for an explanation to the parable of the wheat and the tares.

In this parable, He tells them that the field represents the world in general, not the church in particular. The good seeds represent God's true people, who belong to the invisible church and who are the sons of the kingdom. The one who sows the good seed is the Son of Man, who alone brings salvation.

The weeds and tares represent the false believers and teachers in the world, those who coexist with God's people, and they are those that He calls the sons of the evil one. It is their father, Satan, who sows the bad seed.

Within this parable, we are told that at the end of the age, when all of God's predestined grain is ready, Christ in righteous judgment will send His angels to reap the harvest and to separate His people, who are destined for radiant glory, from those who are destined for the fiery furnace of eternal perdition. Of this glorious day, John Calvin comments,

> What a remarkable consolation! The sons of God, who now lie covered with dust, or are held in no estimation, or even are loaded with reproaches, will then shine in full brightness, as when the sky is serene, and every cloud has been dispelled.

VERSES 44–46

We are presented here with two more parables that have the same meaning. The first parable is about a fortune that is buried in a field, and the second is about an invaluable pearl, and both parables represent the hidden and priceless treasure in the value of the gospel and of our salvation. When the means of salvation that is ours in abiding with Christ has been revealed through the effectual and divine calling of God, there is nothing that we won't do or sacrifice in order to obtain that treasure. This doing and sacrificing in themselves do not merit salvation but denote that we are willing to forsake that which the world holds in high esteem so that we can emulate the life of Christ. This doing and sacrificing is in thankful recognition of the grace and mercy of God, who freely offers it to us.

> Come, everyone who is thirsty, come to the waters; and you without money, come, buy, and eat! Come, buy wine and milk without money and without cost! (Isaiah 55:1 HCSB)

Matthew Henry wrote the following about the value of the kingdom: "Those who discern this treasure in the field, and value it aright, will never be at ease until they have made it their own on any terms."

These two parables are ones which the people to whom Jesus was addressing could identify with. In Jesus's time, there were no banks as we know them.

There was also a great deal of instability and threats of invasion, so treasure was often buried to keep it safe. If someone stumbled across something of value and dug it up, they were required to take it to their master. If they left it in the ground and did not dig it up, they could scrimp and save until they had enough money to buy the field, and then they could retrieve the treasure and it would be theirs. Pearls were highly prized during this era, and the extent of their worth would be equivalent to how we value diamonds today.

Verses 47–50

Jesus now compares the kingdom of heaven to a fishing net that, when cast, helps the fishermen indiscriminately gather every kind of fish. When the net is full, they draw it to the shore and sort out the good fish but throw out the bad. Likewise, at the end of the age, the angels will come and separate the wicked from the just, casting the wicked into the fiery furnace, where there will be wailing and gnashing of teeth.

This parable speaks to another group of people by using their understanding of their trade and skill sets to help them understand Jesus's teachings. The use of a dragnet and the sorting out of the catch was employed by every fisherman on the Sea of Galilee.

The dragnet is one that Jesus will be throwing over the world at the end of the age, and it will be filled with all types of people without distinction, both the regenerate and the reprobate, each of whom will coexist in the world, and in the church, until that time. The angels will come and sort out the evil from the righteous, with the evil being thrown into the fiery furnace, a place of eternal punishment, a place of weeping and gnashing of teeth. Second Thessalonians 1:7–10 tells us that mighty angels will come with Jesus to inflict vengeance on those who do not know God and on those who do not obey the gospel of our Lord Jesus. The last descriptive phrase of verse 50, of wailing and gnashing of teeth, was one that Matthew frequently used to highlight that hell will entail an eternal punishment and that it is not simply annihilation.

VERSES 51–52

The disciples told Jesus that they understood what He had been teaching, and although they affirmed that they understood, no follower of Jesus will fully comprehend what we have been taught until we are with Christ in glory. James Montgomery Boice writes, "Their yes did not actually mean that they understood all that Jesus was teaching, only that they believed all that they did understand and were prepared to act on it."[72]

Jesus then said to them that the scribes and teachers of the law, those who had been trained for the kingdom of heaven, should be like their master. The Greek phrase for "instructed unto the kingdom of heaven" could be rendered as "has become a disciple of the kingdom of heaven." The disciples, in being like their master, would bring out the treasures of their wisdom, which consists of both the things of old as well as those that were new. It was now time for them to begin teaching others what they had previously known from scripture as well as the new teachings and understandings of the kingdom of heaven that they had received during their time with Jesus. These teachings would include the redemptive history of the Old Testament that pointed to Christ as well as the confirmation of His fulfillment of those prophecies through miracles and other signs that were the manifest evidence of the presence of the kingdom which was now upon them.

John MacArthur comments,

> The disciples are not to spurn the old for the sake of the new. Rather, they are to understand the new insights gleaned from Jesus's parables in-light-of the old truths, and vice versa.

VERSES 53–56

Jesus finished teaching these parables, left Capernaum, and journeyed back to His home in Nazareth. As was His custom, He went to the synagogue

---

[72] *Tabletalk Magazine* (Sanford, FL, Ligonier Ministries, Inc., June 19, 2008).

and taught them, and what they heard from Him astonished them. They wondered where this "man" had gotten His wisdom from and how it was possible that He conducted the mighty works that He had performed.

It has been said that familiarity breeds contempt, and seeing Him with their own eyes, eyes that had seen Him as a boy in His formative years and had witnessed Him at work with His earthly father as a carpenter, they saw Him only as a man and not as the incarnate Son of God. They had heard Him speak, they had witnessed miracles, and surely they had heard of many more, yet they remained blind to the truth of His identity.

In their unbelief and amazement, they began naming His mother and all His siblings, citing the fact that each of them continued living in Nazareth, and they remained steadfastly incredulous at the wonder of this "man" and His having attained all that He had.

John Calvin comments about sinners unwilling to believe in what God has sent by saying,

> It is not mere ignorance that hinders men, but that, of their own accord, they search after grounds of offense, to prevent them from following the path to which God invites.

VERSES 57–58

The veil of their superficial knowledge of Jesus as a boy, and the shadow that undoubtably remained around the speculative gossip of Mary's pregnancy and Jesus's birth, played heavily in clouding their perception of Jesus and His divine authority. The villagers took an ardent offense at Jesus and His claims, a person who they believed to be both an ordinary and uneducated man.

Jesus responded, "A prophet is not without honour, save in his own country, and in his own house." In His rejection, Jesus is aligned with the prophets of the Old Testament who proclaimed God's truth yet were consistently rejected by the people of Israel.

Scripture goes on to say, "And he did not do many miracles there because of their lack of faith (NIV)." Jesus refused to conduct many miracles in Nazareth because they were a sign of His deity and without faith, the people of His village wouldn't be able to grasp the true significance of them. This was a judgment on their disbelief as well as a mercy against any further hardening of their hearts.

I paraphrase R. C. Sproul's comments where he said, "Sadly the people of Nazareth missed the treasure, the pearl of great price, as they rejected Jesus as He stood before them."

CHAPTER 14

THE BAPTIST'S DEATH, FEEDS FIVE THOUSAND, WALKS ON WATER

VERSES 1–2

The Herod who was reigning as tetrarch at the time of Jesus's birth was known as Herod Antipas and was the son of Herod the Great. Jesus's fame was so widespread that He was even known to Herod and his household. Herod's guilt and superstition over his having beheaded John the Baptist in exchange for the lustful pleasure of a dance that was performed by his stepdaughter had engendered fear in his heart. Herod attributed Jesus's divine powers to John the Baptist, who he thought had been raised from the dead.

VERSES 3–13

John the Baptist had been an agent of Herod's conscious in that he had publicly rebuked Herod for the sin of illegally divorcing his previous wife, the daughter of a neighboring king, Aretas, and then taking Herodias, his half-brother Philips wife, to be his own.

The act of Herod taking his brother's wife violated Leviticus 18:16 and 20:21. Just to show how incestuously entangled the relationships that Herodias was involved in, we remind you that both Philip and Herod were Herodias's uncles as her father was Aristobulus, another son of Herod the Great.

For his rebuke of their openly rebellious sin, John the Baptist was imprisoned. His being jailed was in lieu of being executed because Herod had feared the people's reaction, for they esteemed him to be a prophet.

On the occasion of Herod's birthday, there was a great celebration that was attended by many dignitaries and those of Herod's court. As the party went on and the wine flowed, Herod made an inviolable oath to his stepdaughter and niece (she was Philip's daughter) that if she would dance for him and his guests, that he would give her up to half of his kingdom. This was no ordinary dance, but one that was designed to entice the wicked appetites of Herod and his guests. It was more than likely a sensual performance that was planned and encouraged by Herodias herself as a way of getting what she wanted. Herodias told her daughter Salome that she was to request the head of John the Baptist on a platter.

Herod was taken aback by such a demand, and although he did not want to execute John, he felt compelled because of the impulsive but unbreakable oath that he had made in front of his guests, an oath that was driven by a carnally impassioned lust. Herod was well-known for his duplicity, so it is unlikely that he would be overly concerned with going back on his oath for any moral or ethical reasons, but he did let pride rule and didn't want to lose face in front of his guests. So entangled in a combination of his oath and his pride, Herod commanded that it be done. This sinful act of murder was a violation of the Mosaic law[73] as there was no trial before he had John's head presented to Salome, and she in turn presented it to her mother.

---

[73] *The Death Penalty in the Mosaic Law,* by Peter Leithart, states, "The death penalty is an essential, foundational principle of biblical theology. Second, the death penalty was carried out only after a trial, only through due process." https://theopolisinstitute. com/the-death-penalty-in-the-mosaic-law.

John's disciples then came and were granted permission to take his body and to bury it. When they had done so, they went and told Jesus what had happened. Scripture tells us that when Jesus heard this news, He withdrew from the area and, getting into a boat, sought out a desolate place so that He and His disciples could find some solitude in order to grieve. In conjunction with finding a place to grieve, there was also the distinct possibility of political unrest after the killing of John the Baptist. Herod was fearful that Jesus was John and out of his fearful speculations was asking questions. Jesus, in consideration of His Father's timing of events and with a thoughtful practicality born out of the situation, may have departed to avoid any potential for escalation. As we have seen before, the ever-watching crowds saw Him leave and followed Him on foot.

VERSES 14–16

Jesus had gone to another shore to find a place of rest, but the crowds that followed gave Him no rest, yet looking upon them, He had compassion. John MacArthur states,

> Here the humanity of Christ allows expression of His attitude toward sinners in human terms: He is moved with compassion. Whereas God, who is immutable, is not subject to the rise and fall of changing emotions. Christ in His incarnation was both fully God and fully man, and with all the attributes and faculties of humanity, was on occasion moved to literal tears over the plight of sinners.

Jesus began to heal those who were among them, and we read in Mark that He began to teach the people as well. He continued ministering to them until evening, when His disciples came to Him to request that He send them away from the desolate place where they had met so that they might go into the villages to buy themselves some food. Jesus then said that the people didn't need to go away, and He commanded His disciples to give them something to eat. He was both testing the faith of His disciples and setting the stage for the miraculous.

Verses 17–21

The miracle Matthew describes in this passage, the feeding of the five thousand, is the only miracle included in each of the four gospels. The disciples tell Jesus that they only have five loaves and two fish, and without a concern for the meagerness of the offering brought before Him, He orders the crowd to sit down on the grass while He looked heavenward and blessed the food that they had. As He broke the bread, He distributed it to the disciples, and they in turn gave to the crowd what Jesus gave to them. Matthew, in his typical shorthand accounts of what transpires, says no more about the fish, but we can note that Jesus blessed them as well, and the implication is, as supported by the other gospel writers, that the fish was distributed. After the people ate and were satisfied, the disciples picked up twelve full baskets of the leftover and broken pieces. Matthew tells us that there were about five thousand men, besides the women and children. There are some who estimate the total people who were fed to be as many as between fifteen or twenty thousand people.

Verses 22–24

After this, Jesus made His disciples get into the boat and told them to go to the other side while He sent the people away. The translations that use the phrase "constrained his disciples" seem to give some urgency to His sending them away, and in John's gospel, we read that Jesus wanted to disperse the crowd so that they wouldn't continue clinging to Him with an expectation of making Him their king in their hope of His being a warrior king like David and overthrow the Roman oppression. There is further speculation that the disciples were beginning to be swept up in the crowd's enthusiasm, and that is why Jesus so quickly sent them to the boat and told them to go. Matthew does tell us that He wanted to be alone to pray. After all, that is what He went there for in the first place, so He went up on the mountain and prayed. We have read that when Jesus started His prayers, it was still evening, a time span that could range anywhere from a few minutes before the sun set until the first three stars appeared in the night sky.[74] We are not sure exactly what time Jesus began to pray, but we do know that the next event recorded of His activity is during the fourth watch, which was anywhere between three and six in the morning. The point of this observation is that if Jesus, who is sinless and always within His Father's will, spends that much time in prayer, what does that say about our need to be in deeper communion with our heavenly Father?[75]

We now find that He is alone and that the boat is a long way off but that it was being beaten by the waves and that the wind was against them. The primary means of navigating through the water for these fishing boats was by raising sails, but with the wind against them, the sails were useless, and they had to man the oars to try to make it to the other side. We further read that they were being beaten by the waves so they would have had to struggle with every ounce of strength just to maintain their position, let alone make any forward progress.

VERSES 25–27

Matthew tells us that around the fourth watch, Jesus was walking on the sea as He came toward them, but as soon as they saw Him, they were terrified and cried out in fear because they thought that He was a ghost. In Jesus's day, the sea was thought to be symbolic of chaos and hell, with cultural lore depicting the sea as a monstrous beast and a place where Baal would battle other gods. As they had been battling against the raging seas most of the night, they were physically exhausted, and it is then they saw Jesus walking on the water. They didn't immediately recognize Him and attributed His presence to that of a ghost coming up from the abyss of the sea.

To assuage their fears, Jesus said to them, "Be of good cheer; it is I; be not afraid." The Greek for "it is I" is "ego eimi," and it literally translates as the words "I AM." That was the same descriptive terminology that God had

---

[74] Found within the definition of the term "relative hour" as it pertains to rabbinic Jewish law https://en.wikipedia.org/wiki/Relative_hour.

[75] Paraphrased from *Tabletalk Magazine* (Sanford, FL, Ligonier Ministries, Inc., June 25, 2008).

used when He revealed Himself to Moses in Exodus 3:14 and the same divine reference that Jesus used to describe Himself in the seven "I AM" statements found in the book of John.

VERSES 28–33

Peter hears Jesus's voice and he knows it; he has heard it countless times while they walked together, during meals, and while He spoke as He taught. Jesus tells us, "My sheep hear my voice" (John 10:27), yet Peter says, "Lord, if it be thou," which gives an indication of some level of doubt within him. Even at this, Peter continues by saying to Jesus, "Bid me come unto thee on the water," and Jesus simply replies with a single word: "Come." With a renewed and strengthened faith, Peter steps out of the boat, walks on water, and goes toward Jesus. But then Peter does what many of us do when we are surrounded by the tempests of life: we take our eyes off Jesus. Peter saw the wind and was afraid. He began to sink and cried out, "Lord, save me." It was a cry we would do well to voice ourselves when we find that we are in troubled waters.

Jesus reaches out, takes hold of him, and says, "O thou of little faith, wherefore didst thou doubt?" They got into the boat, and the wind ceased. Those in the boat worshipped Him and said, "Of a truth thou art the Son of God."

Matthew leaves out a phenomenally striking detail from his narrative, and we learn from John's gospel that as soon as Jesus got into the boat, it was miraculously found to be on the other side. John 6:21 reads as such: "Then they willingly received him into the ship: and immediately the ship was at the land whither they went."

It is no wonder that they worshipped Him, and in that spirit of worship, they proclaimed that He was the Son of God. It was obvious that a person who was merely a man could not walk on water, nor could an ordinary man calm the sea by merely getting into the boat, let alone have it supernaturally transported to where they were going. They may not have known it, but they had also witnessed testimony of His deity in the fulfillment of several Old Testament prophecies. In Isaiah 43:16, we read,

"Thus saith the LORD, which maketh a way in the sea, and a path in the mighty waters …" Psalm 77:19 says, "Thy way is in the sea, and thy path in the great waters, and thy footsteps are not known." And Job 9:8 says, "Which alone spreadeth out the heavens, and treadeth upon the waves of the sea" It was Jesus who created the sea and set its boundaries, with all creation being subject to the authority of His commands.

VERSES 34–36

They crossed over and were in the region of Gennesaret, on the western shore just south of Capernaum. Gennesaret has the Hebrew meaning of "princely gardens" because the soil is a deeply rich loam and exceedingly fertile. The men recognized Jesus, and they knew of His healing power. They quickly had everyone in the surrounding region bring to Him all who needed healing. Mark 6:55–56 (HCSB) contains a parallel account and tells us that they

> began to carry the sick on mats to wherever they heard He was. Wherever He would go, into villages, towns, or the country, they laid the sick in the marketplaces and begged Him that they might touch just the tassel of His robe. And everyone who touched it was made well.

They begged Him that He allow all who came to just touch the hem of His robe, and as many as touched it were made perfectly well.

CHAPTER 15

TRADITIONS, DEFILES, CRUMBS FROM TABLE, FEEDS FOUR THOUSAND

VERSES 1–2

The Pharisees and the scribes spoken of in these verses were more than likely an official delegation sent to hear what Jesus was teaching and to watch how the people reacted to Him. The journey between Jerusalem and Galilee would have taken a little under two weeks. Even though it is a straight-line distance of only about 78.9 miles, the trek would be more circuitous as you traversed over the rugged terrain, and it was not a journey without its dangers.

On this day, they questioned Him about transgressing their ceremonial tradition of washing; it was not an inquiry that was based upon a command found in scripture. They were offended that Christ's disciples eschewed the rigid and extensive ritual washing that this delegation was bound to perform before their meals could be eaten. They weren't concerned with hygiene with their line of questioning; they were specifically asking about a ritual, a solely ceremonial cleansing. The Jewish rabbi Jose is quoted to have said, "He sins as much who eats with unwashed hands, as he that lies with a harlot."

One commentary I read had the following step-by-step outline of the extremes surrounding the traditional washing that many of the Pharisees ceremoniously performed. The process began with the use of consecrated stone vessels of water because ordinary water might be unclean. They started by taking at least enough of this water to fill one and a half eggshells. Then you poured the water over your hands, starting at your fingertips and running down toward your wrist. Then you cleansed each palm by rubbing the fist of your other hand into it. Then you poured water over your hands again, this time from the wrist toward the fingers. An extremely strict Jew would do this not only before the meal but also between each course. This cleansing ritual was so seriously ingrained in them and so important that they said that eating bread with unwashed hands was no better than eating excrement. With this last statement in mind, it is no wonder that they questioned why the disciples ate with defiled hands.

Tradition and ceremony had become such an overpowering aspect of their religious trappings they had lost all semblance of the reality of daily life. For the religious leaders, their traditions had supplanted or usurped scripture to the point of being legalistically binding but without a basis in God's Word. The extent of their delusional elevation of tradition over scripture was to such an extreme degree that it had become treacherous. Warren Wiersbe tells us just how deeply it had affected their minds.

> Rabbi Eleazer said, "He who expounds the Scriptures in opposition to the tradition has no share in the world to come" … The Mishna, a collection of Jewish traditions in the Talmud, records, "It is a greater offense to teach anything contrary to the voice of the Rabbis than to contradict Scripture itself."

VERSES 3–9

Jesus didn't give an answer to them but in turn questioned them as to why they held tradition so highly even when they transgressed God's commandments. Their accusatory questioning was based upon tradition and not on scripture, and Jesus wanted to know why they felt justified in holding their traditions in higher regard than scripture. Jesus doesn't give them an open-ended question but immediately gives them the specific example of one of their traditions where a man could stand upon that tradition to forsake his duty to care for his parents, and that was the tradition of corban.

Unlike the Pharisees, Jesus continued His use of scripture to support what He was saying. He used the example of Moses and the Fifth Commandment, "Honor thy father and mother …" (Exodus 20:12) and "Anyone who curses their father or mother is to be put to death" (Exodus 21:17 NIV). These are clear Old Testament responsibilities for children of any age to honor their parents. Part of that honoring was to care for them and to provide for them financially. However, Jewish tradition allowed for money that had been committed or otherwise saved for their care to be reallocated as corban, which is a Hebrew term for any gift or sacrifice of money or goods a person vowed as dedicated to God upon his death. This loophole used by the one who dedicated his money as corban nullified the Word of God, setting it aside and replacing it with a tradition, and neither this man's parents nor God was honored.

The dishonor was multiplied when, under the guise of being ultra-religious in his pledge, that person no longer had the financial obligation to do anything for his parents, even though he had full access and use of his proceeds until he died, at which time it was given over to the temple. Jesus said that this practice, and many other similar things they did to get around the law of God, were hypocritical to the faith that they supposedly espoused. "They feigned obedience to the law, but it was an obedience to their extrabiblical customs that they treated as law, while their actions were contemptable to the Law of God."[76]

Again, quoting the Old Testament, Jesus references Isaiah 29:13 (HCSB) to rebuke the Pharisees and scribes when He said,

> In this way, you have revoked God's word because of your tradition. Hypocrites! Isaiah prophesied correctly about you when he said, These people honor Me with their lips, but their heart is far from Me. They worship Me in vain, teaching as doctrines the commands of men.

Their actions were external and not from the heart, and their teachings were not from God but merely reflected human tradition; it is primarily for these two reasons they were called hypocrites.

VERSES 10–11

Jesus shifts back to the subject of defilement, and He called the people to Him, telling them to both hear and to understand. He wanted them to pay attention. In contrast to the Pharisees' washing and cleansing tradition, He tells them that nothing outside a person that goes into a person would be defiling to them. He taught that true cleanliness doesn't pertain to what we put into our bodies but that which comes from within. The things that come out of a person are what defile him as it reveals their unclean hearts. A defiled heart is much more serious than that which can be removed by a ceremonial washing. In scripture the heart depicts one's entire being it is at the very core of who we are as humans and includes the mind, emotions, and will. Jeremiah 17:9 tells us, "The heart is deceitful above all things, and desperately wicked; who can know it?" This is the point that Jesus was making: God demands holiness, a cleanliness that only He can provide, and scripture tells us that He will do this by giving us a new heart and a new spirit (Ezekiel 36:26). No amount of external washing can produce righteousness. It is just a futile work that is done for show with no merit to it whatsoever.

---

[76] Paraphrased from *Tabletalk Magazine* (Sanford, FL, Ligonier Ministries, Inc., May 18, 2016).

Their extreme concern with outward acts as opposed to the intent of God's law revealed their legalistic blindness to the ultimate source of impurity and that is why Jesus reminded them that the heart is the true source of corruption, not the hands.[77]

VERSES 12–14

His disciples asked if He was aware that He had offended the Pharisees, and not only did Jesus know that He offended them, He had intended to offend them because of their false sense of value in their holding their traditions in a position of supremacy over and above scripture. God had not planted the weeds and tares of tradition, but He will root them out.

Jesus told His disciples not to be worried about the Pharisees and the scribes. He said, "Let them alone," because in their hardheartedness, they weren't worth arguing with. This spoke judgment against them, they were being abandoned by God, and He called them blind guides. Although they had access to scripture and were teachers of the law, they didn't understand what they read, nor did they ascribe what they knew about the coming Messiah to Jesus. They had suppressed the truth.

Paul and the other New Testament writers would have called them false teachers, and in their concern for their churches, they admonished them to make sure to do as the Bereans had done. They were to search the Word daily to see if what they had been taught was scriptural. The people of Jesus's earthly ministry depended upon the leaders of the synagogues and the Pharisees and scribes to search the scriptures and to lead them, but to their guilt, the people were led astray and were kept blinded to the truth. The blind truly were leading the blind, and it is the pit of hell that awaits their fall.

---

[77] Paraphrased from *Tabletalk Magazine* (Sanford, FL, Ligonier Ministries, Inc., June 26, 2008).

VERSES 15–20

The disciples still don't understand the big picture and once again ask Jesus to explain what He has just taught. Jesus finds it almost incredulous that they still don't get it and begins to break down His teaching so that they can more easily see what He is saying. He tells them the obvious, that whatever they eat goes into the mouth, is digested, and then is excreted. On the other hand, what comes out of the mouth, or manifests in an evil action, those things that originate from a corrupt heart which entertains the inner most thoughts of a sinful man and his debased disposition about life, these are what defile a man, not what is eaten with unwashed hands.

VERSES 21–28

Jesus then traveled about fifty miles northwest of Galilee to the region of the Gentile cities of Tyre and Sidon, located about twenty miles apart on the coast of the Mediterranean Sea. R. C. Sproul's commentary indicates that this is the only time that Jesus left the ancient borders of Israel and sojourned into a pagan land.

Once there, He was confronted by a Gentile woman who begged for Christ's mercy as her daughter was severely oppressed by a demon. In her plea, she calls Jesus Lord and remarkably identifies Him as the Son of David, each testifying to her honor of Him even though she probably didn't fully grasp the full significance of what she was saying.

Jesus doesn't answer her right away, and in that momentary pause, His disciples came and begged Him to send her away, and this was more than likely with the meaning that they desired for Him to give her what she wanted so that they could be done with her. Ignoring His disciples' protests against this woman, He turns to her and tells her that He was sent only to the lost sheep of the house of Israel. Kneeling before Him, she called Him Lord and remained persistent in her plea. He continues by telling her that it isn't right to take the children's bread and give it to the dogs. And here, Jesus is not talking about the wild scavenging dogs that are hated by the Jews but to smaller, domesticated house pets, which presents a decisively more compassionate and tender approach. Many commentators see from this that He is not trying to insult her but is testing her faith.

Picking up on His metaphor, she continues the use of it to further entreat Him by saying that even the dogs eat the crumbs that fall from the table. Her poignant reply was one that clearly showed her acknowledgment that she was not one of Jesus's people, but it also showed that she was aware that He owed her nothing. There was no sense of entitlement about her. She was only asking for Jesus to help her by giving her the grace of a few crumbs for her daughter from the Lord's table. Jesus's final response is to extol her for her great faith, and as a result of this strength of faith, He tells her, "Be it done for you as you desire" (ESV), and in that instant, her daughter was healed.

VERSES 29–31

He left the region of Tyre and Sidon, skirted the Sea of Galilee, went up a mountain, and sat down. In Mark 7:31, we see that Jesus was now ministering in an area called the Decapolis, a region of ten predominantly Gentile cities east of the Sea of Galilee. Although they were Gentiles, the great crowds that came to Him knew of Jesus's curative powers and brought to Him many who needed healing and laid them at His feet. Their conditions were varied and ranged from being lame or crippled to being blind or mute and included many other types of disorders that Matthew didn't name. Although there is no mention of great faith, those who brought friends and family with needs had a confident belief in what they had heard about Jesus, and He healed them all. This predominantly pagan crowd wondered at all that He had done, and they glorified the God of Israel.

VERSES 32–39

After having healed all that they had brought to Him, Jesus called His disciples to Him. He told them that the people had been with Him for three days and needed to be fed. It is important to note that this is not the same event as the feeding of the five thousand.

Jesus told His disciples that in His compassion for the people, He was unwilling to send them away hungry because in a weakened state they might faint along the way. The disciples told Him of their concerns; they were in an isolated and desolate place and could not conceive of how they would find enough bread to feed so many. It isn't any wonder why Jesus called them men of little faith. He had recently fed the five thousand and still they doubted. Some speculate that because the crowd was made up of unclean Gentiles the disciples had no expectation that Jesus would grace them with the same type of miracle. What they also didn't conceive of was that this act of Christ's benevolence was merely a foreshadow of the future expansion of God's kingdom that would include the Gentile nations.

Jesus asked the disciples what they had, and they in turn replied that they had seven loaves of bread and a few small fish. Jesus then directed the crowd, which was comprised of four thousand men, not including their wives and children, and He had them all sit down. In another display of His deity, He gave thanks for the food that had been provided and then took the loaves and fish, broke them, and gave them to the disciples, who in turn gave them to the crowds. Matthew then tells us that not only had everyone eaten and become satisfied but that they picked up seven large baskets full of broken pieces that were left over. "The number seven symbolizes perfection or completion, and here it can be representative of the blessing and fullness of God's provision for all people, including the Gentiles."[78] Although what food that they had to begin with was meager, God had provided out of His abundance.

Once they were well fed, Jesus sent the crowd away, and He and His disciples went to the region of Magadan, which is located a little over six miles south of Capernaum on the western shore of the Sea of Galilee.

---

[78] Paraphrased from the footnotes in the ESV Study Bible (Wheaton, IL, Crossway, 2008) 1854.

CHAPTER 16

SIGNS DEMANDED, YOU ARE THE CHRIST, FORETELLS DEATH

VERSES 1–4

No longer do we read of Jesus's antagonists as being just the Pharisees and the scribes. There is now another powerful element added to the delegation, the Sadducees. The significance of this is that the Pharisees and Sadducees were long-standing enemies and often bitterly opposed to one another because of their many disparate beliefs. And the fact that they had united around their common hatred and fear of Jesus showed just how much of a threat He was to their tenaciously held traditions and the focus of their teachings.

Stubbornly unconvinced of the miraculous signs that Jesus had already demonstrated, they asked for another sign from Him, one that they would subjectively recognize as being a sign from heaven.

> Their traditions had deluded their thinking and those traditions held that a sign done on the earth could be a counterfeit from Satan, whereas a sign from heaven, one

that came down from the sky, were assumed to be from God.[79]

There was no lack of evidence as to Jesus's deity in what they had already witnessed, but there was a hardened unwillingness to accept the significance of what was so obvious that even the pagans in Decapolis glorified the God of Israel. Therefore, in their obstinance, they sought nothing less than an irrefutable sign of astronomical proportions. They wanted to see "the heavens shall be rolled together as a scroll" that Isaiah wrote about (Isaiah 34:4).

Jesus responded by calling them hypocrites and pointing to their being able to discern the weather based upon the color of the sky at dusk and at dawn, but they could not discern the sign of the times. The sign of the times was in the fulfilled prophecy with reference to the wonders and miracles that the Messiah would perform at His coming, and that it was He who was accomplishing their fulfillment right before their very eyes. He further calls them a wicked and adulterous generation because they continued to seek signs, and that other than the sign of Jonah, none would be given. This last sign, the only one that would be given, repeats what He had already explained (Matthew 12:39–41), and the testimony of this yet future event would manifest itself as the greatest sign of His Messiahship. After this, Jesus left them.

VERSES 5–12

Once they had reached the other side, Jesus began teaching them again. In speaking about the Pharisees and the Sadducees, He used the metaphor of leaven, which is often, but not always (see 13:33), used in reference to sin, corruption, evil influence, and all other elements that defile. The disciples missed the teaching altogether because instead of hearing the message He was teaching they were busy discussing among themselves that they had forgotten to bring bread. More than likely in exasperation, Jesus proclaims their lack of faith and reminds them of the feeding of the five thousand and

---

[79] Paraphrased from www.blueletterbible.org study notes on Matthew 16 by David Guzik.

the feeding of the four thousand along with all the baskets of scrap that they had gathered after all were fed. He further questions how they could possibly think He was talking about bread and how they continued to fail in their understanding. After His rebuke, they finally got it. Jesus was warning them to beware of the doctrine and the teachings of the Pharisees and the Sadducees, which were more focused on tradition than scripture itself. The leaven of their position of power, their pride in external ritual, and the elevation of tradition over scripture had permeated and corrupted the whole loaf of their teaching.

VERSES 13–16

Jesus and His disciples were now in an area known as Caesarea Philippi, which was located about twenty-five miles northeast of the Sea of Galilee, near the base of Mount Hermon, and outside the domain of Herod Antipas. The populace there was mainly Gentile, and its location distanced Him from the demanding crowds that followed throughout the Jewish regions around the Sea of Galilee.

> It was also an area that was steeped in a history of idolatry and myth surrounding rival deities. There were no fewer than fourteen pagan temples in the near neighborhood. This was an area where the breath of ancient religion was in the very atmosphere. It is said that it was the birthplace of Pan, and there was a great temple of white marble built to the godhead of Caesar.[80]

Yet it was here that He could find some rest and be able to focus on mentoring the apostles.

In stark contrast to the darkness that pervaded this area, the light of the truth of His glory must have shone ever more brightly. It was within the

---

[80] William Barclay's Commentary: (1907–1978) Church of Scotland minister and professor of divinity and biblical criticism at the University of Glasgow. Within his commentary, he quotes the ancient Jewish historian Josephus. https://www.studylight.org/commentaries/dsb/matthew-16.html.

shadows of, and in juxtaposition to, these pagan temples and myths that He sought to engender a teachable moment when He asked them (NIV), "Who do people say the Son of Man is?"

In response, they set forth several of the prophets' names—John the Baptist, Elijah, and Jeremiah—as well as an overarching response of "or one of the prophets." Each of those mentioned was laudable up to a certain degree, but each reply was an extreme underestimation of Jesus, falling far short of the truth of His identity as the Messiah.

After listening to these varied responses, He asks them (HCSB), "Who do you say that I am?" Whereupon Peter replied, "Thou art the Christ, the Son of the living God." And this was the answer that Jesus, their mentor, Rabbi, Lord, and Master, had been striving for them to come to. This realization, and the confession of faith that had been proclaimed, would be required of them as an encouragement and the strength that they would need as they moved forward with the mission that Jesus had been preparing them for. Not only had Peter proclaimed his acknowledgment of Jesus as being the Messiah, but based upon historical Jewish thinking, his use of the term "the Son of the living God" was a confession that Jesus was deity, God incarnate.

VERSES 17–20

The Lord tells Peter that it wasn't human wisdom or the intimate relationship that they had together that brought him to the conclusion that Jesus was the Christ. It was nothing less than divine inspiration from God the Father who had opened Peter's heart, and in his confession of faith and his acknowledgment of who Jesus is, Peter was blessed. Peter had been traveling with Jesus for a long time by now, he had heard all of His teachings and seen countless miracles, but to this point, he hadn't grasped the fullness of who Jesus was. It took divine revelation for it to finally sink in. This concept was captured by Jonathan Edwards in his sermon "A Divine and Supernatural Light." In that sermon, Edwards explained and expanded upon the idea that in our fallen humanity, we are blind to the truths of God, and unless God the Holy Spirit opens our spiritual eyes, we cannot see the power and the splendor of Christ.

Jesus then tells Peter that upon this rock, He will build His church. Peter's name, Petros, transliterates into the Greek word "stone," and Peter's other name, Cephas, is Aramaic and translates into the Greek word *kephas*, which means "rock." But it is unlikely that Peter was the rock that Jesus said that He would build His church upon. It is true that the prophets and the apostles are the foundation of the church (Ephesians 2:20). However, Jesus alone is the cornerstone and the power that holds it all together, and it is through Jesus alone that all spiritual sacrifices are acceptable to God (1 Peter 2:5). Peter, the other apostles, and all who are spiritually united with Jesus are each emblematic of the greater Rock that is Christ. It is the view of Protestants that the confession of faith that Peter made, along with the confession of faith that every believer has made, is that He, Jesus Christ, is the rock that He continues to build His church upon.

There is no scriptural evidence that Peter was the first pope, and even while Peter rises to become a spokesman for the apostles (first portion of Acts), he is still being sent by the other apostles (Acts 8:14) to Samaria and remains accountable to the church in Jerusalem for his actions (Acts 11:1–18). In Acts 15:7–13, we also see that the final word for the church belonged to James and not to Peter.

Jesus goes on to make a promise that the gates of hell shall not prevail against the church. Satan and the wages of sin, death, and destruction have no power to overcome or conquer the church. John Calvin comments,

> Against all the power of Satan the firmness of the Church will prove to be invincible because the truth of God, on which the faith of the Church rests, will ever remain unshaken.

Jesus in this verse imparts the keys to the kingdom, and when we get to Matthew 18:18, we will see that this was an authority given to all the apostles, not just to Peter. In this verse, and in the parables that it follows, Jesus is speaking to all the apostles when He repeats, "Verily I say unto you, Whatsoever ye shall bind on earth shall be bound in heaven: and whatsoever ye shall loose on earth shall be loosed in heaven." The power for binding and loosing is something that the Jewish rabbis of that day used. They bound or loosed an individual in the application of a particular point of the law. Jesus promises that Peter—and the other apostles—would be able to set the boundaries authoritatively for the New Covenant community."[81] Simply put, this is representative of the church's authority in the administration of church discipline.

Jesus now commands His disciples that they are not to reveal to anyone that He was the Christ.

VERSES 21–23

"From that time" is a transitional phrase or expression that marks the end of Jesus's Galilean ministry and begins His journey to Jerusalem and His ultimate earthly destiny as He moved ever closer to the cross on Calvary.

After Peter's confession of faith, Jesus confirmed that He was the Christ, and with that confirmation, the disciples must have been experiencing a whole range of thoughts and emotions, none of which fit into what they were now hearing Jesus tell them about suffering, death, and resurrection. Their expectations still centered around a conquering king, not the one who was about to fulfill Isaiah 53. And still, Jesus taught them why He must fulfill the purpose of His coming: in submission to the Father's will, to atone for man's sin, and to show God's great love and forbearance.

In their astonishment of what they were hearing, even though it wasn't the first time Jesus had taught on this subject, they continued to miss the significance of His being raised on the third day. Peter, in all of his audacity, takes the situation in hand, draws Jesus aside, and begins to rebuke Him, telling Jesus that this cannot be and that it wasn't going to happen. The next words that Jesus spoke must have stopped Peter dead in his tracks, and he became dumbstruck when he heard said of himself, "Get behind me, Satan! You are a hindrance to me. For you are not setting your

---

[81] www.blueletterbible.org study notes on Matthew 16 by David Guzik.

mind on the things of God, but on the things of man" (ESV). Once Peter stopped reeling from this scathing reproach, he must have wondered if he had heard correctly: that Jesus had just referred to him as Satan and said that he was a hindrance.

This was a such a monumental dichotomy from having just been told that he was blessed because of his confession of Jesus as the true Christ that it makes you wonder if Peter even heard anything about his mind being set on the things of man instead of on those of God. Peter had made the mistake of taking His eyes off Jesus and letting his mind settle upon the things of men. He did not intentionally fall into Satan's grasp or overtly reject the things of God, but what he did do was to allow himself to be caught up in the human perspective of a limited worldview; he did not remain focused on the eternal purpose of Christ, his Lord and Master. He had become a stumbling block, an impediment to God's sovereign plan for salvation. Peter and the others still did not understand that the kingdom of God must come through the portal of Jesus's suffering, death, and resurrection and that this narrow gate was the only path that would lead His followers to heaven's gate.

VERSES 24–28

The idea of crucifixion on a cross was abhorrent to those who suffered under Roman oppression, and they were aware of the unrelenting and cruelly torturous death for those who were cursed enough to be hanged on a tree (Galatians 3:13). But now the disciples are hearing from Jesus that they must deny themselves and that they too must take up their cross if they wanted to follow Him. This is a supreme test of faith in that we are to deny ourselves, which means giving ourselves totally to Christ, and in this case, He is telling us we must take up our cross and die to Him and with Him. On this side of the cross, we see the resurrection power that He had proclaimed prior to His execution, but the disciples were asked to believe in that power by faith.

Jesus follows this command to take up our cross and follow Him by stating that if we wanted to save our life, we would lose it, but if we lose our lives for His sake, we will find it. They must have pondered what seemed to be a riddle over and again in their minds. Jesus was talking about the difference between our mortal and our eternal lives and the fact that we cannot save ourselves. To gain eternal life, we must be willing to lay down our mortal lives and everything that constitutes our worldly existence. We must die to this world and live for Christ in order to gain the resurrected life that is ours in Him. John Calvin says that self-denial is extensive, calling us

> to give up our natural inclinations, and part with all the affections of the flesh, and thus give our consent to be reduced to nothing, provided that God lives and reigns in us.

Christ goes on to ask what eternal value there is in the gaining of everything that this world offers if it is at the cost of our eternal salvation. We are but fading flowers and all that is of this world is subject to moth, rust, and decay with none having any eternal value. We are reminded of the rich man in Hades who would give anything for Lazarus to be able to comfort him with but a drop of water from the tip of his finger. He had lost his soul and in his plea, we can almost hear the echo of what Jesus was teaching. "What shall a man give in exchange for his soul?"

Jesus promises His disciples that some of them would not see death until they saw the Son of Man coming into His kingdom. In the near-term context of this statement, it seems more than likely that this was fulfilled on the mount of transfiguration, an event which directly follows this discourse. In addition to the immediate timing of the transfiguration to the promise, another compelling argument is that the word *kingdom* can be translated as "royal splendor." However, it should be noted that several other events have been interpreted as the fulfillment of this promise. They are His resurrection, the coming of the Holy Spirit at Pentecost, the spread of His kingdom through the preaching of the early church, and the destruction of Jerusalem in AD 70.

We too have a promise of seeing the glory of His kingdom. Hebrews 9:26–28 (NIV) tells us that Christ has appeared once for all at the culmination of the ages to do away with sin by the sacrifice of himself. Just as people are destined to die once, and after that to face judgment, so Christ was sacrificed once to take away the sins of many; and he will appear a second time, not to bear sin, but to bring salvation to those who are waiting for him.

We will have found eternal life once we have died to Christ, and when He comes again in His glory, we will join in His exaltation and be rewarded for our steadfastness and in accordance with our works.

CHAPTER 17

TRANSFIGURATION, HEALS BOY, FORETELLS DEATH, TEMPLE TAX

VERSES 1–2

Matthew tells us that six days had passed since Jesus had made the declaration that "there be some standing here, which shall not taste of death, till they see the Son of man coming in his kingdom" (Matthew 16:28). In a parallel account found in Luke 9:28, we read, "And it came to pass about an eight-days after these sayings, he took Peter and John and James, and went up into a mountain to pray." Some have used this seemingly difference in the time frame as a reason to scoff at the accuracy of scripture, but if you look more deeply you will find that there is no difference. Matthew says after six days, and Luke used the Greek way of speaking when he wrote "about eight days later." The Greek rendering of the timing of the event actually means "about a week later." With this note, we can see that the phrases "after six days" and "about a week later" have the same intent when describing the lapse of time between the two events. Another point to be made is that this exacting time reference is extremely rare in the gospels, and it is believed that was included to show the close connection between Peter's confession of faith and the confirmation of Christ's deity as evidenced by the transfiguration's unveiling of His glory.

Peter uses this wonderous event as a proof for the authority of the apostle's teachings when he said,

> For we have not followed cunningly devised fables, when we made known unto you the power and coming of our Lord Jesus Christ but were eyewitnesses of his majesty. (2 Peter 1:16)

Jesus took three of His closest disciples with Him, His inner circle if you will, and led them up a high mountain. Which mountain they ascended is still being debated, but it has no real bearing on the glorious event that transpired there. One might even speculate that exact location was purposefully withheld because of sinful man's propensity to idolize whatever they deem to be holy, such as the bronze serpent Moses had crafted at the Lord's command. God had sent fiery serpents in retribution for the people's sin, and in His mercy, He had used the bronze serpent so that those who had been bitten and looked upon it would live (Numbers 21:4–9). Later we find that when King Hezekiah was removing all of the high places, he broke into pieces the bronze serpent that Moses had made because the people of Israel had made offerings to it (2 Kings 18:4).

Once they had arrived, Jesus was transfigured before them. This has the meaning of a dramatic change that went beyond His external appearance. It was a wholly comprehensive metamorphosis, a transformation of Jesus's entire being whereas He outwardly exhibited a brilliance that was nearly blinding. Of this, John later wrote, "And the Word was made flesh, and dwelt among us (and we beheld his glory, the glory as of the only begotten of the Father,) full of grace and truth" (John 1:14). Matthew goes on to tell us, "His face did shine as the sun, and his raiment was white as the light." Mark 9:2–3 (HCSB) tells us, "He was transformed in front of them, and His clothes became dazzling—extremely white as no launderer on earth could whiten them." Luke's observation was this: "And as he prayed, the fashion of his countenance was altered, and his raiment was white and glistering" (9:29).

The refulgent light of Christ was reminiscent of the glory that Jesus had set aside when He humbled Himself to become a man, and it prefigured His future exaltation and the glorious radiance of deity that has always been His. Revelation 1:16 echoes these verses where we read, "And his countenance was as the sun shineth in his strength."

VERSES 3–4

Suddenly Moses and Elijah appeared and were talking with Jesus. Many see Moses as representing the law and Elijah the prophets, and together, their teachings are the sum total of Old Testament revelation. Today, and on this mountain, they came as a testimony of who Jesus was and to confirm His fulfillment of the revelation found throughout the pages of the Old Testament. They were encouraging Jesus to remain steadfast in His obedience to the Father, steeling and strengthening Him for what was to come. In fact, Luke 9:31 tells us that they were speaking about His departure and what was to be accomplished on the cross at Jerusalem. This was to be the culmination of what had been foretold throughout the Old Testament as it continually pointed to Christ and His ministry.

Undoubtably the apostles were given the spiritual insight to discern who these other men were. In his excitement at the privilege of witnessing the dialogue between Jesus, Moses, and Elijah, Peter somehow hoped that this encounter would not end, and for that reason, as they were departing from them, he tells Jesus that it is good to be there and goes on to offer to make tents or tabernacles for the three of them. It is in this offer that it can be seen that although Peter had correctly identified Jesus as the Messiah, in his limited perception, he had put Christ's servants, Moses and Elijah, on an equal level with their Creator and their Lord. No matter how revered these men were, they were nonetheless men just like Peter and the other apostles, and that it is Christ alone who is preeminent. Luke tells us that Peter didn't know what he was saying, it appears that he was just caught up in the glory of the moment.

VERSES 5–8

Scripture tells us that Peter was still speaking, but in midsentence, he is interrupted by a divine message. Matthew uses the transitive verb "behold" to move us to the manifestation of God in the form of a bright cloud, the shekinah glory, and they heard a voice say, "This is my beloved Son, in whom I am well pleased; hear ye him." These words are reminiscent of the Father's words at the beginning of Christ's ministry when He had just been baptized, but now, toward the end of Jesus's earthly ministry, God adds that they should listen to Him. In Charles Spurgeon's commentary on this verse, he listed several godly men and then said, "But if we be disciples of Jesus, then let us follow Jesus, and follow him with other men only so far as we perceive they followed Christ."

God has pronounced the uniqueness of Jesus, identifying Him as His beloved Son and setting Him above both the law and the prophets. He is superior to Moses and Elijah, and above all others, it is He who should be heard. The apostles are to understand that Jesus is preeminent, and as the Messiah, His purpose must be achieved.

At hearing God's voice, they fell on their faces and were terrified. Up to now, they were in awe of seeing Jesus's transfiguration and at being in the presence of Christ, Moses, and Elijah, an experience they wanted to savor in its continuance, but once they encountered the immediate presence of God the Father, they fell prostrate as they were overcome with an abject fear. For us, having the advantage of scripture (Isaiah 6:5; Ezekiel 1:28; Revelation 1:17), we see this as a normal reaction by anyone who has encountered the sovereign power and supreme authority of God, but for these men, it was a terrifyingly personal and shattering encounter that triggered a physical and sensory overload at the very core of their being that went well beyond anything they had ever experienced.

Jesus comes to them and comforts them with a touch, and at the same time, He tells them to arise and to not be afraid. The passage says that they lifted up their eyes and saw no one but Jesus. The Shekinah glory had lifted, and Moses and Elijah had departed. Once more their attention is focused solely upon Jesus. We too are to lift up our eyes, and our focus should be on Him alone, giving Him honor and glory in all that we do. This is what it is to live a Christ-centered life.

VERSES 9–13

As they came down from the mountain, Jesus commanded them not to speak of His transfiguration until His resurrection. The hidden wisdom of this exhortation was that those who weren't there to see it for themselves may have doubted what had happened, and in this doubt, their faith may have been tested. However, once Jesus rose from the dead, the testimony of His transfiguration would be readily accepted in light of the greater miracle of the resurrection itself, the ultimate proof of His deity. That was why the full revelation of His glory could only come after the cross.

The disciples then ask Jesus about Elijah's coming as it had been told in the Old Testament passage of Malachi 4:5 that says, "Behold, I will send you Elijah the prophet before the coming of the great and dreadful day of the LORD." This was the last prophecy recorded in the Old Testament some four hundred years before, and they were trying to piece together what they knew to be true, that Jesus was the Messiah, with what they knew of scripture. It was a good question as far as their understanding of Malachi's prophecy, but what they overlooked was the full measure of its meaning. This, like so many Old Testament prophecies, had both a more near-term fulfillment as well as an end-time and final completion. The near-term was fulfilled by John the Baptist as foretold in Luke 1 when the angel Gabriel spoke to John's father, Zechariah, and told him that his son would go before the Lord their God in the spirit and the power of Elijah. The end-time fulfillment of the prophecy was more than likely a reference to the appearance of the two witnesses of Revelation prior to the Second Coming of Christ.

Jesus then continues by telling his disciples that in essence Elijah had already come, he wasn't recognized, and they did what they wanted to him. Jesus further told them that He too would surely suffer by their hands. Through their discipleship under the teachings of Jesus, they had grown in their understanding and now perceived that He was talking about the ministry of John the Baptist.

VERSES 14–18

When Jesus and the three had returned, there was crowd awaiting them and a man knelt at His feet begging mercy for his son. He describes his son as suffering from seizures so terrible that he falls into the fire and often into water. Some of the other gospels say that he was an epileptic and that his disease was caused by demons. The man had brought his son to the disciples for healing, but they were unable to help or to heal him. Other gospel writers tell us that there were scribes with the man, with many thinking that this man and his son were known to them and were brought before the disciples as a test. Mark 9 tells us much more about the boy's condition, that he was both deaf and mute. He also tells us that the scribes were belittling the disciples at their failure to cure him, while they themselves did nothing to help. Perhaps they had not wanted to try to heal the boy because Jewish exorcists believed that it is extremely difficult, if not impossible, to eradicate a demon unless you knew its name and thereby gain power and control over them. If it were a mute spirit, you couldn't find out its name. This is the same type of thinking and approach that demons take when they call out the name of Jesus and identify Him as the Holy One of God; it is their feeble and misguided attempt at trying to gain control over Christ.

Jesus said to them "You unbelieving and perverse generation, how long shall I stay with you? (NIV)" He had the boy brought to Him, and immediately after Jesus rebuked the demon it came out of Him. The boy may have been deaf and mute, and the demon may have been unable to hear Jesus's command to come out, or to tell Jesus its name, but nothing is beyond the absolute power and authority of God incarnate.

VERSES 19–20[82]

The disciples came to Jesus privately to question Him as they were bewildered as to why they couldn't cast out the demon. Their perplexity more than likely stemmed from their former successes at casting out demons on the recent mission trip where Christ had commissioned them to do these types of miracles. They now wondered why they could not cast this one out. Perhaps they had been too pridefully dependent on their previous successes and less dependent on the power of Jesus from whom all power emanates, and perhaps they were putting too much faith in themselves and not enough in Jesus. He told them that they failed because of their little faith and pointed out to them that even if the faith they had was like a grain of a mustard seed, they could move mountains and that nothing would be impossible for them. In Jesus's time, the phrase "moving a mountain" was a common Jewish metaphor for accomplishing, through one's trust in the power of God, what was seemingly impossible to do. What He was telling them was that a little faith in the object of their faith goes a long way. Jesus should always be both the object and the subject of our faith. He is our all in all. He alone is always in the perfect will of the Father; any invocation that we make should always be within God's will.

VERSES 22–23

While they were in Galilee, Jesus reminds His disciples again of His pending death at the hands of men and that on the third day He will be raised back to life. They had heard this before but had always either disbelieved, rebuked Him for saying it, or forgotten it altogether until after His resurrection. What was different this time was the fact that He would be delivered into the hands of men. This is the first indication of the insidious and imminent betrayal by Judas.

We are told that at this latest reminder that they were exceedingly sorrowful. They were in such distress that they couldn't comprehend the glory of His

---

[82] Some manuscripts contain another sentence where Jesus says, "But this kind never comes out except by prayer and fasting." Although absent in Matthew, it does appear in Mark 9:29.

overcoming death, not only for Himself but for all those who are His elect past, present, and future. In the case of our Lord and Savior, they are told that He will rise again on the third day, and considering both facts, should they not have been rejoicing? But we won't see that type of emotional response until His ascension, of which we read in Luke 24:51–53.

> While he blessed them, he was parted from them, and carried up into heaven. And they worshipped him and returned to Jerusalem with great joy: And were continually in the temple, praising and blessing God. Amen.

In addition to their sorrow, there may have been a great deal of fear about Jesus's death at the hands of His Jewish enemies and the Roman authorities. In that period of history, the fate of someone's followers was often tied to the fate of their leader, and Jesus was predicting His own death.

They continued to wrestle with their understanding of all that Jesus had taught them, and even though they had witnessed Jesus raising Lazarus, they struggled with coming to a plausible comprehension of His death, a death that would be followed by His being resurrected. All that Jesus had taught and shown them, especially the three who had witnessed His transfiguration, should have bolstered their belief, but it was being quenched by their prior notions of Messiahship and their new and untried perception of a Messiah who was a suffering servant. John Calvin says, "So great is the influence of preconceived opinion, that it brings darkness over the mind in the midst of the clearest light."

VERSES 24–27

This event about the temple tax is only recorded by Matthew, and it is thought that it may have caught his attention in that he himself was a former tax collector. These passages also display Jesus's deity in that He spoke to Peter about the tax before Peter had told Him about his encounter with the collector, as well as in His instruction to Peter regarding the fish and the shekel.

They had arrived at Capernaum, the hometown of Peter. A tax collector approached Peter about the temple tax and whether Jesus would pay it, at which Peter replied yes. Some believe that the tax collector went to Peter instead of Jesus out of deference to the great esteem that He had as a teacher. Others state that he approached Peter because Jesus lived in his home during much of His ministry and it was impolite to approach another's guest directly. Peter then went into the house and before he could say anything, Jesus poses a question to Peter. "On who are the taxes to be imposed?" And upon his replying, "Others," Jesus states, "Then the children are free." There is a subtlety to this in that Jesus, being the Son of God, the Son of the King (as well as rightfully being a King Himself), was exempt from the tax. "Christ, who is greater than the temple and fulfills its intent, has come and true worship will be centered in and toward Him."[83]

This is an example of what Paul later teaches as being a Christian liberty, a right that has been set aside so that another might not stumble. Therefore, instead of causing any offense, Jesus directs Peter to go fishing, but not in the normal sense of him taking his boat and nets out to sea for a normal catch. He simply instructs him to cast a hook and take the first fish that he catches. He is then to open its mouth where he is told that he will find a shekel. It is not in the fish's belly but conveniently in its mouth. No less miraculous as all this is, unsurprisingly, a shekel is a silver coin that is worth four drachmas, which is just enough for Peter to pay the annual temple tax for both himself and for Jesus.

---

[83] Paraphrased from *Tabletalk Magazine* (Sanford, FL, Ligonier Ministries, Inc., July 22, 2008).

CHAPTER 18

WHO'S GREATEST, TEMPTATIONS, PARABLES, SINNED AGAINST

VERSES 1–6

The disciples often debated among themselves as to who was the most favored, the most loved, or who would be chosen as worthy to sit at Jesus's side when Jesus came into His kingdom. This last question escalated to the point where, as we will see in a few more chapters, James and John's mother knelt before Jesus and asked Him to say that they would sit one on the right and one on the left of Him in His kingdom. They continued to fix their eyes on the gain that they would obtain when Jesus was firmly enthroned in His kingdom. They viewed these gains as similar to the spoils of war. There seems to be among the disciples an unending grasping for power and status in Christ's kingdom, and John Calvin says that "they strove with wicked ambition to excel each other."

While they were still in Galilee, they came with the question of who was the greatest in the kingdom of heaven. The disciples remained locked into defining greatness in worldly terms, in their human aspirations, strivings, and accomplishments. Jesus, in His infinite patience, calls a child to be brought in among them. Although He could have rightfully identified Himself as the greatest in heaven, He leaves the question of who is the greatest and shows them that unless they turn or change and become like children and possess a childlike faith, they won't even enter heaven. Without my going into a lot of detail, do not skip over Jesus's use of the word "except" because it is a significant and necessary condition of their ever being able to enter heaven.

Jesus was drawing their attention to the fact that within the nature of sinful man is the innate need for significance, to leave a legacy, and to somehow be seen as important, whereas, a child comes having an implicit faith. With an open heart that is trusting, they are lowly and vulnerable, with each trait being an objective reality of being a child. And because of these characteristics, they willingly answer the call when Jesus beckons them to come. He then tells them that whoever humbles himself as this little child, and displays their ultimate dependence of God, is the greatest in the kingdom. This, of course, obviates any form of false humility but focuses upon living in the knowledge, obedience, and willing acceptance of the sufficiency of Christ, and as Paul taught us in Romans 12:3,

> For I say, through the grace given unto me, to every man
> that is among you, not to think of himself more highly
> than he ought to think; but to think soberly, according as
> God hath dealt to every man the measure of faith.

The nature of this child, as well as His true followers that He also calls little ones, and their open acceptance, is tantamount to the acceptance of Jesus Himself, and this will not go unrewarded. Earlier in Matthew 10:42, we read, "And whosoever shall give to drink unto one of these little ones a cup of cold water only in the name of a disciple, verily I say unto you, he shall in no wise lose his reward." Although Jesus speaks of little children, He is talking about those who have converted and have come to believe in Him with the faith of a child.

In verse 6 of chapter 18, Jesus in effect adds a "woe" to anyone who causes one of these little ones who believe in Him to sin, that it would be better for a millstone to be put around their neck and to be drowned. This put an emphasis on the seriousness of this sin in that this was a form of execution that the Gentiles used, and it was a method of execution that was utterly repulsive to the Jews.

VERSES 7–9

In these verses, we find two distinct woes. The first is for the entire world that faces the inevitable temptations that will come as a part of the unavoidable outcome of man's fallen nature. It is man's sinful nature that manifests itself in a universal depravity, one which Christians should have no part. The second woe specifically targets the man who brings temptation to others. They are guilty before God and have no excuse for their encouragement of sin. They will stand in judgment for their offense.

Jesus's teaching lays out drastic measures for dealing with our sin, and His use of hyperbole is not a call for self-mutilation but a graphically strong representation of the high cost of sin as well as a powerful analogy to encourage us to purge ourselves from sin before it overcomes us. John MacArthur says, "Sin must be dealt with drastically because of its deadly effects."

For these verses to be taken literally would leave our remaining limbs, minds, hearts, and every other aspect of our humanity to readily fill in the void, and we would still remain in our sin. Sin is a part of the nature of fallen man, and Jesus is emphasizing its seriousness and the need to take whatever action that is required to deal with it, no matter how drastic it seems.

Jesus continues His teaching by telling us that it would be better to enter maimed and disfigured into the eternal life of heaven than having two hands and go to hell. This would have been a radically shocking teaching for a Jew to hear because bodily mutilation was strictly forbidden, and it disqualified one from entering the synagogue for worship (Deuteronomy 14:1, 23:1; Leviticus 19:28).

Bearing our cross, we are to live sacrificial lives, forsaking sin, and other worldly entrapments, rather than to enjoy all that the world has to offer at the cost of our souls. Personal sacrifice and the avoidance of sin in obedience to God's mandates is eternally better than going to hell. Scripture tells us that the fire shall never be quenched; it is an everlasting and conscious torture that does not consume; it is perpetual anguish, a place of weeping and the gnashing of teeth, and all the while, most miserably, it is an eternal absence from the presence of the Lord.

VERSES 10–14[84]

Jesus reiterates how highly regarded these little ones are to God and that we are not to despise or ridicule them but treat them well. In our dealings with people throughout our lives, we are in contact with a wide variety of people with a huge disparity in their beliefs, or in at least how they are acting upon those beliefs. To the consternation of the religious elite, Jesus spent a lot of time with those who were seen as sinners and outcast. Jesus was doing what a Good Shepherd is supposed to do. He was looking for strays to bring into the fold, and that is the way we are to look at our own efforts as we proclaim Christ. "We must all grieve when we see brothers or sisters stumble and do all that we can to rescue them."[85] Only Jesus can save them, but we can point them to Him and, when they are drawn to Him, rejoice in the truth of what Jesus says in John 10:27. "My sheep hear my voice, and I know them, and they follow me."

Those described as "little ones" have angels in heaven that are always in direct and continuous communication with our heavenly Father, and this speaks of their principal care and vigilance over those whom they have been charged to watch over. Hebrews 1:14 calls them "ministering spirits," and this should be a great encouragement to us as Christians when we find ourselves immersed in the distress of a crisis in our lives.

---

[84] Some manuscripts add verse 11: "For the Son of Man came to save the lost."

[85] *Tabletalk Magazine* (Sanford, FL, Ligonier Ministries, Inc., July 28, 2008, Coram Deo).

The disciples must also take responsibility and share with Jesus the heart that He has for every individual His Father had given over to Him. With this statement, He segues into the parable of the lost sheep and the value God places on each and every one of us that are a part of His flock, those who are members of the invisible church. Jesus asks a rhetorical question about a large flock of hundred sheep. If one goes astray, won't the ninety-nine who are secure be left while the one that has strayed is being searched for? The stray is the backslidden Christian, the one who now finds himself on the precipice and is in danger of falling into the chasm of sin. The Good Shepherd, filled with pastoral compassion, searches relentlessly for the one who has gone astray and, upon his rescue, rejoices greatly at his return to the fold. His joy, and ours at our brother's restoration, is reflective of our heavenly Father's decretive will that none of His chosen should be lost. It should be remembered that Jesus was talking about the "little ones" that are His true followers. There are those who are lost in that they have never been a part of the flock, such as Judas Iscariot, and in their case, they will remain lost as "the devil, as a roaring lion, walketh about, seeking whom he may devour" (1 Peter 5:8).

VERSE 15

Having just concluded a lesson on not giving offense, this verse begins a teaching on what must be done in the inevitability of having been on the receiving end of an offense. This teaching is on church discipline and therefore "necessarily means confrontation and is established in Christ's call for us to care for the spiritual growth of one another."[86] As a point of clarity, church discipline deals with professing believers who are members of the church and who have sinned against another. As seen in these verses, it is a multiple stepped process.

If we feel that we have been grievously sinned against, or seriously wronged in some way, we are not to talk to our friends or acquaintances about it and we are not to bring it up at a prayer meeting. Rather, we are to go quietly and privately to the one who we feel afflicted us and talk directly with them about it. There should be no garnering of support for our cause

---

[86] *Tabletalk Magazine* (Sanford, FL, Ligonier Ministries, Inc., July 29 2008).

and no opportunity given for various factions to begin taking sides on the issue and thereby bringing disunity to the body.

We have another choice. We can decide to drop the matter altogether, especially if we are talking about a simple slight or some other insignificant and petty annoyance. In this case, we are to remember Peter's admonition. "And above all things have fervent charity among yourselves: for charity shall cover the multitude of sins" (1 Peter 4:8). In any case, if we are to follow Paul's urgings from Ephesians 4:2–3, we must truly drop the matter for the sake of unity and our own conscience. The verses say, "With all lowliness and meekness, with longsuffering, forbearing one another in love endeavoring to keep the unity of the Spirit in the bond of peace." Although this is true, it must be understood that there are some types of sin that merit church discipline. These consist of flagrant sins that may destroy the peace and purity of the body of Christ.

If it is subjective sin and you cannot let it go and it continues to fester within you and there is no peace about it, then you need to lovingly go to your brother and work through the issue. It may be that he wasn't even aware of the offense and upon hearing of it sincerely apologizes, or if he was aware, he may repent of his offense. And then again, you may find that you both were in the wrong in the way the matter was originally handled and come to an equitable settlement of it. In any case, you have gained your brother. He has heard you, which means he has listened, and that is what Jesus requires in this teaching. You have also gained him in the sense that he now sees that you handled the situation in a delicate and biblical manner, with your objective being repentance and not reproach.

VERSES 16–18

If he doesn't listen and remains in sin, Matthew Henry tells us that "we must not be weary of well-doing." In our endeavor at reaching him, we are to follow the law concerning witnesses as it is written in Deuteronomy 19:15, where we read,

> One witness shall not rise up against a man for any iniquity, or for any sin, in any sin that he sinneth: at

the mouth of two witnesses, or at the mouth of three witnesses, shall the matter be established.

This has the benefit of "clearer heads" and many eyes seeing more than one can when it comes to ascertaining the responsibility for what has occurred. They may very well see things differently than the person who was originally offended, as is exampled on Proverbs 18:17–19 (HCSB), which teaches that

> he first to state his case seems right until another comes and cross-examines him. Casting the lot ends quarrels and separates powerful opponents. An offended brother is harder to reach than a fortified city, and quarrels are like the bars of a fortress.

The witnesses also may see the validity of the one who was offended, and if the brother who had made the offense is still unrepentant, the issue is to be brought before the church, which is next step in any escalation of disciplinary action. Some translations say the entire or whole church, and there are many who believe that this refers to the elder board as they are the church leaders who have been charged with shepherding and are the representative head of the congregation as a whole. They are also the body of people who have the power to excommunicate if need be and then to restore the offender when the goal of repentance and reconciliation has been met. With this goal, we can readily see that this is not punishment, retribution, or a total shunning but a loving discipline that keeps the leaven of sin from spreading throughout the congregation. John MacArthur says that he should now be viewed as an evangelistic prospect rather than as a brother. Along this train of thought, Augustine of Hippo wrote that we were not to neglect the offender's salvation, "for every heathen, that is, the Gentiles and Pagans, we do not reckon among the number of brethren, but yet we are ever seeking their salvation." John Calvin, in his *Institutes,* says that it is the best help to sound doctrine, order, and unity. Calvin's comment could be rephrased in such a way as to state that the primary reasons for excommunication would be concern for the soul of the individual and concern for the health of the church.

With these important elements of personal and corporate health and unity, shouldn't every church actively demonstrate and validate these concerns by including biblical discipline as a defining characteristic of their church? As God's people, we are called to be holy, and our being set apart leaves no leeway for even the appearance of a tacit approval of flagrant sin and false teachings. It is for the sake of safeguarding the integrity, purity, and peace of Christ's church that we should embrace church discipline as the righteous judgment and restoration of God for His people.

Unfortunately, many churches do not practice any form of discipline in their misguided fear of appearing unforgiving and merciless.

> Yet refusing to apply church discipline in careful obedience to scripture is the most unloving and merciless thing the church can do. When the church does not call out impenitent people, it gives them the false assurance that they are justified in their sin, and it becomes the cause of disunity and disharmony within the body.[87]

As we have just said, the goal of excommunication is repentance, upon which restoration can occur. Excommunication is not for every sin that one could commit. It is only for the sin of impenitence.

This biblical pattern of discipline in the exercise of godly judgment is a dutifully performed and binding act which denies the unrepentant party fellowship with other believers, as well as the partaking of the sacrament of communion. This earthly binding, and the potential for loosening after evidence of the prayed for repentance that will bring about restoration, are actions that are in complete harmony with those executed in heaven. Church authority is inseparable to the Word of God, and therefore righteous judgment and absolution are proper and heavenly sanctioned uses of the keys of the kingdom.

---

[87] Paraphrased from *Tabletalk Magazine* (Sanford, FL, Ligonier Ministries, Inc., August 15, 2012).

VERSES 19–20

Jesus continues His teaching by restating what He had taught in Matthew 18:19–20, that

> if two of you shall agree on earth as touching anything that they shall ask, it shall be done for them of my Father which is in heaven. For where two or three are gathered together in my name, there am I in the midst of them.

This shows God's willingness to answer the prayers of His church, and within the context of the preceding verses, we can see that this agreement is not just any agreement but an agreement that is within the will of God. And it is in reference to the issue of church discipline. The two or three who are asking are doing so in a prayerful spirit of humble petition while they are gathered in Jesus's name. This is a conditional and specific promise that Jesus makes. It has nothing to do with the radical misinterpretation that some have presumed, that somehow it has become a pledge to grant everyone all of their wishes and dreams.

> Verse 20 promises that He backs up the church's authority when it makes decisions in accord with the Bible, not that He will do whatever a group of Christians asks of Him.[88]

He says that if they ask in His name, He will be with them and guiding them in the decision process, and that is representative of just how strongly He feels about the unity and purity of His church.

VERSES 21–22

At the conclusion of Jesus's teaching on church discipline, Peter questions how often he should forgive a brother of sin against him. He wanted to know what the upper boundary of his obligation was so He asks Jesus if he should forgive that person up to seven times.

---

[88] *Tabletalk Magazine* (Sanford, FL, Ligonier Ministries, Inc., July 31, 2008).

The number of times that Peter suggested has significance. The first being that, according to rabbinical teachings, forgiving someone three times was an acceptable and sufficient amount. And the second was that in Jewish tradition the number seven was considered to be the number representative of perfection. In either case, Peter felt that he would be lovingly generous in forgiving anyone that many times. Peter was probably more than surprised when Jesus replied that he should forgive someone seventy-seven times (English Standard Version and the New International Version). The King James Version and New American Standard Versions state it as seventy times seven. Whatever number Jesus actually responded with is simply representative of the infinite number of times that forgiveness should be given to someone. Forgiveness is always given in the spirit of love, and 1 Corinthians 13:7 tells us that love bears and endures all things. In Luke 17:4, we read that Jesus taught His disciples, "And if he trespass against thee seven times in a day, and seven times in a day turn again to thee, saying, I repent; thou shalt forgive him." Again, there is no stipulated formula where you can plug in a constant number to develop a quantified amount of times you must forgive someone, because the answer always comes up as an infinite number of times. A Christian's life is characterized by love and forgiveness.

VERSES 23–27

As was His pattern, Jesus seamlessly slips into the use of a parable to make His point. There was a man who owed the king ten thousand talents, an insurmountable amount of money to come up with, and this figure was common parlance that signified an infinite number. The value of the debt that this man owed in today's market has been widely estimated and to be as much as nearly $6 billion. Again, the exact worth of the debt is not the point of the parable; it is the exorbitant amount that is to be viewed.

The king ordered him and his whole family sold into slavery and the debt to be paid. We aren't told what this debtor's net worth was, but on the slave market, a captive of royal linage might bring a price of one talent, but the average value of a male slave was closer to forty shekels. Assuming the man was sold for one talent, the value of that amount of money would equal to about twenty years wages for a laborer. This would be a proverbial drop in the ocean of debt that was owed.

The man then begged his Master to have patience with him, and that he would pay it all back. This was an utterly ridiculous pleading as it would be impossible to ever repay his debt. Yet the master of this man was moved to release him and to forgive him of his debt.

This of course is another of Jesus's timeless teachings, and this one brings to us a dramatic illustration of the massive debt of sin that we have accumulated and are unable to pay. This parable resonates with God's mercy and grace at the high cost of our sin and the inestimable price that Jesus paid to become our propitiation. His eternal plan for our salvation set the stage for Him to display His love for us, and out of our fervent prayers, our cries for mercy, and our repentance, our heavenly Father has compassionately forgiven our sins based upon the finished work of Christ. Our debt has been paid even though what we deserved was the full wrath of God and the penalty of death that comes with sin. Our Master's mercy has freed us from the debt of sin and an eternal imprisonment in hell. This grace begets the further blessing of our being able to glorify Him forever as we cast our crowns at His feet in awe and in worship of His majesty.

VERSES 28–30

Here we have the same forgiven servant, a man who has not only been saved from him and his family being sold into bondage as slaves but was also freed from an unsurmountable debt that he could never pay. He should have been walking on the clouds with no worldly cares or concerns, but in the wickedness of his heart, he went out and found one of his fellow servants who owed him one hundred denarii. He grabs the man by the throat and demands to be repaid. We next read that this debtor pleads with the one he owes and uses identical words as he begs for the first man to be patient with him and says that he would pay all that he owes. Even though he himself had been forgiven for a much greater debt, he didn't have the same compassion on the one who was in his debt. This smaller debt amounted to enough money to pay a man's wages for one hundred days, or about four month's wages, so it was not an insignificant amount, but by comparison to what the first man owed, it was nothing. The first man showed no mercy and threw the second man into debtor's prison.

VERSES 31–35

There were other servants who had observed all that went on, and they found what the greater debtor had done to the lesser debtor to be abhorrent. They saw the injustice in this man's actions, something that he was too blind to see for himself. They then went to their master and told him all that had happened. Their master called in the unforgiving servant and called him wicked. He had given this man a great mercy and asked him why he thought that he shouldn't show his fellow servant the same kindness and mercy. In his anger, the master handed him over to the jailer, until he should pay all of his debt, and in this case, his would have been equivalent to multiple life sentences. The man received the justice that he deserved, not the mercy that he had previously obtained.

Jesus concludes His parable by saying (ESV), "So also my heavenly Father will do to every one of you, if you do not forgive your brother from your heart." Christ points to God's offer of forgiveness for the immeasurable magnitude of humankind's debt of sin, and if we fail to grasp the enormity of our debt, along with our inability to pay it, how can we forgive others? The crux of the parable is that we who have been regenerated and have been given transformed hearts should be merciful just as our Father is merciful. As Christians, we are to model ourselves after our Master and King, and in imitation of His mercy and grace, we are to extend that same mercy and grace to others. Matthew Henry reminds us that

> God multiplies his pardons, and so should we. We should make it our constant practice to forgive injuries and should accustom ourselves to it until it becomes habitual.

When we have forgiven others in this way, we can be assured that our Father's forgiveness will overwhelm us in the splendor and majesty of His grace toward us.

CHAPTER 19

ABOUT DEMONS, CHILDREN COME, RICH YOUNG MAN

VERSES 1–2

Jesus had concluded His teachings in Galilee and now traveled to Judea.

Jesus's fame, popularity, and the people's knowledge of the power of His healings was widespread and reached regions well beyond His Galilean ministry. The distance from Galilee to Judea, depending upon where you start and end your journey within these two areas, is from about ninety to 125 miles. Based upon the fitness level of the traveler, it would take somewhere between six days to just under two weeks to make the journey. In these verses, we are told that even in Judea great multitudes sought Him out, followed Him, and that Jesus healed them.

> Jesus taught for several months in Perea, along the eastern shore of the Jordan River, and that area was not technically a part of Judea, but because it was a territory that had been

ruled by Herod the Great it was commonly referred to as Judea.[89]

VERSES 3–9

The ever-present Pharisees with their endless testing come to Jesus with another question that was designed to back Jesus into a corner. On this occasion, the question centered around the highly controversial question surrounding the lawfulness of divorce. There was a great divide even among the leading rabbinical schools, both factions based their arguments around their interpretation of the Mosaic law (Deuteronomy 24:1). One of the hinge points is bordered around the single word translated as "indecency," which can also be translated as "uncleanliness," and just what constitutes or defines these terms.

On the liberal and twisted side of the issue was Rabbi Hillel, who taught that there were many and varied reasons that allowed for a man to put aside his wife. Some of those reasons included spoiling a meal, spinning yarn in the streets, talking loudly enough to be heard by the neighbors, talking to a strange man, or speaking disrespectfully of her husband within his hearing. Another from this liberal school of thought was Rabbi Akiba, who went as far as to say that a divorce could be sanctioned "if a man found a woman who was fairer in his eyes than his wife was." The hardness of the people's hearts quite naturally made this the most popular and acceptable teaching on divorce.

On the other side of the debate is a more conservative view, and Rabbi Shammai's understanding was that the idea of indecency and uncleanliness was to be more narrowly defined as sexual immorality and said that this was the only valid reason for divorce.[90]

---

[89] Paraphrased from John MacArthur, *The MacArthur Bible Commentary* (Nashville, TN: Thomas Nelson Inc, 2005), 1159.

[90] The rabbi's various points of view are paraphrased from excerpts from www.blueletterbible.org study notes on Mark by David Guzik as well as R. C. Sproul's *St. Andrew's Expositional Commentary on Mark* (Wheaton, IL, Crossway, 2013).

The Pharisees were well aware of the contentiousness surrounding the subject of divorce and were only baiting Jesus. It was another effort to trap Him into standing in opposition to the Mosaic law or in saying something that would be unpopular with the people and therefore discredit Him in their eyes. Another possibility for this question may have been the fact that Herod Antipas governed this area. John the Baptist had been extremely vocal against Herod's incestuous marriage to his former sister-in-law Herodias, and Herod had John executed. Perhaps the Pharisees were hoping for some type of intervention from Herod if Jesus took a similar stance on divorce.

They still hadn't accepted that Jesus was the Law Giver and that He had no interest in Herod's opinion, the public's opinion, or theirs for that matter. Jesus's mission was to preach God's truth without concerning Himself about how it would be perceived.

Jesus always defaults to scripture. It alone dictates how we should handle our lives, not rabbinical traditions or misinterpretations that tickled the ears of many. Jesus went to scripture as the common ground for discussion, as it was something that the Pharisees should have had a deeply profound knowledge of.

Jesus then tells them that the reason Moses granted the writing of the certificate of divorce was because of man's hardheartedness. It wasn't a command; it was a concession. He emphasized that marriage is a permanent relationship between a man and a woman. Jesus further explained why the popular view of the day was wrong, and He demonstrated this by going back to God's act of creation. He reminds them of what Genesis 1:27 and 2:24 say. So God created man in his own image, in the image of God created he him; male and female created he them" and "Therefore shall a man leave his father and his mother, and shall cleave unto his wife: and they shall be one flesh." Jesus continued to move toward the logical extension of God's creative design and said "Therefore, what God has joined together, man must not separate (HCSB)."

Jesus wasn't interested in the cultural understanding of the time that they were living in. He wasn't pressured by the social normative espoused by the religious leaders of the day. He went back to God's original intent for marriage and family. God's pattern, or design, for marriage hadn't changed. He is immutable and there is an eternal perfection in His design.

When they are wed, a couple are not only joined together through a betrothal and a ceremony that consecrates the covenant of marriage; it goes much deeper than that. They are bonded together as one flesh, "bone of my bones, and flesh of my flesh" (Genesis 2:23). A man and a woman are joined together physically, emotionally, and spiritually; therefore, divorce is a radical surgery. It is an attempt to sever two out of the spiritually conjoined who have become one. Jesus concludes with the statement that if a man divorces his wife, with the exception of a case of sexual immorality, and then marries another woman, he commits adultery.

VERSES 10–12

In His teaching about divorce and remarriage being an adulterous situation, Jesus introduces the fact that sexual immorality is a legitimate reason for divorce, and in this statement, there is the implication that He substantiated Rabbi Shammai's understanding that uncleanliness, or indecency, was defined by sexual immorality and was the only valid reason for divorce. We later find that under his apostolic authority, Paul adds the case of abandonment by an unbelieving spouse to sexual immorality as having scriptural grounds for divorce (1 Corinthians 7:15).

The disciples conclude that if this is the case, it is better not to marry, whereas Jesus goes on by telling them that He recognizes that what was said was a hard teaching, that it is better not to marry, and that not everyone can accept it. Nor should they. We must keep in mind that in Genesis, once Eve was given to Adam, God blessed them and told them to be fruitful and multiply. Jesus's Word on these matters should not be misunderstood as His calling everyone to a life of either celibacy or of marriage. He talks of eunuchs and our modern Western culture immediately leaps to the emasculated man who is in charge of a sultan's harem, but there are other forms of one being considered a eunuch. Jesus tells us that there are some who are born without the capacity for sexual union in marriage. There are also those who are made eunuchs by men, such as the overseer in a harem. And the final category includes those who choose to live a life of celibacy and forego marriage for the sake of service to God, such as Jesus Himself. Jesus says that these are not easily acceptable conditions and can only be received by those who will acknowledge the certainty of those conditions.

VERSES 13–15

The people brought their children to Jesus so that He would bless them. The disciples were reluctant to allow the children, who were more than likely infants, to be brought to Jesus as they thought perhaps that they would be a hinderance to His teaching. Although Jewish culture prized children, they had a fairly insignificant role in first-century society. The disciples felt that their Master shouldn't needlessly be disturbed by their presence. Jesus rebukes the disciples for turning them away and tells them not to hinder the children. Jesus then proclaimed that "for of such is the kingdom of heaven." Jesus's teaching now moved beyond merely the children who were being brought to Him, and the "for of such" He spoke of are indicative of all who came to Him with a childlike faith, with no hidden agendas or preconceived notions, and from that point of view, the children were pure at heart. This does not mean these children were devoid of the inherent guilt and sin that are ours as a result of Adam's fall, but that they did not have the culpability that comes with intentionally willful sin. What they did possess were the childlike qualities of absolute dependence, and in the simplicity of their trust, they could turn from their sin and be peacefully sheltered in His loving arms.

This teaching was a metaphor for the spiritual humility that is needed for entrance into the kingdom of heaven, and even at that, it is because God, in His infinite grace, has chosen to redeem them.

Scripture tells us that He laid His hands on the children, which is a biblical euphemism for His having blessed them as this was the traditional manner of blessing children in Israel, especially when the blessing is one that is handed down from one generation to the next.

VERSES 16–19

A young man came to Jesus and called Him teacher. The other gospels tell us he knelt at Jesus's feet and called Him "Good Master," whereas Jesus told him that "there is none good but one, that is, God." Other rabbis would never use the title of Good Teacher as everyone recognized the uniqueness of that title because of the implication of sinlessness; therefore, only God was called "good" by ancient rabbis. Jesus's questioning of the man's use of the title "Good Master" was a subtle and an almost imperceptible demand that the Pharisees look to the truth of words of adoration that the young ruler had just spoken.

This young man's world viewpoint is strikingly obvious in the manner of his questioning concerning what he could do to have eternal life. The connotation is that he can somehow make it happen if only someone would give him the esoteric means or knowledge that would allow him to unlock, through his own works righteousness, the pearly gates. This same mentality is still prevalent today.

Jesus taught everyone that He encountered that salvation was a gift of God, but this young ruler asked, "What good thing shall I do, that I may have eternal life?" This man had not, in a spiritual sense, heard Jesus's message and had fallen into the trap of works as a means to obtain righteousness. He wanted to perform some sort of religious deed that would grant him eternal life. Being wealthy, he may have thought that a large contribution might buy him what he sought. He wasn't focused on a relationship; he wanted to be in a position of earning, or in some way, deserving his salvation.

Because all Jews know the Ten Commandments, Jesus quoted the man the second portion of the Decalogue, the part that dealt with relationships and how we treat one another.

VERSES 20–22

The man, either out of arrogance or a misunderstanding of the full purity and depth of the meaning of these commandments, told Jesus that he had kept them all from his youth. From a shallow worldly perspective, his declaration would seem to be true, but from a more complete understanding that comes with the faith we receive after regeneration, it is seen to be blatantly false and impossible as true obedience calls for absolute perfection.

Jesus didn't refute his claim to having kept all the commandments but viewed him with loving compassion. This look wasn't a superficial gaze; it was a piercing look into the man's heart and at his motives. If this man couldn't accept the free gift of salvation and wanted to know what he could do, Jesus would give him something to do. Jesus simply told him "If you want to be perfect, go, sell your possessions and give to the poor, and you will have treasure in heaven. Then come, follow me (NIV)." Jesus gave him a promise that he would have treasure in heaven. Jesus's promises are always fulfilled, but this man chose to cling to his fleeting earthly wealth instead of the eternal wealth that Jesus had assured him of. In dismay, he counted the cost from a worldly perspective, and in sorrow, he went on his way. In his tacit refusal to follow Christ, he not only didn't divest himself of his wealth, he also denied the poor of the blessings that would have come from his charitable act of giving.

Jesus's exchange with the rich, young ruler was not a call to a life of poverty or self-denial as a means for salvation. It was asked to unmask his true affections. Would he, as Matthew had done when he walked away from his career and his wealth, leave everything and submit to Jesus as his Master? Or would he embrace his possessions and forsake what Christ had to offer, which was the eternal life that he had been seeking? Although he had claimed not to break any commandment, he walked away from Jesus after having broken the greatest commandment. "And thou shalt love the LORD thy God with all thine heart, and with all thy soul, and with all thy might" (Deuteronomy 6:5). Jesus had discerned that this man's god was money, and it was clear that he had also broken the first commandment as well. "Thou shalt have no other gods before me."

VERSES 23–26

Jesus, in His perfection and as the consummate teacher, never missed an opportunity to instruct His disciples. In His telling them that it was hard for the rich to enter the kingdom of God, they were perplexed as they more than likely thought that riches were a sign of blessings and could only bring about good. This idea was probably based on scriptures such as Deuteronomy 28:11 where they would have read,

> And the LORD will make you abound in prosperity, in the fruit of your womb and in the fruit of your livestock and in the fruit of your ground, within the land that the LORD swore to your fathers to give you (ESV).

Unfortunately, the part of scripture that they had glossed over was found at the end of verse 9, where they would have read that this promise followed a conditional clause, which stated, "If thou shalt keep the commandments of the Lord thy God and walk in his ways." We are often so attracted to God's promises we forget about, or somehow overlook, their inseparable link to a condition.

At the disciple's reaction, Jesus repeated His statement. "Again I say unto you, It is easier for a camel to go through the eye of a needle, than for a rich man to enter into the kingdom of God."

We tend to forget that as compared to those who were thought to be rich in Jesus's time, most of us live a more comfortable life and have luxuries that they never dreamed of. Our complacency to the comforts of life can be the very impediment that creates in us a false sense of self-sufficiency and a satisfaction with the goodness of our lives. There are inherent spiritual dangers that come with wealth or any degree of it. The same danger exists for anyone, rich or poor, who loves and strives for money more than they strive for Christ. Money and material wealth are not the problem. In and of themselves, they are neutral. It is the condition of one's heart that matters.

The danger is in being lulled into living a life that is seemingly independent of our need for God and therefore fosters within us a lack a yearning for the kingdom to come. Our only hope is that God sovereignly intervenes and through the Holy Spirit convicts us to awaken to the greatest need that we have—that of our salvation.

The disciples are now not only perplexed but astonished at the magnitude of Jesus's impossible comparison, and in an almost pleading manner they asked, "Who then can be saved?" With their misconception about the rich having an advantage over the poor when it came to salvation, they feel at a loss as to how anyone else could be saved.

Jesus looked at them reassuringly and replied, "With men this is impossible; but with God all things are possible." He was telling them that man is incapable of realizing their own salvation and God's grace is both necessary and sufficient to save anyone, rich or poor.

VERSES 27–30

Peter, the ever practical, states that they had left everything to follow Jesus. He was somewhat consternated by the fact that the rich could enjoy their earthly wealth and through God's saving grace also enjoy heavenly rewards. He was trying to figure out how things would balance out once they received their eternal reward. Jesus replied that when He, the Son of Man, sits upon His throne, they would each sit on thrones and judge the twelve tribes of Israel. They would be a part of His heavenly administration with the special role in the future judgment that was to come. In addition, they will be highly honored in that the wall of the New Jerusalem will have twelve foundations, and on them will be the names of the twelve apostles of the Lamb (Revelation 21:14).

Jesus again resorts to hyperbole by stating that "everyone that hath forsaken houses, or brethren, or sisters, or father, or mother, or wife, or children, or lands, for my name's sake, shall receive a hundredfold." But most importantly, they "shall inherit everlasting life."

And as a final note, Jesus reminds them again, "But many that are first shall be last; and the last shall be first." This could be viewed as a mild admonishment to Peter's questioning of future gains for following Christ. It should be sufficient to follow and serve Him out of thankfulness for His salvific ministry and the promise of eternal life. There should be no comparison of one's accomplishments or perceived merits based upon some level or another of sacrifice by one person over another. Christ came to serve, and they were not greater than their Master. It is the grace of God that should drive us to thankful service and obedience.

> Many who are great in the eyes of the world will be last, and others who are deemed as less than worthy and are overlooked in the world will be first in the kingdom of God.[91]

Another aspect of this saying is that, although the apostles were the inner circle of Jesus's friends and therefore could be thought to be the first to receive special accolades, there may be those yet to come who may very well be last in some sort of chronological scheme of things but may still be first from an eternal perspective. Peter and the others should not be concerned about the sovereignty of God. He is always just, and each of His chosen will come into the same eternal glory.

Jesus never denied that there are degrees of heavenly reward, which can be seen in the parable that follows. With Peter's awareness of the full abundance of God's grace and generosity, it may have been prudent for him to have acknowledged that they would all receive more than they ever deserved or dreamed of.

---

[91] Paraphrased from R. C. Sproul, *St. Andrew's Expositional Commentary on Matthew* (Wheaton, IL, Crossway, 2013), 582.

CHAPTER 20

LABORERS PAID, A MOTHER'S REQUEST, TWO BLIND MEN HEALED

VERSES 1–2

This teaching is an extenuation of the last several verses in chapter 19, where Jesus gave a promise of reward and told them that in God's economy, the distribution of rewards is not the same as man's way of giving them out. In His presentation of this parable, Jesus will illustrate God's principle when rewarding men.

In this teaching, He used another parable that centered around agriculture as it was a familiar theme for those He was addressing. Jesus begins telling about a master who goes out early one morning to hire workers for his vineyard. They agree upon being paid a denarius, which was the usual wage for a day's work, and he sends them to his vineyard to begin working. The marketplace was commonly where day laborers came and waited for someone to hire them, and they usually were there and ready to work by 6:00 a.m.

VERSES 3–7

A typical workday was divided into four three-hour intervals, and at each interval, the master goes to the marketplace and continues to hire groups of men to work in his vineyard. Presumably, he had been monitoring the progress being made and continued to hire on the basis of the need to complete a certain amount of work within the course of that day. We are told that he returned to the marketplace four more times, even right up to the eleventh hour, which was about 5 p.m., to hire additional workers.

> Grapes were one of the most valuable commodities in ancient Israel because they could be transformed into fine wines. So important were the vineyards that the prophets often describe the salvation of God's people as including the restoration of the vineyards of the Promised Land (Amos 9:14). Vinedressers and vineyard owners know, however, that the profitability of their vineyard depends on harvesting the grapes at just the right time.[92]

VERSES 8–10

The day's work had concluded, and in the evening, the owner of the vineyard had his foreman call them to be paid. He also instructed him to start by paying those who had come last and continue up to those who had come first. Those who had come to work at the eleventh hour each received the full day's wage of a denarius, and when those who were hired first came for their pay, they had an expectation that they would be paid more, but each of them was given the same wage of one denarius as those who had worked for only one hour.

VERSES 11–16

Those who had been the first to begin the work had watched as each group consecutively received their wages. When they finally got paid, they were disappointed because it was an equal amount of money as had been given

---

[92] *Tabletalk Magazine* (Sanford, FL, Ligonier Ministries, Inc., March 24, 2016).

to those who had only worked an hour. These earliest workers were upset at what they viewed as a gross inequity. They grudgingly spoke of their long hours of work in the heat of the day and compared their toil to that of those who had only put in a short amount of time but had received an equal amount of pay.

When the landowner replied to the complaint, it was without malice, and he called the man he was addressing friend. He reminded them that they had set an agreed-upon wage of one denarius and this was the amount that they had been paid. He told them that they had received what they had initially been hired for, and in paying that amount, he had done them no wrong. He continued by saying that they should take what belongs to them and to go. He resumed in his gentle rebuke by further pointing out that it was his right, and his choice, to be generous with his own money and they shouldn't begrudge that fact.

Jesus now gives His disciples an application of the principle of God's grace and sovereignty in rewarding those that He has chosen, "so, the last shall be first, and the first last." God's gracious rewards for His people will always be fair, but they also may be surprising.

We are to serve God within the fullness of our individual capacities without comparing our accomplishments with any others. Our serving should be with our hearts filled with gratitude for His grace and not a spiteful envy for what others may have received. One example of this is that we all will get to heaven by God's grace. Some will have served faithfully for many years, and others, such as the thief on the cross, have or will receive God's mercy, grace, and full blessing as a disciple of Christ even though following Him for a much shorter period. Our reward of salvation remains the same, indifferent to what happens to others.

In both the Old Testament and New Testament, a vineyard is a metaphor for Israel, with God being the landowner. This parable is about God's grace. Each of the early laborers had received a just reward for their efforts. There was no injustice in their having received their agreed-upon wage. In every group of workers that came later we see mercy and grace in that they received a full wage. The owner of the vineyard in the parable said "Don't I have the right to do what I want with my business? Are you jealous because I'm generous (HCSB)?" Likewise, although not all are chosen, as God's creation, we are all His people to do with as is His good pleasure, and God said to Moses, "I will have mercy on whom I will have mercy, and I will have compassion on whom I will have compassion" (Romans 9:15).

Not unlike the first group of workers, in our fallen condition, we sometimes think that God owes us more than what we have received. The reality is that God owes us nothing and we owe Him everything. We deserve nothing but His wrath, but by grace, we are saved because of a righteousness that is not our own. If God were to pour out His justice upon us, we would not stand, but by His grace, we are saved. We stand before God and are declared just, we are righteous because of the finished work of Christ, and this is true no matter how long we have been laboring in His vineyard.

VERSES 17–19

They were on the way to Jerusalem, drawing ever closer to the cross, and Jesus took the twelve aside to give them some more insight. They were more than likely traveling with larger groups of pilgrims who were making their way to Jerusalem for the Passover and His message was not for everyone. Jesus told them where they were going and that He would be betrayed and delivered over to the chief priests and scribes. At this point, there was no response from His disciples. On the one hand, they were aware that they were headed in the direction of Jerusalem, and in that it was nearly Passover, they weren't too surprised at their destination. What is puzzling was that Jesus had once again told them that He would be betrayed, yet they didn't ask Him a single question about who would betray Him, nor did they say anything about Him being condemned to death, turned over to the Romans, mocked, flogged, and then crucified. They didn't even question His claim that He would be resurrected after three days. This was the third and most detailed prediction of His passion and resurrection, and it was the first indication that the Gentiles would play a major role in the events that were about to unfold.

As painful as it must have been for them to hear, there was no response or probing questions. You have to wonder if the disciples were even listening. Charles Spurgeon said that they may have imagined that this was a parable that they couldn't grasp the meaning of. They may have felt that it had some deep mystery, and they tried to fathom meaning where there was no depth, and that the truth lay on the very surface of what Christ had told them.

VERSES 20–21

Sadly, right after Jesus had spoken of the events that would soon come to pass, His predicted fulfillment of destiny as the suffering servant, James and John's mother comes with a personal request reflective of the ongoing debate within the close followers of Jesus. Salome knelt before Him and asked that her sons, who were two of Jesus's closest disciples, be elevated to positions just to the left and right side of Him in His kingdom. Jesus had already promised His apostles that they would have twelve thrones in heaven, and now, on the cusp of Jesus's passion, they are covetously jockeying for position, even to the point of assigning their mother the task of going before Jesus to plead for these places of honor. Salome is a faithful follower of Jesus, and based upon other scriptural references (Mark 15:40, 16:1; John 19:25), it is believed by many that she is the sister of Jesus's mother, Mary; therefore, James and John are His cousins. If this is the case, she may have been relying on this familial connection to ensure these cherished seats of power were her sons.

VERSES 22–23

The word used for "you" or "ye" in these verses is plural, so we see that Jesus responds to James and John directly and tells them they have no idea what they are asking of Him. He goes on to question them and asks if they are able to drink the cup that He is about to drink. The cup that Jesus was about to drink contained of fullness of God's wrath stored up for the sin of all humankind. The magnitude of the horror contained within this cup would later cause Jesus to fall on His face and pray "Father, if it be possible, let this cup pass from me" (Matthew 26:39).

Their reply of yes, that they were able, was both emphatic and a little too quickly made, for they had no clue as to what was before them. Matthew Henry tells us, "We do not know what we ask, when we ask for the glory of wearing the crown and do not ask for grace to bear the cross on our way to it."

No one but Jesus could drink the fullness of what He was about to endure, and He simply replied that they would indeed drink of His cup as it was common that the followers of a master shared in his fate. All believers will in some small measure take up the cup of suffering, but they will never have to experience the wrath of God for their sins. Jesus alone has paid the price for our inequity, and we have become heirs of His glory and covered in His righteousness. Jesus continues by asking them if they are prepared to be baptized as He is about to be baptized. This is the baptism of suffering, and in fact, they will suffer but to a lesser degree. James will be the first apostle to be martyred (Acts 12:2), and John, although not martyred, will be severely persecuted throughout his life. Another quote from the pen of Matthew Henry informs us, "Religion, if it is worth anything, is worth everything; but it is worth little, if it is not worth suffering for."

Jesus further told them that it was not His to grant the positions that they had asked for, but that they were appointed to those that the Father had prepared them for. Although He was of the same essence of the Father and equal in power and glory, He willingly submitted to the Father's will and defers to Him in all things. Each person of the Trinity is always in agreement because, although they are distinct in personhood, they are indivisible as the one true God. Charles Spurgeon put it this way:

> He comes to do not his own will, but the will of him that sent him, and so he correctly says of rank in his kingdom that it was not His to give. How thoroughly did our Lord take a lowly place for our sakes! In this laying aside of authority, he gives a silent rebuke to our self-seeking.

VERSES 24–28

The other ten apostles heard all that was going on and what Jesus had said to James and John, and they were indignant at the two brothers. Their concern more than likely centered around the brothers having used their mother in an attempt to gain some sort of unfair advantage in acquiring what they too wanted for themselves. Some Bible translations say that the ten were greatly displeased, and this has the meaning of a jealous displeasure toward the two in their pursuit of personal rights and privilege.

Jesus called them to His side and began His teaching with an example of how Gentile rulers lord their power and become autocratic and dictatorial over the people. Jesus followed this example with an admonishment that this wasn't the way it was going to be with them. He continues to correct their thinking by telling them that whoever would be great among them must be their servant, and whoever would be first among them must be their slave. These were two of the lowest positions in Jewish society, but Jesus elevates these positions with a previously unheard-of dichotomy so that the first and greatest among the disciples must be like the least, humbling themselves in loving service to others.

Jesus finishes this teaching by using Himself as the example that ought to be followed by every Christian. Using His favorite title for Himself, He tells them that the Son of Man didn't come to be served but to save and to give His life as a ransom for many. Spurgeon said that

> his was a life of giving, and the giving of a life ... No
> service is greater than to redeem sinners by his own death,
> no ministry is lowlier than to die in the stead of sinners.

Jesus is our Redeemer, and He alone was qualified to pay God the ransom that was required to satisfy the injustice of our sin and to assuage the wrath of God for our transgressions against His holiness. A ransom is a payment of money and was often used to release a slave or a prisoner from bondage, and in this case, it was to release many of those in bondage and enslavement to sin. Jesus also said that He was giving His life as a ransom for, or in place of, "many," not that He was giving His life to ransom "all."

This is nothing less than what theologians have termed as "substitutionary atonement," and more specifically "limited or particular atonement." Jesus gave His life for those the Father had sovereignly chosen in eternity past as His elect. That being said, it should be further noted that in the perfection of Christ's sacrificial death, it was sufficient for all, but that it was only efficient for some. God's effectual calling preconditions the value of the ransom, and there are those who place their values on things of this world without considering the eternal value of what they have put their trust in.

VERSES 29–34

We find Jesus and His disciples leaving Jericho. This was not the Jericho of the Old Testament, but a new city built in the same general area. This potentially confusing fact may be the reason that one gospel account says that they "were drawing near" to Jericho whereas this account says that they were leaving.

As Jesus and His disciples continued on their pilgrimage to Jerusalem, which is now only about a day's journey to the southwest, we are told that a great crowd followed Him and that by the roadside were two blind men. When these men heard that Jesus was passing by, they cried out to the Son of David for His mercy. Scripture tells us that the crowd rebuked these men and told them to be silent. We have become used to seeing the disciples discouraging and trying to silence those who would come to Jesus, and it may very well be that the crowd that was following Jesus was wholly comprised of His disciples. Nonetheless, these two blind men cried out all the louder. They had no doubt heard of Jesus's miraculous healings, and in fear of missing this great opportunity to avail themselves of His healing power, they paid no attention to the crowd as their only focus was on Jesus. Perhaps we are too complacent in our Christianity, but shouldn't our fervor for Christ resound with the same level of desperation that drove these men to continue pleading for His mercy as they gave glory to His name by calling Him Lord and the Son of David?

For some time now, Jesus had been relentlessly steadfast on His quest to return to Jerusalem, but upon hearing the persistent pleas for His mercy,

He stopped and stood still, and He beckoned them to come. He then asks them what they want Him to do for them, at which they replied, "Lord, that our eyes may be opened." Jesus, the ever compassionate and loving shepherd that He is, took pity on these men. Even with the weight of the cross already on His shoulders, He had stopped to heal them with a touch, and having recovered their sight, they followed Him.

CHAPTER 21

TRIUMPHAL ENTRY, FIG TREE, AUTHORITY CHALLENGED, PARABLES

VERSES 1–6

Jesus was aware of what was waiting for Him in Jerusalem, the condemnation, His arrest, His being turned over to the Romans, and His crucifixion. To put it succinctly, Jesus's arrival in Jerusalem on Palm Sunday marked the beginning of the final events that would lead to His exaltation. At this juncture in His journey, He sent two of His disciples into Bethphage with very explicit and detailed instructions. Once they arrived, they would find a donkey and her colt, untie them, and bring them back to Jesus. He even told them the specific response they were to give if anyone asked what they were doing, and the words "the Lord needs them" was included in that response. Jesus had referred to Himself as Lord. He did not send them with the message that Jesus of Nazareth needed them but that the Lord needed them. This event was a display of His divine omniscience, in His foreknowledge of the animal's location, as well as the ready acquiescence of those who owned them.

All this was to set the stage for His triumphal entry into Jerusalem, all in fulfillment of the coming king that had been prophesized (Zechariah 9:9). R. C. Sproul's commentary indicates that Jesus was consciously aware that He was fulfilling messianic prophecy and that He was doing it in submission to God's eternal plan for our salvation.

Mark's gospel message tells us that the colt had never been ridden, and this combined with the noise and press of the crowds would have normally made this young animal wild and unfit to ride. However, Jesus mounts and rides the colt with ease; the Creator was in full dominion of His unassertively yielding creation. His riding into Jerusalem on a colt not only fulfilled what was prophesized but was in keeping with what was customary for royalty, to humbly ride a colt in dignity just as the kings of old had done (Judges 10:4, 12:14; 1 Kings 1:33, 38, 44). Up to this point in His earthly ministry, He had continually warned people not to disclose His true identity, but now in the fullness of time, through the continuance of unmistakable fulfillment of prophecy, and in undeniable messianic overtones, He is preparing to ride into Jerusalem in an unambiguous yet humble declaration of His kingship.

VERSES 7–11

They brought the donkey as an effort to sooth its unbroken foal, draped their cloaks over them, and Jesus sat upon the colt and on top of their garments. As they moved toward and into Jerusalem, most the crowd began to spread their cloaks on the road, an ancient right of homage to royalty, with some cutting branches off the trees and laying them on the road as well, which was symbolic of victory and success, a foreshadow of the event written of in Revelation 7:9–10.[93] The multitude of people was such that many went before Him and others followed along behind, and in His honor, each was shouting out, "Hosanna to the son of David: Blessed

---

[93] Revelation 7:9–10 says, "After this I beheld, and, lo, a great multitude, which no man could number, of all nations, and kindreds, and people, and tongues, stood before the throne, and before the Lamb, clothed with white robes, and palms in their hands; And cried with a loud voice, saying, Salvation to our God which sitteth upon the throne, and unto the Lamb."

is he that cometh in the name of the Lord; Hosanna in the highest!" They gave glory to Jesus in the use of these titles, each of which was befitting of the Messiah. Hosanna means "save now," which can be seen as the salvation Christ brought, as well as a petition that some cried out in hope of an earthly reign that would soon overthrow their oppressors. Many still did not understand that Jesus had not come to be crowned as an earthly and conquering king but that He came as a suffering servant whose intent was to utterly destroy their true enemies of sin and death. Even so, the fact that they recognized Jesus as having been sent by God was made unmistakable in their resounding chorus of "Blessed is He who comes in the name of the Lord."

Luke's account (19:41–44) tells us that as Jesus looked over the city, He wept in His knowing the fearful judgment that would come upon Jerusalem.

As Jesus entered Jerusalem, the raucous display and the cries of adulation aroused the whole city, and some wondered aloud, "Who is this?" The crowd responded, "This is Jesus the prophet of Nazareth of Galilee." It seems evident that neither the questioner nor the respondent was a follower of Jesus. Even while they were jubilantly crying out words of blessing toward Him, there were still those who only acknowledged Him by one of His titles, that of prophet, while leaving out His other messianic titles, those which in conjunction with that of being a prophet would have more completely identified Him as being prophet, priest, and king, further highlighting that He was the long-anticipated Messiah.

Going to the book of Luke again (19:39–40), we see that he added the fact that some of the Pharisees who were in the crowd urged Jesus to rebuke His disciples for the intensity and their fervency in proclaiming Him as Messiah. Jesus boldly replied that "if these should hold their peace, the stones would immediately cry out."

VERSES 12–13

In John's gospel (2:13–17) when he records that Jesus cleansed the temple in Jerusalem, the event takes place early in Jesus's ministry, sometime between the wedding at Cana where He performed His first miracle and the meeting He had with Nicodemus and His teaching about being born again. In John's account, there was an immediate confrontation with the temple officials, and this is absent from the other gospel accounts. In Matthew (21:12–13), Mark (11:15–17), and Luke (19:45–46), a similar event takes place late in His ministry, sometime after His triumphant entry into Jerusalem and within a week of His arrest. This second cleansing has no recorded contact with the temple officials, only Jesus's interaction with those buying and selling within the temple grounds. Even so, there remain differing opinions on it being the same or different events, but the fact remains that the purpose would have been the same, to drive out those who desecrated the Lord's house.

Not only was there desecration, they were extorting large sums of money from the pilgrims, exploiting those who came to sacrifice. Some chose not to bring animals on their arduous journey from their homeland and bought animals once they arrived. Others brought their own animals and the priests would determine if an animal was fit for sacrifice, and if it wasn't, the merchants were more than ready to sell them an animal that would be. R. C. Sproul's commentary said that the price for a pair of doves was nearly fifty times higher if purchased inside the temple than if they were purchased elsewhere. The same was true with the money changers. Roman coins bearing the emperor's image and other forms of currency were unacceptable for the temple offering. Shekels were the only coinage accepted as an offering, but they were not always used in everyday commerce. So if you didn't have shekels, the money changers were there, and for a handsome profit because of the excessive exchange rate, they were eager to trade a person's unacceptable coins for shekels. In all of these transactions, there would have been some level of kickback that went to the temple or its representatives ("but ye have made it a den of thieves").

The other aspect of this is with the great number of animals brought in for the required sacrifices and the need for them to be housed. The animals, while waiting to be sold, along with the money changers conducting their business, were all located in the Gentile court. Marks gospel tells us that Jesus went back to scripture and told them what Isaiah had said. "Is it not written; My house shall be called of all nations the house of prayer?" (Isaiah 56:7). And the only place of prayer for the Gentiles was the court of the Gentiles, which was now a corral filled with livestock; therefore, it was defiled and not conducive for prayer and worship. It is no wonder that Jesus drove out those engaged in these activities, overturning the tables of the money changers and the seats of those who sold pigeons.

VERSES 14–17

His righteous indignation may have upset the temple officials, but it did nothing to discourage the needy from seeking Him out and coming to Him. The blind and the lame were also thought to be restricted from the temple grounds, or at least relegated to the Gentile court, and were more than likely present as Jesus drove out the merchants and money changers. When things had settled down, Jesus turned to these outcasts in His loving compassion to minister to their want of healing, once again displaying the power of God that was His to wield to those suffering the hardship of their infirmity.

The chief priests and the scribes witnessed all the wondrous things that were going on and saw the children playing and crying out in the temple praises toward Jesus as they sang out, "Hosanna to the Son of David." They were indignant to say the least, and in their mortification, they asked, "Do You hear what these are saying?" Jesus drew upon scripture once again and replied, "Have ye never read, Out of the mouth of babes and sucklings thou hast perfected praise?" (the Greek translation of Psalm 8:2). "This is another assertion of His deity as Psalm 8:2 speaks of praise offered to God, and Jesus used this verse as a claim to the right to be worshipped as God."[94]

> Pride in their own status and power motivates the authorities to reject Jesus as the Messiah, despite all the proof of His anointing. Matthew Henry writes, "Proud men cannot bear that honor should be done to any but to

[94] Paraphrased from John MacArthur, *The MacArthur Bible Commentary* (Nashville, TN: Thomas Nelson Inc, 2005), 1164.

themselves, and they are uneasy at nothing more than at the just praises of deserving men.[95]

And with that, He left Jerusalem and went back to Bethany, where He was likely a guest in the home of Lazarus and his sisters Mary and Martha.

VERSES 18–22

We read that Jesus became hungry on the way to the temple, and it is probable that He had risen early and went to a quiet place to pray before going back to Jerusalem and had not taken the time to eat before He left Martha and Mary's.

He saw a fig tree along the wayside, which was in full leaf, and this type of fig tree generally produced fruit during the same time that it had its leaves. However, when Jesus went to it, there weren't any figs. (This is reminiscent of Jeremiah 8:13.) He then cursed it with the words "Let no fruit grow on thee henceforward forever," and presently the fig tree withered away.

As he tends to do, Matthew's report of this event is in the form of a literary compression where the timing of an event is condensed so as to just relate what is deemed to be the most important aspects of what occurred, whereas Mark's version (11:20–21) was more chronologically oriented. Mark told of Jesus cursing the tree on Monday morning and the disciples seeing the withered tree on Tuesday on the way back to the temple.

Astounded, the disciples wondered how it could have withered so quickly. Once more Jesus used hyperbole when He told them that if they had unwavering faith, they could not only do what was done to the fig tree but that they could say to the mountain "Go, throw yourself into the sea (NIV)" and that it would happen. He further told them that whatever they asked in prayer they would receive it, again adding "if you have faith." Jesus's point was that if they had this kind of faith, trusting in God fully, He would hear them also. This type of faith and trust is such that those praying in the Spirit are praying within the will of God for His divine

---

[95] *Tabletalk Magazine* (Sanford, FL, Ligonier Ministries, Inc., September 3, 2008).

purpose and not out of their own selfishness. It is in this type of doubtless praying, and in the possession of the full confidence of God's power, that the impossible and the improbable happen.

Jesus had used this same relationship between strong faith and the moving of a mountain in His earlier parable about the mustard seed (17:20). John MacArthur comments that these are examples of when Jesus "speaks figuratively about the immeasurable power of God, unleashed in the lives of those with true faith."

The important symbolism of this parable is that it alludes to the hypocrisy of the people who have the appearance that they bear fruit and belong to the invisible church, but they do not, as they are not true disciples. It has been suggested that a possible basis of these recent actions on Jesus's part is found in Hosea 9:10–17.

With this type of understanding of why Jesus may have cursed the fig tree, we can see that it was not done out of anger or some form of petulance but as another teachable moment for His disciples. Christ's curse is a foreshadow of what will happen to hypocrites, those who are like the fig tree with leaves and have the promise of fruit but are found to be empty and barren. They will hear Him say, depart from Me, I never knew you.

VERSES 23–27

Jesus had no reservation or fear as He returned to the temple, even though this was the day after He had overturned the money changer's tables and had driven out those selling the sacrificial animals. The people gathered around Him, and He began to teach.

The chief priests and the elders of the people came and interrupted His teaching as they demanded to know by what authority He did all these things and who gave Him the authority to do them. This line of questioning implied an unspoken acknowledgment that Jesus in fact possessed the authority that He had been exerting throughout His ministry. You have to believe that the "all these things" that they were questioning Him about was comprehensive in scope and would have included His healings, teachings, and the cleansing of the temple courts.

Jesus, ever in control of the situation, chose not to answer them right away but told them that if they answered His question, He would answer theirs about where His authority rested and who had given Him that authority. In all of their previous questions throughout Jesus's ministry, they never gave Jesus reason to hesitate. He always had a reply that was based upon the Word of God. On the other hand, when Jesus asks them questions, they are either mute or claim not to know, and so was the case on this occasion. Jesus asks them, "The baptism of John, whence was it? from heaven, or of men?" They were once again afraid to give an honest answer to the obvious because everyone knew that John was a prophet from God. This had turned into a losing proposition for them. They were now in a damage control mode and huddled together to decide on the best political answer. They had to formulate a response that would be the most favorably acceptable to their position and the least unfavorable to the crowd. They could confess that John was a prophet from God, and by extension they would have to confess Jesus as the Christ because God's prophet had testified to this fact. Or they could say that John was not of God and have to face the wrath of the crowd because they strongly believed that he was God's prophet and that he had been sent to proclaim the coming of the Messiah. Every Jew recognized that John was a prophet of God and that he was the first prophet in over four centuries to speak in God's name in all of Israel. The chief priests and elders found that Jesus had turned the tables on them, and when faced with this dilemma, they feigned ignorance and said that they did not know. If these learned men of God did not know where John was from, how could they be in a position to examine and judge where Jesus had derived His authority from? Because of their calculated response, Jesus replied that He wouldn't give them an answer to their question.

VERSES 28–32

As we have seen before, Jesus returns to the use of parables as a teaching tool. He begins the first of three consecutive parables to condemn the faithless Israelite. He again uses a parable that centers around a vineyard and the work that needs to be done. There is a father as master of the vineyard, his two sons who are presumably heirs, and then we have their individual responses to his exhortation for them to go to work. He goes to the first son who says that he won't go but later thinks it over and submits to his father's will. The second son respectfully says that he will go but never makes the effort to get to the work that needs to be done.

The vineyard can be seen as God's kingdom, and the work that of following our heavenly Father's will. The first son rebelliously says that he wouldn't go but subsequently repents and in a belated obedience bends to the will of the Father. The second son in quick recognition of the honor that the Father is due calls Him sir and says that he will be about his Father's work, saying that he will go, but never makes the effort to follow through. There is no repentance in his heart.

Both sons knew the Father's will, both had heard the call to be doers of God's Word, but that call was only effectual for the first son. Our mandate is to live in obedience to our calling, such as is seen in the first son, and not to be hypocritical by saying the right words and in the end just be giving lip service. The second son modeled the attitude that Isaiah 29:13 tells us. "This people draw near me with their mouth, and with their lips do honour me, but have removed their heart far from me …" This second son represents the authorities in Jerusalem. "Just as in the parable of the Prodigal son, this parable also ends with the father's acceptance of the wayward son. It is those who finally submit to God who are His faithful children."[96]

Jesus asks which son did the will of his father, and they correctly responded that it was the first son. At their response, Jesus replies by starting out with the word "verily," which has the meaning of amen, truly, most assuredly, and so be it. In this case, Jesus is saying that most assuredly that tax collectors and prostitutes will go into the kingdom of God before the Pharisees, scribes, and other religious leaders would. He goes back to

---

[96] Paraphrased from *Tabletalk Magazine* (Sanford, FL, Ligonier Ministries, Inc., September 8, 2008).

their discussion on John the Baptist and his coming in righteousness, and their having not believed in him. He goes on to tell them that even in their spiritual poverty, the tax collectors and prostitutes also heard, and with open hearts they believed. The religious elite had witnessed their repentance and the events that brought about their repentance, and that some had even become ardent and faithful followers of Jesus, yet these same temple leaders continued in their disbelief. He pointed out that even when they saw the miracles and wonders that John had prophesized and that Christ subsequently performed, they still didn't change their minds. And if anything, they dug in their heels and hardened their hearts.

> Being able to discern the faithful son is actually an act of self-indictment on the part of the leaders. If they can rightly choose as faithful the son who left his disobedience, surely they must also be able to discern in themselves their own lack of righteousness and their need of the Savior's mercy and grace, yet they never acknowledge their guilt.[97]

VERSES 33–41

Jesus teaches another parable about a landowner and vineyard, and in this one, Jesus is alluding to Isaiah 5:1–7, which would have been familiar to these Jewish leaders. In Jesus's use of the parable, a man plants a vineyard, develops the property, digs a winepress, and builds a tower. It is now fully operational, and he puts it up for lease as he is relocating to a distant country. This was a common practice among foreigners and wealthy Jewish landowners who would lease their lands as investment properties.

In this parable, we can see God's covenant relationship with Israel, and Isaiah 5:7 specifically tells us that "the vineyard of the Lord of hosts is the house of Israel." God has now put His vineyard/kingdom under the dominion and rule of ethnic Israelites, the religious leaders.

---

[97] Paraphrased from *Tabletalk Magazine* (Sanford, FL, Ligonier Ministries, Inc., September 8, 2008 Coram Deo).

In this parable, we read that several times the landowner sent messengers to collect what he was due. However, they were beaten or killed by those managing the vineyard, and these messengers are representative of the prophets God had sent throughout Old Testament history. Finally, in the parable, the man sends his own son, whom they also killed, and in reality, this is exactly what the Pharisees, Sadducees, and other religious leaders were planning to do to Christ Himself.

In their arrogant presumption, they had staked claim on the temple and the law, and now Jesus had come to reconcile the discrepancies between their traditions and God's Word. They want Jesus out of the way so that they can run things just as they have always done, but without what they perceived as outside interference. They looked at Jesus as their competition and refused to recognize His deity and the legitimate rights and sovereignty of God the Father, the owner of the vineyard.

Jesus asks them about what will happen to these wicked men, and the Pharisees said that they would be put to a miserable death and the property leased to others who will give the landowner the fruits of the harvest. In this answer, they condemned themselves and pronounced their own judgment. Their old-guard leadership of God's Word would be taken from them and given over to the apostles and the newly converted Jews and the Gentiles who are being grafted in and would make up the church that would be built with its cornerstone being none other than Christ Himself.

VERSES 42–46

Transitioning from parables back to scripture, Jesus asks them if they had ever read Psalm 118:22–23. "The stone which the builders refused is become the head stone of the corner. This is the LORD's doing; it is marvelous in our eyes."

He asked this question to make the point that in every instance that He quotes scripture to them, it is because they have ignored the teachings that those scriptures have presented, and they by their actions have either disregarded them or, to their advantage they have superseded scriptural truth with their own tradition.

Jesus was referring to Himself as the rejected stone and to the religious leaders as those who were rejecting God as well as Jesus's Messiahship. Not only does He allude to Himself as the cornerstone, but also as the stone of offense and the rock of stumbling found in Isaiah 8:13–15 where we read,

> You are to regard only the LORD of Hosts as holy. Only He should be feared; only He should be held in awe. He will be a sanctuary;

> but for the two houses of Israel, He will be a stone to stumble over and a rock to trip over, and a trap and a snare to the inhabitants of Jerusalem. Many will stumble over these; they will fall and be broken; they will be snared and captured (HCSB).

Jesus goes on to tell them that the kingdom of God will be taken away from them and given to others who would produce the good fruit of faithful service to God. God's church would consist of a new people from all different nations and ethnic backgrounds, Jews and Gentiles coming together in praise and worship under the banner of Christ. This is not a nation in the geographic sense, but it is in that they are a people for God's own possession, a holy nation, just as we read in 1 Peter 2:9.

The chief priests and the Pharisees could not fail to recognize themselves in the parables and in what Jesus was saying. In their recognition, they could have turned in repentance, but they remained recalcitrant and thought to arrest Him, but they feared the crowd's reaction because they all regarded Jesus as a prophet.

CHAPTER 22

TAXES, RESURRECTION QUESTIONS, GREAT COMMANDMENT

VERSES 1–3

Jesus continues in His use of a parable to highlight the danger that they are in by continuing to reject Him. A king had arranged a great wedding for his son and heir. Weddings are a highpoint in life and a cause for celebration, and as this wedding was to be hosted by the king, to be invited was an honor to be coveted. But to the king's surprise and dismay, they would not come. This parable in analogous of entering into the kingdom of heaven and those who have no interest in the things of God. Just as the king in the parable was insulted because there is no logical reason that they would not come, so too it makes us wonder why the religious elite of God's chosen people would not heed the general call to the wedding feast of Jesus as the bride of Christ. John Calvin said,

> when God kindly and gently invited them, they rejected his grace with disdain ... God bestowed on the Jews distinguished honor, by providing for them, as it were, a hospitable table; but they despised the honor which had been conferred upon them.

VERSES 4–7

The king sent other servants with a second invitation to those who were invited, telling them that all was ready and to come to the wedding feast. In the parable, "tell them which are bidden" is a reference to the Jews who God had previously called as His covenant people. God's continual invitation shows His mercy and grace that even in our repeated rejection He reaches out in love.

Those who the king had invited to his son's wedding paid no attention to him and went about the routine business of living, while some others seized his servants, treated them with disdain, and then killed them. What this lapse of interest in the things of God points out is that the Jews were so devoted to the things of the world that they desired these fleeting things over the riches of the kingdom of God. The comparison here is that we see God the Father persisting to implore the Israelites to worship Him even after being continually rebuffed, and when He sent His prophets with His messages of exile and impending sorrows, they either dismissed, persecuted, or even killed them.

In the parable, the king was angry and sent his army to kill the murderers and burn their city. The dialogue in Jesus's parable was prophetic as to what would happen to Jerusalem in AD 70, a city whose leaders had so contemptuously rejected and killed Jesus.

VERSES 8–10

The wedding was ready, but those who had been invited were not worthy. The king sent his servants to go out to the highways and invite as many as they could find. In this, we see that Israel was not prepared to accept Jesus, not ready to come to Him, and God would now extend the grace of His invitation outside the covenant He had with Israel. God would include the Gentile nations, to all those who would hear, and they would be grafted in.

VERSES 11–14

Ancient kings often provided the proper attire to the guests at their feasts, and this group of invitees from the highways and byways certainly would have had a need for the appropriate clothing. The king had seen the obvious refusal by one guest to accept and to adorn himself in the proper clothing.

He was there, like the many who had received the miraculous feedings by Christ, to take advantage of the king's hospitality of food and not out of honor for the host. And by his way of dress, he displayed a lack of common courtesy, decency, and the respect that should have been shown, for in his heart he had no love or concern for the king or his son. He is likened to persons who are members of the visible church who have externally accepted the mantle of Christ but have refused to actually wear the cloak of righteousness that had been offered to them. They are in the visible church, but not a part of the invisible or true church. Matthew Henry comments, "Those, and those only, who put on the Lord Jesus, and to whom He is all in all, have wedding clothes."

There are a couple of viewpoints on the type of garment that would have been expected and acceptable. The first was embraced by Augustine of Hippo, and that was to be clothed in the righteousness of Christ that He imputes on all believers. The second view is that of a clean garment which would be symbolic of the righteous works being performed by a regenerate believer in gratitude for their salvation. Together, these teach us about justification and sanctification. The first is ours through the finished work of Christ, and the second is the working out of our already possessed salvation by serving others and becoming more Christlike. Although these are distinct, they are inseparably linked in the life of a believer.

When the unwanted guest was approached and questioned, he was speechless. He had nothing to say in his own defense as it was inexcusable. This is the same response everyone will give when they stand before God on the Day of Judgment; none of us will have an excuse. This man was bound and cast out, and those who refuse to accept the call of God's invitation will also be tethered in the bondage of their own sin and be cast into hell, where there is "inconsolable grief and unremitting torment."[98] This passage says, "For many are called, but few are chosen." This teaches that although there is a common or general call in the gospel message that summons everyone to come to Christ, only those of the elect are chosen and will respond to an inward call and believe. This is known as the effectual or irresistible call of God, and it is given to those who have been chosen by the grace of God from eternity past to respond in true faith and accept Jesus as their Lord and Master.

John Calvin writes,

> Let us not flatter ourselves with the empty title of faith, but let every man seriously examine himself, that at the final review he may be pronounced to be one of the lawful guests … for the words of Christ mean nothing more than this, that the external profession of faith is not a sufficient proof that God will acknowledge as his people all who appear to have accepted of his invitation.

VERSES 15–22

Here we find the Pharisees and the Herodians, two diametrically opposed groups, banding together in a common cause. They had joined forces to devise a plan on how best to destroy Jesus. They were already resolved to killing Him, and this was a meeting to determine the best way to implement that decision. The Pharisees represented the religious elite, and the Herodians were a secular group of Jews, a political party, who were associates and supporters of Herod Antipas's ruling power under the authority of Rome. Normally these two factions would have nothing to do with one another, but to this end, they had banded together against their perceived enemy, Jesus. John Calvin's commentary puts the Pharisees' unusual alliance with the Herodians this way:

---

[98] John MacArthur, *The MacArthur Bible Commentary* (Nashville, TN: Thomas Nelson Inc, 2005), 1166.

> Now they regarded the Herodians with the fiercest hatred;
> for their eagerness to be considered the guardians and
> protectors of public liberty made it necessary for them to
> make an open profession of mortal hatred to the ministers
> of that tyrant [Herod].

They begin their dialogue with Jesus with disingenuous flattery. Although what they said was true, the motive behind it wasn't in the spirit of a sincere compliment but a weak attempt at getting Jesus to let His guard down.

Their question was about Roman taxation and whether it was lawful to pay taxes to Caesar, which had been the practice since AD 6. The Romans collected three separate taxes. The first was called a ground tax, which amounted to 10 percent on all grain and 20 percent on all wine and fruit. The second was an income tax and was 1 percent of a man's wages. The third was a poll tax of one denarius each year paid by men between the ages of twelve and sixty-five and women between fourteen and sixty-five. The poll tax amounted to about a day's wage for a laborer.

The first part of the question was whether it was lawful to pay the tax to Caesar, and the implication was whether they should pay it or not. They were trying to trap Jesus. If He answered that the taxes should be paid, they would say that He was denying the sovereignty of God over Israel and He would lose the support of the people. If He said that the taxes should not be paid, He would be labeled as an insurrectionist and an enemy of Rome.

Jesus knew what they were up to and asked why they were testing Him. When He said, "why put Me to the test", it was almost as if He was inferring that they shouldn't bother to continue with their charades and their small mindedness. He next asked that they bring Him a denarius so that He could look at it. They brought one to Him, and as another object lesson, He asked them whose inscription was on it. He had seen coins like this innumerable times. What He was after was their verbalization so that everyone could hear them. They replied that Caesar's appearance was on the coin, whereas Jesus countered that they should "render therefore unto

Caesar the things which are Caesar's; and unto God the things that are God's."

The Greek word translated as "render" means to pay or give back, which implies that they needed to give back to Caesar what they owed him—and to give back to God what they owed Him.

Once more they were astounded and marveled at His answer. Of course, this won't stop them from twisting Jesus's words when they testify against Him in front of Pilate; accusing Jesus of forbidding the payment of taxes to Caesar.

This was the coin of the realm, and in using it, they had already acquiesced through their participation in the Roman social order and its power and authority. A ruling government, whether it is just or not, has certain authorities as well as responsibilities. One of Rome's responsibilities was to maintain the peace, a system of roads, aqueducts, and other benefits that each person benefited from. Their taxes helped support these civic obligations. They were to submit to the governing authority, but only if their religious beliefs weren't infringed upon, and one aspect of their submission was to pay their taxes.

The remaining part of Jesus's reply was that we are to render to God the things that are God's. There is a limit to Caesar's rights, and the government should never overstep the authority of their earthly boundaries and into the heavenly realm, both which have been established by God. It was another teachable moment, and "Christ took the opportunity to teach that believers can both fulfill what God demands and do what the state rightly demands …"[99]

VERSES 23–28

The Sadducees looked only to the Pentateuch as being scriptural. They believed that the books that Moses wrote did not teach of a literal resurrection. They also ignored oral law, tradition, and the Pharisees'

---

[99] *Tabletalk Magazine* (Sanford, FL, Ligonier Ministries, Inc., September 8, 2016).

scribal laws. MacArthur tells us that all the high priests, chief priests, and the majority of Sanhedrin were Sadducees. They also were some of the wealthiest and most influential of all the Jewish sects. They fully cooperated with the Roman government, and this enabled them to maintain their privileged status and position.

In the law of Moses (Deuteronomy 25:5–6), there was established what came to be called the levirate marriage *(levir* is the Latin for brother-in-law), which was a practice that if a man died childless, his brother would take the widow as his own wife. The idea was that they would provide a son and heir for his deceased brother and ensure the preservation of tribal names, families, and inheritances. This same premise is seen in Boaz being the kinsman-redeemer in the book of Ruth.

So here are influential Jews who do not believe in the resurrection, and they are asking a question that flies in the face of their beliefs. The question is not being asked that they might gain knowledge. It is merely another attempt at trying to discredit Jesus. They went to the extreme of citing seven different brothers all marrying the wife of the first brother who had died, and then each of them dies without succeeding in producing an heir. They then ask a theoretical question about whose wife she will be after the resurrection, which again is a reality that they didn't even believe in.

VERSES 29–33

Jesus essentially tells them that they are ignorant and didn't have a firm grasp of the truths of scripture; nor did they understand the power of God. In their misguided reasoning, they had put limitations on God, restraining His power to what they believed was feasible. They had turned things around, and in their own minds, they had created God in their own image.

Not believing in the resurrection, they didn't have any understanding of its reality. Jesus pointed out that in our resurrected bodies, marriage is unnecessary; our relationships would be like those of the angels. The Sadducees also denied the existence of angels, which further showed their lack of knowledge when it comes to scriptural truths as well as their lack of understanding about the omnipotence of God. The Old Testament would have also given them a better understanding of God's plan for marriage on earth. First it was not good for man to be alone, so God created a woman as a helpmate and companion. They also would have read,

> And God blessed them, and God said unto them, Be fruitful, and multiply, and replenish the earth, and subdue it: and have dominion over the fish of the sea, and over the fowl of the air, and over every living thing that moveth upon the earth. (Genesis 1:28)

They would have seen that for the seven brothers, none of these commands that God had given would be necessary in heaven.

Knowing that they limited their theology on what Moses had written, Jesus points them to a specific incident, the burning bush passage, and what God had said to Moses. "I am the God of Abraham, and the God of Isaac, and the God of Jacob." Jesus is demonstrating that the resurrection is assured in that God would not have used the present tense when He spoke to Moses about them and declared, "I *am* the God of ..." Jesus told them emphatically that they were not only wrong but quite wrong and that God is not the God of the dead but of the living. And once again, "when the multitude heard this, they were astonished at his doctrine."

VERSES 34–40

As soon as Jesus had finished denouncing the Sadducees' view of the resurrection, a Pharisee who was a scribe (a lawyer), stepped forward with his question. He may have thought his question was more subtle than the last, hoping that he could show that in some way Jesus had either left out or ignored an important facet of the Mosaic law. He asked Jesus, "Which is the great commandment in the law? He was asking Jesus what command of God's was of the most fundamental importance and central to all.

One thing to keep in mind, and this may have been the underlying premise of the question, is that there are 613 commandments within the Pentateuch, which were categorized as either more binding or less binding than another. A total of 365 are in the negative form of "thou shalt not," and 248 are in the positive form of "thou shall." There were disagreements between the rabbis and the scribes on how they should be prioritized. The religious leaders probably leaned forward in anticipation to Jesus's reply.

Without hesitation, Jesus, the One who had given the law to Moses, replied not only with the most important command but that which was second as well. The response that Jesus gave would later be called the "royal law" in James 2:8. Jesus then said, "On these two commandments hang all the law and the prophets." In other words, they summarize scripture in its entirety.

The first is from Deuteronomy 6:4–5 and in Judaism is called the Shema. It is said to be their fundamental creedal statement. The most important one is this:

> Hear, O Israel: The LORD our God is one LORD: And thou shalt love the LORD thy God with all thine heart, and with all thy soul, and with all thy might.

Jesus continues by going to Leviticus 19:18, which is of the same nature as the first commandment that He quoted and said, "The second is this: 'You shall love your neighbor as yourself.' There is no other commandment greater than these."

The combining of these two important scriptures, while first and foremost giving priority to loving God, indicates that although Jesus saw them as distinguishable, they were not separable.

VERSES 41–46

When the Pharisees were together, Jesus asks them about the Christ, what they thought of Him, and whose son was He. They replied that the Christ was the Son of David.

Jesus now begins to speak of Himself. The phrase "'The LORD said unto my Lord" uses two different forms of the divine title. In the Hebrew of the psalm, the first "LORD" translates the Hebrew word *Yahweh,* God's covenant name. The second "Lord" translated the Hebrew word *Adonai,* a title usually given to Yahweh in the Old Testament. And in his psalm, David had pictured God speaking to the Messiah, the second person of the Godhead; it was God the Father speaking to God the Son.

Using this specific scripture from Psalm 110, Jesus points out that there is no mention of the Christ as being the Son of David but that David, divinely inspired by the Holy Spirit, proclaimed that the Messiah is the Lord of David. Jesus is not denying the Davidic lineage of the Christ, but that the Son of David as they defined the title, and the destiny of whom they perceived, was not the same as for the Lord that David had proclaimed while he had been in the Spirit. In effect, they had been reading into scripture that which they most desired, a conquering king from the line of David.

This Son of David would have been the wished-for Davidic Messiah and merely a hoped-for political salvation; however, the Lord that David had proclaimed while in the Spirit was Jesus the Messiah. He was more than a Son of David. He was the Son of God and would be seated at the righthand of God's throne, bringing eternal salvation as Lord of all.

The religious leaders didn't have the benefit of the New Testament, where we read in Revelation 22:16 where Jesus says, "I am the root and the offspring of David." And in the blindness of their lofty position and in their arrogance, they felt that they knew everything about the Messiah. Even though scripture clearly pointed to Jesus, and that His ministry was an exact reflection of what scripture had told them to expect, their hard-hearted preconceived notions had blinded them to the truth of the matter.

Jesus ends their questioning by asking them one more question. "If David then call him Lord, how is he his son?" And no one was able to speak a word in reply. From that day, no one dared to ask Him any more questions.

CHAPTER 23

WOES TO SCRIBES AND PHARISEES, JESUS LAMENTS JERUSALEM

VERSES 1–4

In that no one in Jerusalem's religious establishment dare to ask Him any more questions, Jesus has silenced His opponents. He now turns His focus on and begins to assign a series of seven woes to the scribes and the Pharisees.

Jesus finished speaking to the religious leaders and, in a move to denounce them, turned to His disciples and to those in the crowd to give them warnings of the spiritual peril that they would face if they blindly followed all that the Pharisees were teaching. Even in His words of caution about the scribes and the Pharisees, Jesus affords them the respect of their position of responsibility and their God-ordained authority because they sit in Moses's seat, which itself is symbolic of the high position and authority that they were entrusted with for the teaching of the law. John Calvin said, "To sit in the chair of Moses is nothing else than to teach, according to the Law of God, how we ought to live."

Although people were to continue in their honor and respect of these men's positions, as well as the law of God that they represented, Jesus tells the people to observe what they say but not to do the works that they do. Jesus is not completely condemning all their teachings, and in so far as the Pharisees are accurately teaching and following scriptural mandates, they are to be observed. However, the people are not to follow the leadership's false teachings or extrabiblical traditions that they had surrounded scripture with, and to which they had given precedence to in their practices. Furthermore, Jesus explicitly condemns the rulers for their legalism and for placing such huge burdens upon the people that they can hardly stand under the weight. Jesus's condemnation of them included the fact that although the Pharisees taught the law, their self-adulation and feelings of pride and superiority led them to believe that they themselves were above the law.

VERSES 5–10

In their being filled with their own righteousness, and not that of God's, everything that they did was performed in their effort to be seen and esteemed by others. Even in the mode of their dress, they purposed to draw the utmost attention to themselves. In obedience to passages such as Numbers 15:38–40, it was the practice to adorn themselves with phylacteries, which were small leather boxes that contained tiny scrolls of scripture. These were usually tied to their left arm and forehead with leather straps. They also had fringes or tassels of blue cord on the four corners of the border of their garments, which were to help them remember and perform all the commandments of the Lord. The problem is they took these biblical mandates and amplified them to the point of their being ostentatious by increasing the size of the boxes, the breadth of the borders, and the length of the tassels in a presumptuous display of super spirituality. This was done to seek the praise and admiration of men over its intended remembrance of God and His commandments.

In addition to these acts of exaggerated piety, they coveted the seats of honor at banquets and at the synagogue so that they might be placed in a position where they could, under the guise of false humility, noticeably flaunt that they were held in the highest regard. Even in the mundane, such as going to the marketplace, they loved to be noticed and to be greeted as rabbi and reveling in the fawning admiration they received for the greatness of their spirituality.

Jesus emphatically exclaims that there is but one teacher and no one is to be called rabbi, for they are all brothers and no man on earth is to be called father, for we have one Father who is in heaven. He goes on to say that no one should be called teacher, for we have only one instructor, and He is the Christ. John Calvin tells us that "Christ asserts that this honor does not belong to any except Himself; from which it follows that it cannot, without doing injury to Him, be applied to men."

This is not a command against familial recognition of our earthly fathers or those who teach us through formal and informal education, but it is in forbiddance of our giving someone an excessive level of undeserved spiritual honor and authority. He is speaking to the heart of those who would covet these titles, actively pursuing them for personal honor and prestige rather than them having been conferred upon someone in recognition of their true piety and humble service to God. In all this, Jesus is teaching us that we are to worship and adore our Father in heaven and that we are to place all of our faith and trust in Him as we follow His teachings above all others. God alone is worthy of our praise, and His Word alone is our guide and our anchor.

VERSES 11–12

Jesus reminds His disciples of the truth that He has taught them before. They had just heard about the Pharisees seeking man's approval and the best seat in the house so that they would be first in everyone's eyes, so now Jesus teaches His followers once again that in His kingdom things should and will be different. Instead of looking to see how many likes we have or how many followers we have, we are to serve others, honoring them before ourselves. He was the greatest example of what He was teaching. He humbled Himself in His incarnation to be the suffering servant. He was and is the consummate servant as our Savior and as our advocate.

VERSES 13–15

Jesus is now pronouncing an oracle of woe upon the scribes and Pharisees and calling them hypocrites.

> An oracle of woe is a type of prophetic speech. It is a pronouncement of imminent distress, and it is spoken by God. It outlines the coming woe, the reason for the woe, and the prediction of doom.[100]

Likewise, James Boice in his writings (volume 2 of *The Gospel According to Matthew)* states that a woe is "a lament or wail concerning the final end for evil people."

Jesus tells them that the scribes and Pharisees shut up the kingdom of heaven against men, and they do this by making their traditions and rules more important than God's Word. Their religious system, legalism, and self-righteousness obviate the righteousness of Christ and a personal relationship with Him, which are essential elements in order to obtain salvation. Jesus's rebuke is reflective of what is written in Malachi 2:1–9, and He rebukes them for those very reasons. They have become a stumbling block to themselves as well as those to whom they should be shepherding, drawing them away from God instead of to Him. With their knowledge of scripture, the prophecies pertaining to Christ, and Jesus's fulfillment of those prophecies, the Pharisees should have sided with John the Baptist and pointed everyone to Jesus. In speaking of the truth of scripture and the Pharisees' failure to accurately disclose it, Calvin said that "although they were the guardians of the Law of God, they deprived the people of the true understanding of it."

Some Bible translations omit verse 14 of Matthew 23, but it does appear in Mark 12:40 where we read, "Which devour widow's houses, and for a pretense make long prayers: these shall receive greater damnation." One of the duties of a scribe was to maintain various legal documents, and they

---

[100] *Westminster Dictionary of Theological Terms,* 2nd edition (Louisville, KY, Westminster John Knox Press, 2014) 345.

often were the executors and estate planners for widows. In this capacity, they had the opportunity to persuade these distraught widows that it would be in their best interest to support the temple or the scribes' own holy work. They weren't allowed to be paid for their teaching, but they could accept gifts, and they often preyed upon the vulnerable, the weak, and the poor in their attempts to extract these gifts from them, thereby devouring widow's houses.

Jesus tells them that in their zeal to make a single convert, they will go to great lengths and travel great distances. He then adds that when the have accomplished this, they don't make them a child of God but a child of darkness. They bring this person into the fold of their religious dogma, which is either void of God's Word or so obscured by tradition as to be missing altogether. The Pharisees' missionary zeal was laudable, but God's Word was veiled from their converts by customs and traditions that became for them nothing less than slavery to a religious system without the eternal hope that is only found in God's grace and therefore they would become a "child of hell."

VERSES 16–22

Based upon the scriptural mandate that was written in Exodus 20:7, "Thou shalt not take the name of the LORD thy God in vain; for the LORD will not hold him guiltless that taketh his name in vain," the Jewish people would not make an oath using the name of God. Instead, they developed a labyrinth system of oaths that could be made. This was a concoction of oaths by which someone could swear by something, and depending upon what they were swearing by, their oath could be considered more or less binding, or those that could even be altogether disingenuous. This system allowed the Pharisees, and those who followed their guidance, to be deceitful and to lie with impunity.

Jesus points this out as He pronounces this woe when He scornfully gives examples of some of these oaths. "Whosoever shall swear by the temple, it is nothing; but whosoever shall swear by the gold of the temple, he is a debtor!" They held more reverence for the gold than they did for the temple. Christ goes on with many such examples and shows how perversely twisted they are by one's obligation being bound by the lesser of two oaths, such as swearing by the sacrifice as being that which binds rather than by swearing by the altar, which is of greater significance.

Jesus points out that the altar, the temple, and heaven should have precedence in the binding of any obligation because of the intrinsic holiness in what they represent and that it is God Himself who is a witness to all of their oaths. They had trivialized the seriousness of vows and focused on superficial distinctions while at the same time ignoring God's greater principles and the intent of His law.

Within the Sermon on the Mount (Matthew 5:34–37), Jesus had taught on oaths and declared,

> But I say unto you, Swear not at all; neither by heaven; for it is God's throne: Nor by the earth; for it is his footstool: neither by Jerusalem; for it is the city of the great King.

He further said,

> But let your communication be, Yea, yea; Nay, nay: for whatsoever is more than these cometh of evil.

In effect, Jesus told them that every oath is binding and that they will be held accountable to God for any insincerity of heart.

VERSES 23–24

The scribes and the Pharisees were incredibly meticulous and exacting about the tithe that they gave. Unfortunately, it was at the expense of the core and foundational issues that comprised the more significant aspects of the law, such as justice, mercy, and faithfulness. Jesus did not say they were wrong to tithe for these herbs but that they should have done so without neglecting matters of greater significance.

He continues His rebuke by calling them blind guides. He then contrasts the eating of two unclean animals, covering the spectrum of the smallest and the largest of those which were forbidden, to present His illustration. Jesus intentionally exaggerates the extremes that they might bring to bear within their dietary laws. In this example, they would carefully screen out gnats. That is to say they were fastidious about not ingesting anything that had not met the requirements necessary to be deemed kosher, but at the same time, they would figuratively swallow a camel. To drive home His lesson, Jesus's use of hyperbole showed how this widely disproportional rendering of the law exemplified how they were focused on the minute aspects of it and ignored or minimized areas that were immensely more important.

Although their tithing of garden herbs was in obedience to the law, there is a due order in keeping the law, with the weightier matters having a natural precedence but where we maintain a balance by not overlooking those of a lesser degree of importance.

The scribes and the Pharisees had misapplied this truth, which should have been abundantly evident to them and found themselves in a position of being superficially concerned with the letter of the law and not the spirit of the law. John Calvin wrote,

> The Law is kept only when men are just, and kind, and
> true toward each other; for thus they testify that they love
> and fear God and give proper and sufficient evidence of
> sincere piety.

The Jewish religious leaders had forgotten what Micah 6:8 taught. "He hath shewed thee, O man, what is good; and what doth the LORD require of thee, but to do justly, and to love mercy, and to walk humbly with thy God?"

VERSES 25–26

There was a widespread acceptance among the scribes and Pharisees toward externalizing their righteousness to the point that the appearance of it superseded the reality of it. Their blameless honor and respectability had become a façade that masked the self-indulgence of sin and corruption that festered within them. Jesus exhorted them to clean up their act from the inside out. If they cleaned the inside, then their outside cleanliness would manifest itself because true righteousness is a matter of the heart. Matthew Henry put it this way: "If renewing, sanctifying grace make clean the inside, that will have an influence on the outside, for the commanding principle is within."

VERSES 27–28

Being near to the time of the Passover, it was customary for the tombs to be whitewashed so that they were clearly evident and that no one would accidently step on or touch one and become ceremonially unclean (Numbers 19:16). Jesus in His daily travels to and from the city had more than likely noticed them and today used them as another metaphor to compare the outward appearance of the condition of the scribes and Pharisees to what God saw within them. The truth was that the whitewashed external actions of the Pharisees made them seem to be the embodiment of godliness, but their strict outward observances of rituals belied the uncleanliness, hypocrisy, and lawlessness that was buried within their hearts and the astounding fact that they were spiritually dead.

John Chrysostom (AD 347–407) spoke of them as having only "a soul deadened by sins," and in John Calvin's comments on Matthew 23, he said that "the children of God ought to desire to be pure rather than to appear so."

The magnitude and the offensive impact that Jesus's statement had are almost incomprehensible.

> Touching a dead body is among the most defiling acts recorded in the Mosaic law; thus, Jesus is declaring that the most rigorous scribes and Pharisees are some of the most defiled people in Israel.[101]

---

[101] *Tabletalk Magazine* (Sanford, FL, Ligonier Ministries, Inc., October 7, 2008).

Verses 29–36

They venerated the dead prophets of old while rejecting and persecuting the living prophets. R. C. Sproul's commentary explains that in the first century BC, the Jewish people became zealous to honor heroes from the past centuries, especially those who were martyrs for the truth of God. In this effort, they had searched out their burial places and built monuments to declare the greatness of these prophets.

As a part of their honoring the prophets of old who were killed by their fathers, the Pharisees exclaimed that had they lived in the days of their fathers, they would not have shed their blood. Jesus sees this as a confession and a witness against themselves of being the sons of those who had murdered the prophets.

Jesus then tells them to "fill up" or to finish the work that their fathers had started and prophesized that they would reject and persecute Him and His disciples. This persecution would fill the cup of transgression to overflowing, a metaphor that left no doubt that someone had made themselves well suited for God's wrathful judgment. In their plots against, and their eventual crucifixion of Jesus, along with the ongoing persecution of the disciples, they demonstrated that they were indeed following in the footsteps of their murderous ancestors.

He goes on to call them serpents and a brood of vipers, with the meaning that they were of the family of the devil, and in being so, there would be no escape from the fires of hell. As harsh as it sounds, this was actually what we call tough love. Jesus did not want others to be deceived, and in His love, He was sternly warning them against their false guides and of the coming judgment and that it was time to repent.

Jesus goes on to prophesy that He would send to them wise men, prophets, and scribes, and some they will kill, some they will flog, and still others they will persecute from town to town, just as it took place through the hands of men like Saul of Tarsus.

Jesus said that when this occurs, all of the blood of the righteous will be upon them. They will have to face the wrath of God's holy judgment against them. As well-known bookends to a long list of martyrs, Jesus highlights two of these righteous men from the Old Testament. In the Hebrew Bible, the first killed for righteousness sake was Abel. The Lord said to Cain, "The voice of thy brother's blood crieth unto me from the ground" (Genesis 4:10). And in 2 Chronicles 24:22, the final book of the Hebrew Bible, we can read of the last martyr, Zechariah, who had been stoned in the court of the house of the Lord. When he was dying, he said, "The LORD look upon it, and require it." The term "require it" has the meaning of avenging it.

Jesus finished this woe with the words "all these things shall come upon this generation." Jesus was speaking of the divine retribution that would soon befall them. John MacArthur's commentary tells us,

> This generation experienced the utter destruction of Jerusalem and the burning of the temple in AD 70. Jesus's lament over Jerusalem and His removal of the blessing of God from the temple (verses 37–38) strongly suggest that the sacking of Jerusalem in AD 70 was the judgment He is speaking about.

VERSES 37–39

Jesus laments over His people Israel, as figured in their metaphorical embodiment as the city of Jerusalem. Luke 19:41 tells us that as He drew near the city at His triumphal entry, He wept. In these verses, He starts out with a heartbroken and repetitive calling out to the city. His heart was burdened with the sorrow of knowing what lies ahead for His people, this holy city, and the temple. He speaks of His ongoing ministry to gather the people to Him, to have taken them under the wing of His protection, yet they were not willing to repent. There is an air of loving compassion for the people as a whole, which included those who had rejected Him, as they continue to do today. God is never desirous, nor does He find pleasure, in the destruction of the wicked, only in their repentance (Ezekiel 33:11).

We know that God is sovereign and what Jesus is expressing here is in full agreement with God the Father and in the acknowledgment of that which God had not sovereignly willed.

He tells them that their house is left to them desolate. Often the term "house" is reflective of the temple itself, but at times, it refers to the religious leadership. With the destruction of the temple, it will become desolate, as well as their being an emptiness or desolation of religious leadership.

Jesus then tells them that they will see Him no more until they say, "Blessed is He who cometh in the name of the Lord!" This will be after a period of great judgment and suffering, and this is a conditional promise, that to see Him again, they must be willing to accept Him as the Messiah.

CHAPTER 24

FORETELLS TEMPLE DESTRUCTION, ABOMINATION OF DESOLATION

VERSES 1–2

Jesus left the temple and was going away. These words have a far more reaching impact than the fact that He was merely leaving the temple grounds again. Here we have the scene of the Triune God leaving the temple, He is departing it for the last time and would not be returning to it during His earthly ministry; without the presence of God, the temple would surely be desolate. To the shame of the religious leaders, they would not even notice His spiritual absence until the day of His crucifixion when the curtain separating the Holy of Holies would be torn and the foundations would be shaken in a prelude to its coming destruction. For now, it was business as usual with the money changers, the selling of the sacrificial animals, and the facade of religious obligations being performed perfunctorily, all an affront to God's holiness.

The temple had been rebuilt by Zerubbabel and Ezra, and later, after a nearly eighty-year project, it had been greatly expanded by Herod the Great in both its size and splendor. The temple was the center of Jewish life, and as the disciples were leaving with Jesus, they pointed out its magnificence. This beauty was chronicled by the Jewish historian Josephus, who said that the temple was covered with gold plates and when the sun shone on them, it was blinding to look at. Where there was no gold, there were blocks of marble of such a pure white that from a distance, strangers thought there was snow on the temple.

With what could be perceived as an attitude of indifference to the richness of this beauty, Jesus replied emphatically that there would be no stone unturned, no stone left one upon another, that they all would be thrown down. As incredulous as this may have sounded at the time, this prophecy would come to pass in AD 70.

> It is said that at the fall of Jerusalem, the last surviving Jews of the city fled to the temple, because it was the strongest and most secure building in the city. Roman soldiers surrounded it, and one drunken soldier started a fire that soon engulfed the whole building. Ornate gold detail work on the roof melted down into the cracks between the stone walls of the temple, and to retrieve the gold, the Roman commander ordered that the temple be dismantled stone by stone.[102]

This would have been a monumental task because of the size of each of them. Going back to Josephus's description of the temple, he said that each stone was 50 feet long, 24 feet wide, and 16 feet thick, for a total of 19,200 cubic feet. For perspective, this would be a solid block of marble that if placed upon a football field would be about 25 percent wider than the goal post uprights, about four feet shorter than those uprights, and extending from the goal line to about the seventeen-yard line. Google results show the dimension of the stones to be 44.6 feet by 15 feet by 10.8 feet, and although smaller than recorded by Josephus, they were still massive and weighed in at 570 tons each.

---

[102] www.blueletterbible.org study notes on Matthew 24 by David Guzik.

VERSES 3–8

The Mount of Olives is a hill located to the east of Jerusalem, and it directly overlooks the temple and provides a panoramic view of the city. It is an ideal spot for Jesus and His disciples to reflect upon the recent events and to ponder about those that are about to unfold.

Depending on the commentators you read, the disciples gathered around Jesus and asked Him a question, with some saying it was two questions and others putting the tally at three questions. Many believe that they were asking to be informed about when the destruction of the temple would be, what the sign of His return would be, and about the sign of the end of the age, these were all one compound question and indicative of their belief that these events would be simultaneous.

Of the synoptic gospel accounts, only Matthew includes questions about the time of Christ's coming and the end of the world. The accounts of Mark (chapter 13) and Luke (chapter 21) limit the question to the destruction of the temple and when it will come about. Matthew's expanded questioning considers the Jewish view that the temple would stand until the end of time and that its destruction would mark the end of time, and in turn, that would mark Christ's Second Coming. Matthew linked these events because he saw them as inseparable.

It should be noted that among many great theologians, there has been a centuries-old and perennial debate when it comes to defining the term "end of the age" that is being asked about. Some define it as the end of the history of the world that coincides with Jesus's Second Coming and the advent of His millennial kingdom. And others view it as the end of the "Jewish age," which came at the fall of Jerusalem and the dispersion of the Jews. This event was the defining point that ushered in the time of the Gentiles. This is similar to the use of the phrase that is found in Romans 11:25 (HCSB), where Paul speaks of the mystery of Israel's salvation when he uses the phrase "until the fullness of the Gentiles has come in."

This questioning by the disciples will open the door to an expansive discussion by Jesus, which will be developed throughout the remaining portion of the chapter, and it will cover much of the history of the world from His ascension to the destruction of the temple, the abomination of desolation, and His Second Coming.

As Jesus begins His answer, He is emphatic that He is the Messiah by saying, "For many shall come in my name, saying, I am Christ; and shall deceive many." He has warned His followers before about false prophets and those who would claim to be the Messiah, and He now tells them that as long as the church is in the world, these false teachers will continue to expose them to heresy.

He continues in His answer by telling them that they will hear of wars and rumors of wars but that they are not to be alarmed because these things need to take place as nations rise against nations and kingdoms against kingdoms, but this is not the end yet. He speaks of famines and earthquakes and says that these are just the beginning of birth pangs, of the suffering and persecution that will befall a sinful people before the messianic age. Unsurprisingly, birth pangs when noted in the Old Testament was a recurring image of divine judgment. These are just the first convulsions or contractions, and they will continue through the normal course of events in this present age as a part of living in a fallen world. Collectively, and with an increase in their recurring frequency, all of these things will be a prelude to the end of the age and will indicate the certainty of the advent, but not the timing, of the Messiah's coming to judge sinful humanity and to establish His millennial kingdom. The occurrences of these events will span the entire period between His resurrection and the judgment that He will bring at His Second Coming.

Verses 9–14

Jesus has often told them that they would be persecuted, and now He tells them that they will be delivered up to tribulation. They will be hated by all nations for His name's sake, and they will be killed.

Jesus says that many will fall away, hating and betraying one another. The persecution will be too great for some to endure, and they will give up their profession of faith, proving without a doubt that they never really believed.

In an attempt to turn the intensity of investigation and persecution away from themselves, they will give up others who remain true to their faith. Still others will be led astray by false prophets, both from those outside the church and from the heretics who are already within the church. People will be deceived by the sweet promises that will be used to tickle the ears of those who had falsely professed a faith in Christ, one that was never theirs. These things will be just as Jesus had predicted and warned about many times before.

He next tells of a lawlessness to be found in society that will steadily increase, worsening in an escalation of unmistakable intensity. The compassion of humanity for their fellow men will grow cold and their love for one another will be replaced by indifference and intolerance, even to the point of hatred.

Jesus tells us that those who endure, those who persevere through all of these trials and persecutions, are the ones who will be saved. However, the act of perseverance is not what saves them. It is the very fact of their salvation that allows them to persevere as they hold fast to His promises, stand firm in God's grace, and take refuge in the strength of the Holy Spirit.

Jesus has been outlining all that will transpire before His second advent, and none of them are a sign of, or an impediment to, His return. He now speaks of the gospel message and the preaching of God's Word that will be proclaimed throughout the whole world, a testimony to all nations (with the meaning of peoples or races). This is the catalyzing factor, the final ingredient, and it is the culmination of the Great Commission. And now He says the end will come, and this is 'the when' that the disciples were asking about.

VERSES 15–20

The phrase "the abomination of desolation," as used by Jesus, is defined by *The Westminster Dictionary of Theological Terms* as such: "It is seen either as the antichrist, a sign or act of the antichrist figure, or idolatry." In this context, it is seen as the ultimate desecration of a Jewish temple, the placing of an idolatrous image in the holy place that brings the judgment of God. It is the abomination itself that brings desolation.

As we have seen throughout scripture, many prophecies contain both a near-term fulfillment that prefigures or partially fulfills a prophecy as well as a final fulfillment that corresponds to an end-time event. There are those who point to the days of the Maccabees in 167 BC and what was perpetrated by Antiochus Epiphanes, but this happened nearly two hundred years before Jesus's prophecy that points to the near-term destruction of the temple in AD 70 and the final fulfillment in the end-time as is noted elsewhere in scripture, such as 2 Thessalonians 2:4 and Revelation 13:14.

In Daniel 12:11, we read, "From the time that the daily sacrifice shall be taken away, and the abomination that maketh desolate set up, there shall be a thousand two hundred and ninety days." This number of days is three and a half years, and in verse 13, Daniel is told to go his way until the end. The two verses together indicate that this event will likely take place in the middle of the tribulation period leading up to Christ's millennial reign.

When this event does occur, Jesus says that those in Judea are to flee to the mountains. He is adamant that they should go with an immediacy that foregoes even retrieving provisions or personal possessions, not even a cloak. He gives a special warning for women who are pregnant or nursing, as this will only add to the difficulties that they will face. They are to pray that the harsh conditions of winter weather, and their religious convictions of Sabbath keeping are not an impediment to their flight as it is imperative that they go without any hesitation.

VERSES 21–28

It has been pointed out that those who believe that Jesus's prophecy has been fulfilled have a hard time reconciling verse 21. As great an atrocity as the destruction of Jerusalem and the temple was, it cannot be said that it fulfilled Jesus's words that "such as was not since the beginning of the world to this time, no, nor ever shall be." Within the plain meaning of His words, history shows that with the interminable violence of man and in the horror of his cruelty, this criterion has not yet been met.

Jesus's words are reflective of the outpouring of the bowls of wrath found in Revelation. Consequently, the magnitude of God's wrath that will be poured out on humankind will be of such a destructive force that it would utterly destroy all of humankind, except that by His grace it is cut short. This cutting short "suggests that the actual length of time the beast will be permitted to terrorize the world is fixed at three and one-half years."[103] During this time, with the sin of man being so great and pervasive, even the elect would be in danger of being lost as they were caught up in the ferocity of the events.

There will be those who will declare that Christ has come, but the falsity of this statement should be clear in that Jesus tells us that His coming will be no secret. He likens it to a bolt of lightning that turns the darkness of the storm into the brightness of day as it flashes from east to west across the entire sky.

But in the grip of fear and the terror of the tribulation, there will be those who will be deceived by signs and wonders performed to entrap those who they will draw in and lead astray. The false prophets and Satan's forces are so convincing that without the protective hand of God, even the elect would be led away from the path of righteousness. Jesus tells us to remember His warning and that He has told of their wiles beforehand; we are not to be caught up in our own gullibility.

The final aspect of this prophecy is Jesus's referring to the vultures. One interpretation is that just as the flashes of lightning would be a sign, so would the circling vultures as they are able to be seen from a great distance. Another is that the figure of an eagle, which can also be a translation of the same Greek word for vulture, sits atop the Roman legion's banners. In AD 70, "Titus placed his army's standards at the temple's eastern gate and offered sacrifices to the Empire, defiling what was left of the Holy City."[104] Matthew Bunson, in his publication *A Dictionary of the Roman Empire,* states, "The siege ended on 30 August 70 with the burning and

---

[103] John MacArthur, *The MacArthur Bible Commentary* (Nashville, TN: Thomas Nelson Inc, 2005), 1173.

[104] *Tabletalk Magazine* (Sanford, FL, Ligonier Ministries, Inc., October 23, 2008).

destruction of the Second Temple, and the Romans entered and sacked the Lower City." If Bunson's history is correct, the timing of this event, or abomination, was after the destruction of the city, and we need to keep in mind that it is the abomination itself that brings desolation.

VERSES 29–31

Jesus's use of the word *immediately* should not leave one with the impression that this will occur within a time period that would be seen as directly following another event. Although the two events are closely linked to God's purposes, the actual time span between them cannot be discerned by the finite human mind. This is similar to the apostles' understanding that Jesus's return was imminent and would be consummated within their lifetime.

In this passage, Jesus uses descriptive language found in both the Old Testament and New Testament that describes the cosmic disturbances that will be manifested after the tribulation of those days (Matthew 24:29; Joel 2:10; Isaiah 13:10 34:4; Revelation 6:12–14). It should be kept in mind that throughout scripture, the figurative imagery of cosmic disasters was often used to describe a coming and literal judgment. One example is Isaiah 13:10, where astronomical imagery was figuratively used to predict Babylon's fall to the Medes.

Scripture tells us that a sign will appear in heaven but leaves it undefined, and this allows for a lot of speculation about what exactly the sign of the Son of Man will be. John MacArthur sweeps aside all other conjecture and simply states that Christ Himself is the sign. Another theory is that the sign will be the cosmic disturbances. Still others believe that the sign will be the vision found in Revelation 19:11–14, where we read,

> And I saw heaven opened, and behold a white horse; and he that sat upon him was called Faithful and True, and in righteousness he doth judge and make war ... And the armies which were in heaven followed him upon white horses, clothed in fine linen, white and clean.

Whatever the sign is, it will be unmistakable as it heralds in and underscores the effulgent glory of Him who is to come. All humankind will heed this sign, and "they will see the Son of Man coming on the clouds of heaven with power and great glory." This is the same language we find in the ascension. In Acts 1:9, the apostles watched, and "while they beheld, he was taken up; and a cloud received him out of their sight." The description of the ascension and that of the Son of Man coming in power and glory are nearly identical in wording and will be identical in their fruition. The difference that can be made is that while it was the disciples who witnessed the ascension, the Son of Man coming in power and glory will be witnessed by all the tribes of the earth. Calvin says that Jesus "will turn the eyes of the whole world upon Himself … and that the glory of His kingdom will be heavenly."

At the last trumpet call, the angels will gather the elect, and

> even though they were carried away from the earth and scattered in the air, will again be gathered, so to be united in the enjoyment of eternal life under Him as their head, and enjoy the expected inheritance.[105]

And this will mark the culmination of world history and the ushering in of the millennial reign of Christ.

VERSES 32–35

In the agrarian culture of Israel, it is well-known that a positive sign that summer is near is when the fig tree's leaves flourish, and just as this is assured, so it will be that when all of the things Jesus had just taught are seen that His coming is near and He is at the very gates; His return is imminent.

Jesus's next proclamation is one which has spawned endless debate surrounding the question of just what Jesus meant by the use of the word

---

[105] Paraphrased from John Calvin's Commentary https://www.studylight.org/commentaries/cal.html.

"generation." If it is defined by those who were living at the time of the pronouncement, it would include the disciples, and the destruction of the temple in AD 70 would seem to be the fulfillment of the prophecy about the abomination of desolation, and so it may have been.

This, however, does not account for the abomination of desolation that we find in Revelation, the great tribulation period, the gathering of the elect, or the Second Coming. These might better fit with a generation being defined or translated as race, ethnicity, or a people group such as the Jewish nation. Other definitions include a people that possess a certain quality, such as believers throughout the present age, or the evil generation that will remain until Christ returns to establish His kingdom. "It would seem best to interpret Christ's words as meaning the generation that is alive when those final, hard labor pains begin."[106]

In stating that the heavens and earth will pass away but that His words will not pass away, Jesus is proclaiming by divine authority the permanence of His Holy Word and that it will endure throughout eternity.

One's mind staggers under the inexplicable and myriad possibilities surrounding this issue, one that has been greatly deliberated for two thousand years. The answer may very well fall into the category of respectfully agreeing to disagree upon Christ's meaning and in our knowing that His Word is true, even while we cannot grasp the mystery of God's timing in the unfolding of His perfect plan for His creation.

In the following observation from Calvin's commentary, we can find solace as we read,

> From this passage we draw a useful doctrine, that our salvation, because it is founded on the promises of Christ, does not fluctuate according to the various agitations of the world, but remains unshaken, provided only that our

---

[106] John MacArthur, *The MacArthur Bible Commentary* (Nashville, TN: Thomas Nelson Inc, 2005), 1174.

faith rises above heaven and earth, and ascends to Christ himself.

VERSES 36–39

Going back to the disciples' original questions, Jesus replies that "of that day and hour knoweth no man, no, not the angels of heaven, but my Father only." This knowledge was within the hidden will of God; it is only He who knows the timing of this event. The will of Jesus is always in perfect harmony with that of God the Father, and as such, He acquiesces to that will with unyielding obedience. In our recognition of Jesus's divine nature, we cannot allow ourselves to project upon His humanity any characteristic that would take over or engulf the reality of His humanity—those things that generally remain in the realm of the divine. While He retained His divine attributes, the second person of the Trinity humbled Himself and took on a human nature and being fully human consented that His divine nature be held in check. His two natures retained distinctive attributes and are not mixed or confused. Yet there are still events in Jesus's ministry that remain shrouded in mystery, such as how He had the divine knowledge to address the woman at the well with a precise history of her former relationships.

Although the exactness of the timing is unknown to Him, Jesus compares it to the days of Noah. The people's lives continued to be centered around and preoccupied with the daily task of living. In the carnality of their unrepentant and sinful nature, they remained oblivious to the warnings of judgment that Noah was preaching. Nonetheless, God's wrath swept over them literally in a flood, and for them, it came suddenly and unexpectedly.

VERSES 40–44

We are given two examples of two men and two women, and in each case, we have one that is taken and one that is left. In this teaching, Jesus uses the same verb that Paul used when he wrote in 1 Thessalonians 4:17,

Then we which are alive and remain shall be caught up together with them in the clouds, to meet the Lord in the air: and so shall we ever be with the Lord.

The key phrase that Paul uses here is "caught up," and this is the rapture. *Vine's Expository Dictionary of New Testament Words* defines the Greek word *harpazo* as being drawn up or carried away.

Jesus goes on to tell us to "be ye ready," with the meaning of "giving strict attention" to "be cautious" or to be "vigilant" (Strong's Lexicon G1127). We are to be vigilant in that we do not know on what day or hour that our Lord is coming.

VERSES 45–51

We as Christ's servants, and especially the church leaders set over His household, must be about our Father's business so that when He returns, He will find us both diligent and faithful in what is expected of us as Christians. If we are found to be wise in His ways, persevering in our walk with Him and doing what is right, He will grant to us a position of greater rule, and then with joy, He will bestow upon us heavenly rewards for our attentiveness to His precepts.

However, if the attitude prevails that His coming remains to be perceived as a future event, one that is perhaps a long way off, the faithless servant will begin to allow the old man within to reemerge and will revert to living in the sensual darkness of their fallen nature. Our Master will come and find him lacking. This disciple will be a false disciple, one who was never a follower of the true Christ. Jesus tells us that they will be cut in two and then thrown in with the hypocrites, in a place of weeping and gnashing of teeth, and this phrase is one that is always linked with being condemned to the eternal suffering of hell.

CHAPTER 25

PARABLES TEN VIRGINS AND FIVE TALENTS, FINAL JUDGMENT

VERSES 1–6

This parable of Jesus likens the kingdom of heaven to ten virgins and the lamps they took to greet the bridegroom and focuses on our preparedness for Christ's coming. The traditional Jewish marriage was usually initiated and arranged between the fathers of the perspective couples. This was followed by an extended betrothal during which the couple was deemed to be married, but they were still living separately, and the marriage was yet to be consummated. The final stage was the actual wedding, which took place about a year later and after the groom had prepared a home for them to live in. The actual time the groom and his entourage left his home and came to claim his bride at her parents' home could come at any time during the night, often unexpectedly.

The point at which Jesus's parable takes up is after the first two phases of the wedding have been completed. The bridegroom's arrival is being anxiously awaited and the ten virgins ready themselves to go out to meet him.

In the Old Testament, God is the one who is proclaimed as the bridegroom and Israel is the bride. We can see this in Isaiah 54:5, where we read, "For thy Maker is thine husband; the LORD of hosts is his name …" and in Jeremiah 2:2, where we read, "Thus saith the LORD; I remember thee, the kindness of thy youth, the love of thine espousals …" Don't miss the fact that in this parable, Jesus is the bridegroom and therefore this is another means by which Jesus proclaims His deity to all those who would hear.

Half of the wedding contingent of ten had thought through what they might need and came prepared. The other five were not so thoughtful and had not brought any oil. There was more of a delay than was expected so they all slept. At midnight, a cry was heard announcing his arrival, and they were summoned to greet him. Those who had brought oil were ready to join the procession and to greet the groom. Those who had brought their lamps but had failed to bring enough oil gave the appearance of being ready but were not.

VERSES 7–13

There was not enough oil to go around, and the five who came prepared wisely told the others to go and buy some from the merchants so that they themselves could quickly join the wedding party and enjoy it without the fear of running out of oil. In his commentary, R. C. Sproul tells us that "we cannot share the Holy Spirit with someone who is empty of Him." We each must continue to be diligent in our preparation and readiness for His coming.

Jesus clearly taught that this is what the kingdom of God would be like. This parable highlights the need for our being prepared for Christ's coming, no matter how long His return seems to be delayed. We are to be vigilant, watchful, and ready. If we are ready, we will be invited into the marriage feast of the Lamb at the end of the age. However, if we are not ready, the door of opportunity will be closed and no longer open to us, and we too will forlornly hear the dreadfully frightful words that He does not know us. Only those who are spiritually prepared will enter the kingdom.

VERSES 14–18

As His next example as to what the kingdom of heaven is like, Jesus tells of a master who calls in several of his trusted servants to charge them with some responsibility on his behalf before he leaves on a journey. Likewise, Christ has left each of us with gifts, varying levels of ability, and with the weighty responsibility to invest our time and energy toward the best use of them for His glory. We are to be good stewards with what we have been blessed.

According to each servant's ability, the master entrusts each with a varied number of talents to invest as they see fit. A talent is a specific weight, and in ancient Israel, the common talent was about thirty-four kilograms (seventy-five pounds), whereas a Babylonian talent was smaller in weight at 30.2 kilograms. In addition, a talent of bronze, silver, or gold would have different monetary values because of the base metal that it was comprised of. Perhaps the Greek talent would be most useful in understanding the magnitude of value that we are talking about. "The Greek talent, or *talanton*, was generally regarded as being valued at six thousand denarii, which amounted to about twenty years of pay for a day laborer."[107] To say the least, each of these servants was entrusted with a great deal of responsibility.

The most trusted servant was given five talents, the second most trusted was given two talents, and the final servant was given one talent. The one who was given five immediately set to work with his investment strategy and successfully doubled the amount. The servant given two talents also doubled the master's return on his investment. Taking care that his master's money was not lost, the final servant merely buried the single talent that he had received and hid it in the ground. Although this did not gain any type of interest or return, in the ancient world, burying money or valuables was considered a safe and responsible way of handling your treasures. This

---

[107] The definition for the Ancient Israel talent came from footnotes, ESV Study Bible (Wheaton, IL, Crossway, 2008) 1876, and the value for the Greek talent came from www.blueletterbible.org study notes on Matthew 25 by David Guzik.

was the same idea we saw in the parable about the field in which a man uncovered a great treasure, hid it again, and then bought the field.

VERSES 19–23

After a long period of time, the master returns, and it is time to reconcile with each of his servants individually. The length of their master's delay in returning, like our Master's, lulls servants into beginning to think that they would never have to give an account, feeling that surely He would have returned by now. But they and we should not be deceived; we will all be individually accountable in His timing.

The first two servants came forward by order of the magnitude of their accountability, first the one given five talents, followed by the one who had been given two talents. Both were esteemed as good and faithful, and both were given even greater responsibilities, but their greatest reward was to be invited into the joy of their master. Their rewards were the same because they both were faithful in discharging their responsibilities, and that faithfulness, not the amount of return, was the basis of their reward.

Just as in the parable, if we too are faithful, when we stand before our Lord and Master, we will hear the same words of praise. "Well done, good and faithful servant." He will give us even greater responsibilities and stewardship in that we are to judge angels (1 Corinthians 6:3). However, our greatest reward will be in our eternal worship before the throne of God because we have been faithful in gathering fruit for eternal life, so that sower and reaper may rejoice together (John 4:36).

VERSES 24–30

We often see men who are quick to blame someone else for their own shortcomings. In the case of the servant who was given one talent, he came before his master with excuses that appointed the blame of his lack of productivity back upon the master himself. Even if what he said about his master was true, there still would be no justification for his own incompetence. Many today blame God for their lack of success, despite having the same opportunity as others. Their sloth has made them lackadaisical about the Lord's work, leaving it for others to pick up the slack caused by their indolence. This person sees that the harvest is ripe but does little or nothing to reap the harvest. Jesus had told us about him when He taught, "The harvest truly is plenteous, but the labourers are few" (Matthew 9:37).

The man told his master that he knew him to be a hard man and that he had given him back what was his, and after all, there was no loss to the master's principle that had been given. He had no remorse for not making any effort to be a good steward and how he had handled the master's goods. He didn't try to work toward a successful gain; his only effort was in making excuses. If this man truly knew his master, it should have prompted him to be more diligent. The man denounces himself by avowing such knowledge.

At this, the master harshly condemned the man, calling him wicked and lazy, and even though he was very much aware of his master's disposition about matters, he did nothing. He tells the servant that the least that he could have done was to move it into some form of investment so that it might have accrued some interest.

The master orders that the talent be taken from the man and given to the one who had ten talents. He was not a fruitful steward with what the master had entrusted to him, so what he had was taken and given to one who had shown that he would be a wise steward. This steward will now have even more opportunities to serve his master wisely and profitably.

We need to pray for the discernment of the Holy Spirit, through whom we may find that we have talents and gifts that we aren't sufficiently using for the glory of God. We are not using them in the gathering of a greater increase into God's warehouse because of our anemic evangelistic efforts.

The wicked servant was never a true servant of his master and was cast into the outer darkness of hell. This is a picture of what awaits those our Master finds lacking. We are told that for those who are eternally damned, there will be weeping and gnashing of teeth, which is a picture of inconsolable grief and unending torment.

The crux of this parable was Jesus's admonition to His disciples to be as productive as they can be until His return. We must work, putting our gifts to use for His glory, and we are to be good stewards of what we have received, making the most of it according to our God-given abilities, for we will be judged by the wisdom and diligence of our faithful stewardship in all that He has given us. John Calvin says, "There will be no excuse of the indolence of those who both conceal the gifts of God and waste their time in idleness."

In the last three parables, we have been taught that as we await Christ's return, we are to be vigilant, we are to be prepared, and we are to be productive.

VERSES 31–33

Jesus begins this narrative with a description of the future judgment that will come after His second advent. He speaks of coming in His glory along with His holy angels, and He will then be seated on the throne as Judge and King. He tells us that all of the nations will be gathered before Him and He will separate them in a similar fashion as a shepherd separates the sheep from the goats. The goats will be set to His left side, while the sheep will be set to His right side and in the place of favor. The goats represent the unbelievers who receive justice and are destined for death and perdition. The sheep are those who have heard His voice and follow Him. They will receive His grace and mercy in that they will inherit eternal life as their heavenly reward.

VERSES 34–40

With another allusion to God's sovereignty in election, we are told that we, as the blessed of His Father, will inherit the kingdom that was prepared for us from the foundation of the world. He also gives a list of the reasons why we are known to be His in that the works we have done display the fruit of our righteousness that has sprung out of our regeneration. These works do not merit our salvation but are evidence of the salvation that we have already received, the saving faith that is ours in Christ Jesus. When asked when we served Christ in these ways, He points to our having followed

His commandment to love our neighbors, specifically toward our brothers and sisters divided to the right hand of Christ. And when we responded and provided for the needs of the least of these, it was reconciled to us to also have had compassion for Him.

VERSES 41–46

Our attention is now diverted to those to the left hand of Christ, to the goats. To them, Jesus pronounces words of damnation, telling them, "Depart from me, ye cursed, into everlasting fire, prepared for the devil and his angels." These people had done nothing to aid the Christians who were in need, they were indifferent, and because of this sin of omission, they were going to pay the price. They ask Jesus when they didn't help Him, and He replies that because they did nothing to alleviate the suffering of those who were in need, by extension, they did nothing to minister to Him. Jesus uses the identical criteria to form His judgment on those on His left-hand side and renders the verdict that their lack of compassion will result in their being cursed to the punishment of "everlasting fire, prepared for the devil and his angels."

God's judgment is imminent; we are either for Him or against Him, and there are only two destinations that await us: one that offers eternal bliss and the other eternal punishment.

CHAPTER 26

PLOT TO KILL, BETRAYED, LAST SUPPER, ARRESTED, TRIAL

VERSES 1–2

Matthew has now concluded his writings about Jesus's teachings. Christ had spoken of the betrayal that would lead to His crucifixion, He had warned the crowds about their religious leaders' corruption, and He had forewarned His disciples of the pending events that would come to pass over the next few days. The Passover and the Lord's Supper were about to transpire, and for the fourth and final time, He predicts His arrest and crucifixion. He would soon complete the work that was His. He had accepted and would fulfill the covenant of redemption that was planned for in eternity past, the salvation that would be ours, and this could only be accomplished by His substitutionary atonement. The Passover Lamb would shed His blood for our forgiveness, the Lamb whose blood would cover us and cleanse us of all unrighteousness.

VERSES 3–5

Meeting in the home of Caiaphas, most of the religious leaders, with notable exception, had begun to finalize their plans on ridding themselves of Jesus, but out of political expediency, they didn't want to attempt anything during the Passover because of Jesus's popular support and their fear of an uprising. Of course, we know that God's sovereign timing prevailed and Jesus, the Passover Lamb, was executed on the very day they didn't want it to happen. The timing of Christ's death was set by the providence of God and not by those who wished to kill Him. No one took His life. He gave it willingly, and He gave it with an eternal foreknowledge of this redemptive act.

A careful reading of scripture will reveal that both Annas and Caiaphas are referred to as the high priest. The reasoning for this is that in AD 15, the secular authorities had deposed Annas and replaced him with his son-in-law, Caiaphas. According to scripture, this would have been an illegal transfer of power as the position of high priest should have been retained by Annas until the time of his death.

VERSES 6–13

Jesus and His followers were in Bethany at the house of a former leper named Simon. Not much is known about this man other than he entertained our Lord, perhaps in gratitude for his having been healed.

John 12:3 identifies the woman in this passage as Mary, the sister of Martha and Lazarus. Mary comes before the Lord as He is reclining at a table. She opens an alabaster flask containing an expensive ointment and then lovingly pours its contents over His head.

> This Alabaster flask was made of a fine marble that was quarried in Egypt. It contained pure nard, and aromatic oil extracted from an Indian and Arabian root. The sale

of this would have yielded more than three hundred days' wages for a common laborer.[108]

Matthew tells us that when the disciples saw this, they became indignant at the extravagance of this gesture and lamented the fact that it hadn't been sold for the benefit of the poor. John 12:4–6 ascribes this reproach to Judas, who kept the moneybag and suggests that he was more concerned with the money than the poor as he would occasionally dip into the purse for his own personal use.

In His awareness, Jesus asks why they are troubling Mary and tells them that what she did for Him was a beautiful thing. He continues by telling them that they would always have the poor with them but that they would not always have Him. He explains that pouring this ointment on His body was done in preparation for His burial, concluding by saying that assuredly whenever the gospel is proclaimed in the whole world, what she had done would be told in memory of her. Prompted by the Holy Spirit, her anointing of Jesus was an act of pure worship.

Charles Spurgeon said of this event,

> She probably did not know all that her action meant when she anointed her Lord for his burial. The consequences of the simplest action done for Christ may be much greater than we think … She thus showed that there was, at least, one heart in the world that thought nothing was too good for her Lord, and that the best of the very best ought to be given to him.

VERSES 14–16

Judas had given the impression that he was a devoted follower of Christ. He had traveled alongside the other disciples as they grew in the knowledge

---

[108] Paraphrased from a combination of footnotes in the ESV Study Bible (Wheaton, IL, Crossway, 2008) 1880, and John MacArthur, *The MacArthur Bible Commentary* (Nashville, TN: Thomas Nelson Inc, 2005), 1177.

of Christ and of what the kingdom of God is like. He had become an apostle, one of Jesus's primary disciples, and so what was the turning point? What was the impetus of his betrayal? He was not coerced by the religious establishment, but being already lost to perdition, he went to them.

There has always been a tremendous amount of speculation on just why Judas betrayed Jesus, but the only thing that is revealed in God's Word that comes close to an explanation is a simple matter of greed. We know about his helping himself to whatever was in the moneybag, and now he goes to the chief priests and says, "What will you give me?" And they paid him thirty pieces of silver.

The price of a common slave was thirty pieces of silver, a relatively small amount, yet this was the trivial amount that Judas agreed upon to become the most infamous traitor the world has ever known. Judas had been paid, and from that moment, he sought an opportunity to uphold his side of the pact to betray Jesus.

One thing that we can be assured of is that God sovereignly allowed for this betrayal. Although we can't put our finger on a specific reason, or at least one that makes sense to our fragile psyche, we know that as evil as this act of betrayal was, it became the tipping point in the fulfillment of God's preordained timing and plan for our salvation. Up to now, the high priest and others had cautiously proposed to wait until after Passover, but this new opportunity had escalated the timing of their conspiracy. Their wicked scheme, like so many other events in scripture, became an act of concurrence where what was meant for evil by a fallen humanity became the instrument of God's holy purpose. Without the crucifixion of Good Friday, there would have been no resurrection Sunday. In Acts 2:23, we can read Peter's remarks during his sermon at Pentecost, when he says, "Him, being delivered by the determinate counsel and foreknowledge of God, ye have taken, and by wicked hands have crucified and slain."

VERSES 17–20

As it normally is, there are a lot of differing views on the precise time of day that this meal occurred, but scripture tells us that it was evening, He reclined at the table with the twelve. Apparently there are many subtle nuances surrounding the Jewish customs when it comes to the timing of certain celebratory meals, and those who wish to sort through the minutiae are prone to do just that. The larger point of focus should be on it being the last supper that Jesus would have with His disciples before His crucifixion.

Jesus had already instructed His disciples to make the arrangements by going into the city and telling a man that His time was near and that He wanted to keep the Passover at this man's house with His disciples. This was on Thursday, Nisan 14. Mark and Luke further identify this man as a man carrying a pitcher of water, a chore normally reserved for women.

When Thursday evening came (now Nisan 15), He sat down with the twelve. With our remembering that in Jerusalem the Jewish day started at sundown, we can see that Jesus, according to the Jewish calendar, ate the Passover meal and was killed on the same day, which was now Friday afternoon and still Nisan 15. To fully grasp the timing of the sequence of events, we need to take a moment to adjust our concept of when a day starts and ends as compared to the traditional Jewish view of when this happens, and in this case, we are talking about the southern area of Israel, which centered around Jerusalem. This will also help in understanding His being dead for three days with a day not being defined as the periodicity of midnight to midnight but with each day being differentiated by each sundown and with any portion of a day being counted as a full day.

Customarily the Passover meal was eaten at the end of the Jewish day, which would have been after the following morning, and according to the history of events, Jesus the Lamb of God was killed at the same approximate time as the Passover lambs were being sacrificed. Earlier Jesus had said, "My time is at hand," and this continues to show that it was He who was in control of the timing of His death.

VERSES 21–25

As they were eating, Jesus makes the startling announcement that one of them, the chosen apostles of Christ, one of the disciples closest to Him, would betray Him. It was both inconceivable and frighteningly close to home. They were sorrowful at hearing that He would be betrayed and that the traitor was one of the twelve, but each in his turn, and each in his own doubt, had to ask, "Master, is it I?" Judas, having asked, was disingenuous and an affront to God as he had already arranged the betrayal with the chief priest. Interestingly enough, although each of the other apostles addressed Jesus as Lord, Judas is the only one who addressed Him as Rabbi. The ESV Study Bible footnote on this passage said that there is no biblical record where Judas Iscariot ever called Jesus Lord. (John 14:22 has the other Judas, not Iscariot, addressing Jesus as Lord.)

Jesus answered that the one who has dipped his hand in the dish with Him will betray Him. Jesus was not pointing out an individual; He was merely stating that one of His friends was going to betray Him. His description of His betrayer having dipped into the dish with Him was a euphemism that generally spoke of friends sharing a meal together, as each of them would have dipped into the same commonly shared bowl of sauce. John's gospel tells us that he questioned Jesus on exactly who it was, and Jesus told him, "He that dippeth his hand with me in the dish, the same shall betray me." Jesus then dipped the morsel, and handing to Judas, He said, "That thou doest, do quickly" (John 13:27). Judas immediately went out, and no one in the room knew why Jesus had said these words to Judas.

Jesus goes back to scripture by saying that "the Son of Man goeth as it is written of Him." This verse found in Matthew 26:24 is not a new revelation for Jesus in that He was a part of the Triune counsel that had formulated this plan in eternity past. This was no chance circumstance; this was the confluence of man's evil intent with God's sovereign plan; it was what theologians define as concurrence. Jesus also pronounces a woe to the man who will betray Him, saying it would have been better if he had not been born. This woe underscored the certainty of divine judgment that would befall the one who betrays Jesus. John Calvin's commentary explains it this way:

> And yet Christ does not affirm that Judas was freed
> from blame, on the ground that he did nothing but what
> God had appointed. For though God, by his righteous

judgment, appointed for the price of our redemption the death of his Son, yet nevertheless, Judas, in betraying Christ, brought upon himself righteous condemnation, because he was full of treachery and avarice.

VERSES 26–29

Matthew's gospel teaches us that as they were eating, Jesus instituted the Lord's Supper by taking the bread, blessing it, and breaking it. Then He passed it to the disciples. He instructed them to take it and eat it and told them that it represented His body. He then took the cup and gave thanks, and when He gave it to them, He said for them to drink of it, all of you, and explained that this was representative of His blood that would be shed for many and of the new covenant as the remission of sins. He concluded by telling them that He would not drink again from the fruit of the vine until He does so with them and in His Father's kingdom.

> That Christ invests the Passover elements with new meaning depicts His authority. God originally had the people eat unleavened bread because they had to leave Egypt in haste (Deuteronomy 16:3); now Jesus gives bread to His disciples and says, "…this is my body" (Matt. 26:26). In reinterpreting the Passover meal, our Savior is assuming the authority of God who alone can direct His people in their remembrance of His salvation.[109]

For Christ's followers, nothing about the Passover meal would be the same as it would be when it is celebrated by Orthodox Jews. Jesus Himself said this was a new covenant. For Christians, Passover was no longer focused on the suffering in Egypt, the passing over of the homes of the Jews and their firstborn, or even the exodus. It was now about Jesus, the suffering servant who bore our sins. In the newly and radically transformed Passover celebration, Jesus asks us to partake of the elements of the sacrament in remembrance of Him and what He has done to achieve our right standing

---

[109] *Tabletalk Magazine* (Sanford, FL, Ligonier Ministries, Inc., November 11, 2008).

before a holy God. Not only do we have a new covenant in the finished work of Christ, we are also a new creation because of His atoning sacrifice.

Jesus also talks about the blood He shed, and He qualifies it by saying that it was shed for many, not just for the eleven. This points again to the doctrine of election, and Hebrews 9:15 confirms,

> And for this cause he is the mediator of the new testament, that by means of death, for the redemption of the transgressions that were under the first testament, they which are called might receive the promise of eternal inheritance.

> Jesus says that His blood is poured out for "many," not for "all." His death is not effectual for all people who have ever lived; Christ's death is effectual only for His people, securing eternal salvation for all those who trust in the promises of God through Him. Because He has made an atonement for all those in Him, our pursuit of holiness is not in vain, for Christ is transforming us into His image as we work out our salvation (Philippians 2:12–13).[110]

There has always been controversy surrounding the Lord's Supper. These controversies are framed around the presence or spirit of the Lord within the elements themselves and these positions have long been debated and strongly held positions that have divided the religious establishment ever since Jesus instituted them. There is transubstantiation, the Roman Catholic view that ascribes that the substance of the bread and wine are changed by the power of God into the substance of Christ's body, which becomes present while the species (bread and wine) remains the same. Another viewpoint is called consubstantiation and was held by Martin Luther, which espouses that while the bread and the wine are not changed into the body and blood of Christ, they do coexist or are conjoined in union with each other: the bread with the body and the wine with the

---

[110] *Tabletalk Magazine* (Sanford, FL, Ligonier Ministries, Inc., November 11, 2008).

blood. John Calvin's position was that Jesus's presence in the bread and wine is real but only spiritually, not physically.

> In fact, this was the central issue that kept the Reformed and Lutheran branches of the Protestant Reformation from uniting. To this day, various understandings of the Lord's presence in the sacrament persist and divide the church.[111]

Theological debate remains, but the importance of the Lord's Supper, or the sacrament of communion is that which is agreed upon, that it is a celebration of the death of Jesus, and along with the sacrament of baptism, represents our remembrance of Christ's eternal presence with the church and our union with Christ and His future kingdom reign. The sacraments are a sign or an outward form of the real means of grace, the Word of God which contains His promises and are fulfilled in Jesus. Jesus told His followers to take and eat, and to do so in remembrance of Him, and having pled our fidelity to Him alone, that is what we should do as we also look forward to the "marriage supper of the Lamb (Revelation 19:9)" when He will once again drink of the cup in celebration.

VERSES 30–35

They sang a hymn; these four words seem so innocuous in and by themselves, but in the context of when Jesus and His disciples sang them, it seems almost surreal that on the night before His crucifixion Jesus would be singing songs of praise. Normally a Passover meal ended in singing three psalms known as the Hallel. These were psalms 116–118, and any review of these passages gives one an acute sensitivity that they must have given Jesus great comfort in what was to come.

After they had sung, they departed for the Mount of Olives, where Jesus once again shakes their sensibilities with more startling news. He tells them that they will all fall away from Him on this very night. Going back to scripture, He quotes from Zechariah 13:7, which says, "Saith the LORD of

---

[111] *Tabletalk Magazine* (Sanford, FL, Ligonier Ministries, Inc., October 26, 2016).

hosts: smite the shepherd, and the sheep shall be scattered." He knows His destiny and that they, in fulfillment of scripture, will flee at the time of His arrest. In the assurance of His own resurrection, He tells them that once He has been raised up, He would go to Galilee before them. It would be in Galilee that the resurrected Christ would stretch out His hand, restoring His disciples back into fellowship with Him after their having fled from the Garden of Gethsemane in fear of their own arrest and persecution. Calvin comments,

> God does not cease to recognize as his sheep those who are driven out and scattered in every direction for a time … at length [they will] be brought back to the fold.

You can almost see Peter brashly step forward as he adamantly proclaimed that even if the others all fell away, he would remain the last man standing; he wasn't going to abandon Jesus for any reason. Jesus's response was just as adamant, and He prefaced His next statement with the single word "verily." He continued by telling Peter, "I tell you, this very night, before the rooster crows, you will deny me three times (ESV)." That alone should have ended the conversation, but in the boldness he was known for, Peter said to Him, "Though I should die with thee, yet will I not deny thee. Likewise also said all the disciples." Yet this would be an ultimate test of faith that each of them was totally unprepared for. We all need to rely on the strength of the Holy Spirit as we walk by faith through the trials of life.

Peter's unflinching assertions have set him up to suffer in utter despair at the guilt and sorrow of his failure to follow through on the boldness that Jesus knew would come to nothing as the reality of Christ's arrest and persecution became an all too tangible experience.

VERSES 36–39

Jesus and the disciples went to Gethsemane, a place they frequented and was known by Judas. This garden was to the east of Jerusalem, across a ravine, and it had a commanding view of the temple mount.

He told most of His disciples to sit while He went to another area to pray. In His troubled spirit, He desired the comfort and support of good friends, so He took Peter, James, and John, telling them that His soul was very sorrowful, with the Greek transliteration being expressive of the greatest sorrow imaginable. This feeling was more than understandable in that He was aware of both the physical and spiritual agony that He was about to endure. He told the three to remain where they were and to watch with Him. Jesus did not ask these men to pray with Him. This was a time for individual prayer. It was a personal prayer between a Son and His Father, so Jesus went a short distance farther, fell on His face, and prayed to His Father to let this cup pass from Him. But He also prayed that the Father's will would be done, not His own, and this is indicative of a state of complete obedience. The intensity of His prayer and His acknowledgment that for the first and last time throughout all eternity that He would become at enmity with God the Father caused great drops of blood to fall from His face. Jesus was not in fear of men, nor was He in fear of dying. His fear was in experiencing the separation from God the Father as He, the sinless one, took on the sin of all humankind, and this imputation of the world's sin would invoke God's holy wrath and fully focus it upon Jesus as He became the propitiation that cleansed us by His blood.

Because God is perfect, His immutable plans are perfect. The Triune God had formulated the plan of salvation in eternity past, and in its perfection, it was and is the only means of our salvation. Therefore, the passing of the cup of wrath from Jesus's lips would have been outside of God's sovereign will.

> It should be understood that Jesus having prayed for God's will to be done and not His own, in no way implies that there was a conflict between the persons of the Godhead. Rather it reveals graphically how Christ, in His humanity, voluntarily surrenders His will to the will of the Father in all things, precisely so there would be no conflict between the divine will and His desires.[112]

---

[112] Paraphrase from John MacArthur, *The MacArthur Bible Commentary* (Nashville, TN: Thomas Nelson Inc, 2005), 1178.

God's irrevocable plan of salvation was established, and in His compassion, He sent an angel to comfort to Jesus. Luke 22:43 records this event. "And there appeared an angel unto him from heaven, strengthening him."

VERSES 40–46

Jesus, after His earnest prayer for a different means to accomplish what He had been born to complete, found that His closest disciples had fallen asleep. It had been His desire to have them aid and comfort Him in His time of greatest need. He then posed a question to Peter, asking if they couldn't have kept watch with Him for an hour. He told them that they should watch and pray that they might not enter into temptation. They lacked strength within themselves, and He was encouraging them to pray for the power that they needed to overcome their weaknesses, which would soon scatter them and bring words of denial to their lips. He states to them that their spirits are willing to do as He asks but that their flesh was weakened to the point of slumber, which nullified their ability to pray with any level of effectiveness.

He left them and returned to the solitude of His prayers, telling His Father in heaven that He had yielded to what must come to be and for His Father's will to be done. Leaving His prayers, He found His disciples asleep again, and scripture notes that their eyes were too heavy and that they were unable to keep from sleep. He left them for a third time and returned to His prayers. This prayer was a continuation of what He had prayed twice before, and it is an example to us of the necessity to be in continuous prayer for our requirements.

Having His resolve strengthened in prayer, and in a complete and sinless surrender to His Father, Jesus returned for a final time to His weary disciples. Waking them, He told them to sleep and rest later for the hour of His betrayal had come. He, the Son of Man, was being turned over into the hands of sinners, and they were to rise up and go with Him as His betrayer had arrived.

VERSES 47–50

We are told that while Jesus was still speaking, Judas, who had been thought to be one of Jesus's closest followers, and was even an apostle, came to Gethsemane, leading a great crowd carrying swords and clubs. All four gospels use the term "one of the twelve" to describe Judas, and John MacArthur tells us that "the gospel writers seem to use the expression to underscore the insidiousness of Judas's crime, especially here, in the midst of the betrayal."

The mob was a mixture of Roman soldiers and temple guards who had been sent by the chief priests and elders so that Judas could identify Jesus with a kiss, a traitorous means of identification that was insipidly disguised as a bond of friendly affection. The chief priests weren't taking any chances. They did not want to miss this opportunity to arrest Jesus by having the wrong man apprehended in the darkness of the olive grove. They needed Judas's positive identification and used this kiss as a conclusive sign.

Immediately upon entering the garden, he went to Jesus, and after calling Him Rabbi, he kissed Him. Jesus replied, "Do what you came for, friend (NIV)", and the forces at hand seized Jesus and arrested Him.

Although Jesus had used the word "friend" to address Judas, there was no affection intended as the transliteration of the Greek word *hetairos* does not have the meaning of a close associate. Rather, it had the same implication that Jesus had utilized in various parables concerning someone who has taken advantage of a privileged relationship or situation, such as when used by the landowner who had paid each laborer he had hired the same wage (Matthew 20:13) or the king inquiring how a man entered the wedding feast without the proper wedding garment (Matthew 22:12).

Luke 22:48 records Jesus's words as "Judas, betrayest thou the Son of man with a kiss?" This isn't a question about whether Judas would betray Him, but that Judas would feign respect and honor for his Master by a kiss of betrayal that was merely a sign of identification, and it had nothing to do with a deeply held affection. These are not words of wonder on Jesus's part but words of condemnation toward the hypocrisy of Judas's treacherous heart.

VERSES 51–56

Luke's gospel tells us that there were many of Jesus's disciples who were ready to protect Him as they asked, "Lord, shall we smite with the sword?" (22:49). We also know from John's gospel that the one who struck Malchus, the servant of the high priest, was Peter, and probably no one reading scripture was surprised to find that it was him. In John's gospel, Jesus said to Peter, "Put up thy sword into the sheath: the cup which my Father hath given me, shall I not drink it?" (18:11). He told them that if He chose to call upon God the Father, more than twelve legions of angels would come to Him. Peter's single sword was nothing compared to power and might of 72,000 angels. In fact, 2 Kings 19:35 tells us that the angel of the Lord singlehandedly struck down 185,000 Assyrians. Jesus had the power and authority to thwart any of man's feeble efforts, and surely the garden was both filled and encompassed by angels at the ready, just as they had surrounded Elisha. But Jesus restrained from using that power in order that the prophecies of old might be fulfilled.

Jesus now addressed the crowd who had come under the cover of darkness to arrest Him, telling them that He had spoken daily in the temple, yet they had not seized Him. He told them that by their current actions, prophecy was being fulfilled so that His life might be given and that no one was taking it from Him. Those arresting Jesus would not have understood that God's sovereign will was being played out in perfect harmony to His foreordained and eternal plan and that the power of their clubs and swords was not the power that had affected Christ's arrest.

It was at this point that His disciples fled and left Him alone in the fear of their own capture. As sad as this episode was, Jesus's momentary solitude would pale in light of the loneliness of abandonment that He would soon feel when for the only time in all eternity, His Father would forsake Him as He hung dying on the cross. It was this curse alone that Jesus had feared most as He sweat great drops of blood while praying in Gethsemane.

VERSES 57–61

Matthew tells us that Jesus was led to Caiaphas, the high priest, but we read in John that they had already taken Him before Annas. As mentioned earlier, Annas was illegally removed from the office of high priest by the Roman government, who had deposed Annas and replaced him with his son-in-law Caiaphas. The office of high priest was an appointed position that was to be occupied for the life of the sitting high priest, and there were many who remained faithful to the Jewish tradition and still saw Annas as the high priest.

Caiaphas had called together a group of scribes and elders to pass judgment on Jesus, and Peter had followed them at a distance to see what would happen. This assembly of scribes and elders was not the full complement of about seventy men that comprised the whole of the Sanhedrin, but enough of them to meet a quorum of twenty-three. They were the supreme court of Jewish law, but we can be certain that those hastily gathered together did not include any who may have had reservations about the legality of the trial or misgivings about convicting Jesus on trumped-up charges.

Jesus's fate had already been determined, but the events surrounding this determination were conducted at night during a mock trial, which according to Jewish law was forbidden.

> By the Sanhedrin's own rules criminal cases could not even be tried during the Passover season; guilty verdicts had to wait one night to allow for feelings of mercy to arise; all evidence had to be guaranteed by two witnesses, who were examined separately and who have had no contact with one another; false witness was punishable by death, but nothing was done to *many false witnesses* who had come forward; and each trial was to begin by evidence of innocence before evidence of guilt was brought

forward. These are examples of the many inconsistencies and illegalities of the trial.[113]

It was now daylight and the convening of this group was to officially try to condemn Jesus. Although it was their intent to impugn His character, the Sanhedrin brought forth many false witnesses to testify against Jesus, but they were unable to find any credible evidence from these witnesses who couldn't even agree among themselves on their testimonies. They finally found two men to witness that Jesus had said, "I am able to destroy the temple of God, and to rebuild it in three days." We read in John 2:19–21 that Jesus actually said, "Destroy this temple, and in three days I will raise it up … But he spake of the temple of his body." Jesus's teachings about His death and resurrection, which soon would be fulfilled, were being distorted to the purpose of the religious leaders bad intent. Mark 14:58–59 relates their testimony as such:

> We heard him say, I will destroy this temple that is made with hands, and within three days I will build another made without hands. But neither so did their witness agree together.

VERSES 62–64

Jesus, in His resolve of obedience to His Father's will, had said nothing in His own defense. The high priest then got up and asked Jesus if He didn't have a defense to make against these acquisitions and testimonies, and Jesus still remained silent. "He opened not his mouth: he is brought as a lamb to the slaughter, and as a sheep before her shearers is dumb, so he openeth not his mouth" (Isaiah 53:7). The high priest demanded that Jesus tell them if He was the Christ, the Son of God. In an attempt to obligate Jesus to answer him, Caiaphas even invoked the name of God.

Jesus felt no compulsion to defend Himself and simply replied, "Thou hast said." Jesus then adds that from this point on, they would "see the

---

[113] Paraphrased from www.blueletterbible.org study notes on Matthew 26 by David Guzik.

Son of man sitting on the right hand of power and coming in the clouds of heaven." His meaning was clear to Caiaphas that although they sat in judgment over Him, in the future, He would preside over them in the final judgment as He sat at the right hand of power. The word "power" was typically used by the Jewish people as a reverential expression to avoid pronouncing the sacred name of God and thereby committing blasphemy. By these statements, Jesus not only said that He was Messiah but that He was the divine Son of Man who would return in His glory, riding on the clouds in power to reign over the earth.

> In asserting that He will be seated at the right hand of "Power," Jesus puts Himself on God's level, appropriating to Himself Yahweh's power and authority. This would be blasphemy indeed were He incorrect, but Jesus, the incarnate Son of God, has all divine power and authority. Caiaphas and the others could see this if they would look, but their own power and position, which holds first place in their hearts, blinds them to the truth.[114]

VERSES 65–68

The high priest tore his robe, which in itself was an act that was prohibited in scripture (Leviticus 10:6, 21:10). He more than likely justified his action because it was predicated by what he thought to be blasphemy from Jesus's mouth. Jewish tradition, based upon the Talmud, allowed the tearing of the high priest's robe in the case of blasphemy. The Talmud is comprised of the Mishnah and the Gemara. The Mishnah is the original written version of the oral law, and the Gemara is the record of rabbinic discussions that followed the writing of the Mishnah. We see here another example of man-made or derived writings and traditions that usurp God's Word.

The high priest is apoplectic and cuts the trial short by stating that they need no further witness and asks those in judgment for a verdict. They respond that "He deserves death." All judicial decorum has broken down, and they begin spitting in Jesus's face, slapping Him, and mockingly

---

[114] *Tabletalk Magazine* (Sanford, FL, Ligonier Ministries, Inc., November 27, 2008).

asking for Him to prophesy to them, questioning Him as to who had struck Him. Charles Spurgeon said of these actions,

> Be astonished, O heavens, and be horribly afraid. His face is the light of the universe, his person is the glory of heaven, and they "began to spit on him." Alas, my God, that man should be so base!

Spurgeon also says that men figuratively continue to spit in Christ's face today by denying His deity, rejecting His gospel, preferring their own righteousness, and turning away from Jesus.

The humility of Christ from His incarnation through His persecution, arrest, mock trial, and finished work on the cross all point to the love of God for us in that He gave His Son up to such horrendous physical and spiritual trials so that we might be saved. What greater love is there than this?

VERSES 69–75

Throughout all of the events that were going on inside Caiaphas's residence, Peter sat outside in the courtyard in anticipation of what would come. He didn't have to wait long as a servant girl came and said, "Thou also wast with Jesus of Galilee." Peter quickly crumbled under the accusation, and before everyone, he emphatically denied it. He fearfully moved away and toward the entrance, where another servant girl proclaimed to those around them, "This fellow was also with Jesus of Nazareth." And for a second time, Peter denied Christ by saying, "I do not know the man." But this denial was even more emphatic than the first because we are told that he denied it with an oath. He had just compounded his sin by swearing by God (a thing that Jesus had taught him not to do) that the lie he had been telling was the truth. Things seemed to quiet down for a little while, but more of the crowd came up and said, "Surely thou also art one of them; for thy speech betrayeth thee." Losing all composure, and in abject fear, Peter begins to invoke a curse upon himself, which was likely that he called upon the wrath of God to strike him if he was lying. After this, he vehemently swore once again, "I know not the man." And immediately after these words passed through his lips, the rooster crowed, and with a sorrowful conviction, Peter remembered what Jesus had said. "Before the cock crow, thou shalt deny me thrice." Luke 22:61 adds this significant detail: "And the Lord turned and looked upon Peter." Broken by his three successive denials and the knowing look of Christ, he went out and in his shameful anguish wept bitterly. By the grace of God, this sorrowful contrition was the beginning of Peter's repentance and ultimate restoration.

CHAPTER 27

JESUS, PILATE, BARABBAS, MOCKED, CRUCIFIED, TOMB

VERSES 1–2

It is early in the next morning, and now that the illegal trial had concluded, along with their verdict having been rendered, they came together again in the pretense of conducting an official trial. Luke's gospel account tells us that this morning trial was essentially the same as the previous night's informal trial and was just as much of a sham as the first night's.

Having come to the same conclusion on Jesus's guilt, they took Him and delivered Him over to Pontius Pilate. From eternity past, Jesus had resigned Himself to be the sacrificial lamb and had put up no resistance to His arrest, yet the chief priests and elders felt compelled to bind Jesus as they paraded Him through the streets on the way to His trial before Pilate. Scripture says they delivered Him to Pilate, and the Greek word that has been translated as "delivered" is the word *paradidomi,* which is often translated as "betrayed." This more fitting translation is in fulfillment of what Jesus had told the apostles in Matthew 20:19.

The Jewish leaders had no authority to execute anyone, so they had to take Jesus to the Roman prefect, or governor, and present their case against Jesus. They would be pressing Pilate for a verdict against Jesus that would warrant the death penalty, and because of his reputation as a cruel and ruthless man, they had every reason to believe that he would render such a verdict.

VERSES 3–10

Matthew is the only gospel to record Judas's attempt to return the blood money he had received for his betrayal of Christ. Judas, in finding out that Jesus was condemned, felt the pangs of guilt, and we are told that he changed his mind. He took the thirty pieces of silver back to the chief priests and elders, but they had gotten what they paid for and had no concern over Judas or his plight. Judas told them that he had sinned, that he had betrayed innocent blood, but this was the last thing the chief priests wanted to hear as they too were complicit.

Interestingly, Judas is confessing his sin and the chief priests callously reply, "What is that to us?" and further retort that he should "see thou to that." Judas's remorse was not a godly grief, and the Greek verb for Judas's change of mind is not the one normally used for repentance. Instead of running to God in contrition, Judas threw the thirty pieces of silver down in the temple and instead of repentance ran straight to his death and hanged himself. The dichotomy between the guilt of despondency and worldly remorse and the guilt of contrition that leads to repentance is clearly articulated in 2 Corinthians 7:10, where Paul writes, "For godly sorrow worketh repentance to salvation … but the sorrow of the world worketh death."

The priests picked up the money and, knowing that it was blood money, were unable to put it back into the temple treasury. They advised one another to buy a burial plot for the Gentiles, and it became known as the Field of Blood.

This was another fulfillment of prophecy that Matthew attributes to being found in Jeremiah; however, it seems to actually be a paraphrase of Zechariah 11:13, where it is written,

> And the LORD said unto me, Cast it unto the potter: a goodly price that I was prised at of them. And I took the thirty pieces of silver and cast them to the potter in the house of the LORD.

Further research came up with several explanations, one being a copyist error, where the copyist inserted Jeremiah instead of Zechariah; others said that it may have been a prophecy spoken by Jeremiah and that Zechariah recorded it; another explanation is that Matthew combined quotes from both Jeremiah and Zechariah but attributed it to Jeremiah as he was the older and more ranking of the two prophets. In John MacArthur's commentary, he says,

> The Hebrew canon was divided into three sections, Law, Writings, and Prophets. Jeremiah came first in the order of prophetic books, so the prophets were sometimes collectively referred to by his name.

And finally, some have concluded that Matthew was referring to the "scroll" of Jeremiah, which is said to have included the book of Zechariah. These last two explanations seem to be similar and more than likely resolve what may very well be a false dilemma.

VERSES 11–14

Matthew's account begins at Jesus's second appearance before Pilate, and His first appearance can be found in Luke 23:1–6.

As we have said, Pilate was a man known for his cruelty, but as he questions Jesus, we find that he seems to be going out of his way not to condemn Him. He even sends Jesus to Herod to have him make a judgment against Jesus, but Jesus refused to speak to Herod, who in turn sends Jesus back to Pilate. This is the point at which Matthew's gospel takes up.

Because of the Sanhedrin's fervor in their attempts at making Jesus out to be a dangerous insurrectionist and their insinuation that He was a king with a following bent on treason against Rome, Pilate plainly asks Jesus, "Art thou the King of the Jews?" Jesus's response was just as straightforward and candid when He said, "Thou sayest." Jesus, although His replies were short and to the point, was at least communicating with Pilate, whereas whenever the chief priests and elders hurled their accusations, He gave them no answer. Pilate had seen a countless number of men standing before him and their accusers, but something about Jesus was different. Charles Spurgeon comments about Pilate's assessment of Jesus as follows:

> He had seen in captured Jews the fierce courage of fanaticism; but there was no fanaticism in Christ. He had also seen in many prisoners the meanness which will do or say anything to escape from death; but he saw nothing of that about our Lord. He saw in him unusual gentleness and humility combined with majestic dignity. He beheld submission blended with innocence.

Pilate had been observing both Jesus and His adversaries, and in his amazement, he noted that Jesus didn't respond to a single charge against Him. So perhaps in a rhetorical fashion, he asked Jesus whether He had heard the great number of testimonies brought against Him. Jesus had no intention of defending Himself; His mission still lay before Him and nothing would be an impediment to its fulfillment. Despite all the testimony to the contrary, Pilate could find no fault in Jesus.

VERSES 15–18

During the feast it was customary for the governor to release a prisoner of the people's wish and in a last-ditch effort at releasing Jesus, Pilate suggested two possible prisoners. The first one that was offered to the crowd was a murderous man who was despised by all who knew of his wickedness. The crowd's other choice was Jesus, a prophet and a healer, a man who had recently been welcomed by shouts of joy and worship. Pilate brings them before the crowd and asks, "Whom will ye that I release unto you? Barabbas, or Jesus which is called Christ?" Scripture tells us that Pilate knew that it was out of envy that the religious leaders had brought Jesus before him for trial. He had seen behind the façade of their carefully crafted and manipulative words.

VERSES 19–20

Sitting in judgment of Jesus, Pilate knew that there was no guilt to be found in Him. However, being a political man, he weighed the cost of his decision not on justice but upon expediency. He and the religious leadership were unknowingly agents of God's eternal plan. All the political and religious plotting by Jesus's accusers and by Pilate himself were just a means to what God had preordained.

While Pilate was still deliberating, his wife sent an urgent message to him, imploring him that he was to "have thou nothing to do with that just man: for I have suffered many things this day in a dream because of him." Like Pilate, she too had become acutely aware of Christ's innocence.

In the meantime, the chief priests and elders held sway over the crowd. It was still early morning and those who had traveled from Galilee more than likely had stayed outside the city in encampments and had not yet come back into Jerusalem and would not have been aware of what was happening. These travelers would have known Jesus, heard His message, and seen His miracles, and they would have been prone to be in favor of Jesus being released. Their absence in the crowd played into the advantage of the religious elite as the current crowd would have been comprised of a more local contingent of temple worshippers who would be inclined to side with the priests that they knew and who they either trusted to make the right decision or they would have been intimidated to go up against for fear of some sort of reprisal. In any case, the multitude was persuaded to ask for Barabbas's release and for the crucifixion of Christ.

VERSES 21–23

Pilate again goes before the crowd and asks which of his two prisoners he should release: the infamous Barabbas or Jesus. The crowd, under the influence of the chief priests and scribes, calls for the release of Barabbas.

At their demand for Barabbas's release, Pilate asks them, "What shall I do then with Jesus which is called Christ?" But before we talk about the crowd's response, we should look within our own hearts; we should take this probing question and address it in light of our current standing with our Savior. This is especially true of those who are feeling, perhaps for the first time, that they need to come to a saving faith in Jesus. It is a question to which the answer has eternal consequences. With this significance in mind, one should fervently pray for the answer you are already leaning toward, the answer that will position you for the eternal riches of heavenly reward as you worship God as you stand alongside the angels or are counted among those destined for the eternal damnation that awaits those who remain on the road to perdition. Ask yourself this same question: what should I do with Jesus Christ, and how will I come to know Him better?

At Pilate's question, the crowd shouts out, "Let Him be crucified!" Pilate was more than likely astonished that they had let a murderous insurrectionist go, and he asks the multitude why. He wants to know what evil Jesus had done to deserve crucifixion, but the crowd, now seemingly in a fever pitch, cries out all the more, "Let Him be crucified!" Pilate had surely heard about the jubilant shouts of exaltation that the crowd had ushered Jesus into Jerusalem with just a short time ago. Somewhat confused, and perhaps dismayed, he had to have wondered why they were now clamoring for His execution.

This is a thing to be marveled at; crucifixion is a torturous and barbaric means of Roman execution and for most Jews is seen as abhorrent. Jews normally subjected those who were to be put to death by stoning them. What we must remember is that Jesus was preordained to the cross. The Old Testament had proclaimed, "His body shall not remain all night upon the tree, but thou shalt in any wise bury him that day; (for he that is hanged is accursed of God (Deuteronomy 21:23)" and "the assembly of the wicked have enclosed me: they pierced my hands and my feet" (Psalm 22:16). In fulfillment of this prophecy, Jesus took our sin upon Himself and as our propitiation felt God's wrath as He hung from the cross, cursed for our inequity.

VERSES 24–26

The crowd was becoming riotous, and to placate them, after a meaningless act of purifying himself by washing his hands of the whole ordeal, he releases Barabbas. As he symbolically washed his hands, he told the crowd that he was "innocent of the blood of this just person: see ye to it." We see from this statement that Pilate pronounces Jesus as being innocent, yet he still scourges Him and sends Him to be crucified.

Scourging itself was a part of every Roman execution, with only women and Roman senators or soldiers being exempt. The idea behind scourging was to weaken the person to a state of near death and thereby speeding up the finality of death of those being crucified.

Taking responsibility for Jesus's execution, the crowd responded by saying, "His blood be on us, and on our children." Neither Pilate nor the Jewish establishment and their followers are innocent of Christ's blood, and if we are honest with ourselves, neither are we for Christ died for our sins as well. We should praise God for the covering of Jesus's blood and for the finished work of the cross.

VERSES 27–31

The number of soldiers present has been estimated at between one hundred fifty and two hundred, and they were the governor's bodyguards. Their complement was about a third of a cohort, which at full strength comprised a total of six hundred men. This group of soldiers took Jesus into a courtyard of sorts and then stripped off His garments, put the cloak of a Roman soldier around Him, which mimicked the scarlet robe of royalty, and then a crown of thorns was placed upon His head. They continued to demean and humiliate our Lord by taunting Him with false praises, such as "Hail to the king." And they feigned worship as they mockingly kneeled before Him. They spit on Him, beat Him with their fists, scourged Him with whips of heavy leather straps that had bone and glass affixed to them, and finally led Him away to be crucified.

John Calvin writes,

> Our filthiness deserves that God should hold it in abhorrence, and that all the angels should spit upon us; but Christ ... to present us pure and unspotted in [the] presence of the Father, resolved to be spat upon, and to be dishonored by every kind of reproach.

Jesus, like the others who were crucified by the Romans, was required to carry His own cross to the place of execution. The entire cross weighed about three hundred pounds, but most of the time, the victims were only required to carry the cross bar which ranged in weight between seventy-five and one hundred twenty-five pounds. Portrayals of Jesus's journey along the via Delarosa generally show Him dragging the entire cross, but the upright beam of these instruments of torture was usually placed in a fixed location with the crossbar being attached when those being executed arrived at the actual spot outside the city walls where the upright had been positioned.

VERSES 32–34

Jesus, in the waning strength of His humanity after having been beaten and flogged, struggled under the weight of the cross. The Romans grabbed a man out of the crowd of onlookers and forced him to carry Jesus's cross. This conscription of Simon, who was from the North African city of Cyrene, was sanctioned by a Roman law that allowed any Roman soldier to stop a Jew on the road and compel him or her to drop what they were carrying and to assist the Roman soldier in bearing his load for up to one mile. It was this law that Jesus had referred to in Matthew 5:41, where He taught "whosoever shall compel thee to go a mile, go with him twain."

When they finally got to Golgotha, the place of Jesus's crucifixion, they offered Him a mixture of wine and gall.

> The drink offered to our Lord was vinegar (made of light wine rendered acidic, the common drink of Roman soldiers) "mingled with gall," or, according to Mark 15:23, "mingled with myrrh;" both expressions meaning the same thing, namely, that the vinegar was made bitter by the infusion of wormwood or some other bitter substance, usually given, according to a merciful custom, as an anodyne to those who were crucified, to render them insensible to pain. Our Lord, knowing this, refuses to drink it. He would take nothing to cloud His faculties or blunt the pain of dying. He chooses to suffer every element of woe in the bitter cup of agony given Him by the Father (John 18:11).[115]

VERSES 35–37

From Mark 15:25, we are told that the crucifixion took place at the third hour, which would have been at nine o'clock in the morning; therefore, Jesus remained on the cross for about six hours.

To get a graphic explanation of what it meant to be crucified, you can research an article written in 1986 by Dr. William Edwards for the *Journal of American Medical Association* and titled "On the Physical Death of Jesus Christ."

The gruesomeness and horror of a person being executed by crucifixion was well-known in the first century; therefore, Matthew could simply write "they crucified Him" without going into any type of description or explanation. The use of the word "crucifixion" would flood the reader with ghastly images that were beyond any description that would adequately

---

[115] *Easton's Bible Dictionary*, https://www.blueletterbible.org/search/Dictionary/viewTopic.cfm?topic=ET0001419.

convey the shattering reality of the tortuous punishment inflicted on another human being.

> The Jews under Rome's rule regard the cross as particularly abhorrent, and the rabbis later forbid its use in self-governing Jewish communities. In Jesus's case, however, the religious leaders are elated to see Him disgraced on the cross.[116]

Knowing what was before Him, and the more devastating fact that He would be forsaken by God the Father, it is no wonder that Jesus was sorrowful, even to death, falling on His face and having sweat great drops of blood as He prayed at Gethsemane.

While watching and waiting for Jesus's death as it was unfolding, the soldiers unknowingly fulfilled Psalm 22:18, where we read, "They part my garments among them and cast lots upon my vesture." John's gospel highlights the extent of this fulfillment in greater detail, where he writes,

> Then the soldiers, when they had crucified Jesus, took his garments, and made four parts, to every soldier a part; and also his coat: now the coat was without seam, woven from the top throughout. They said therefore among themselves, Let us not rend it, but cast lots for it, whose it shall be.

On this passage, John Calvin appropriately comments,

> God determined that His own Son should be stripped of his raiment, that we, clothed with his righteousness and with abundance of all good things, may appear with boldness in company with the angels.

As a part of being crucified, the charges of the victim's crime were normally carried by him as he was marched through the streets on the way to his

---

[116] *Tabletalk Magazine* (Sanford, FL, Ligonier Ministries, Inc., December 17, 2008).

execution and then affixed to the cross as a witness to his crime. This placard was a warning notice to anyone who would dare consider some form of rebellious act against Rome. Jesus's placard stated, "This is Jesus, the King of the Jews," and John 19:20–22 tells us that "it was written in Hebrew, and Greek, and Latin." The wording of this inscription was highly contested by the Jewish religious leaders, but Pilate answered, "What I have written I have written."

VERSES 38–44

They placed the two robbers on either side of Jesus during their crucifixions, and some say that this is representative of Jesus being surrounded by all sinful humanity, and others that it signified that Jesus was deemed the most reprehensible of the three. John Calvin states,

> It was the finishing stroke of the lowest disgrace when Christ was executed between two robbers; for they assigned him the most prominent place, as if he had been the prince of robbers.

But it remains that there is no biblical evidence of these assertions. Nonetheless, their being executed next to Jesus was in fact another fulfillment of a prophecy found in Isaiah 53:12, which said that "he was numbered with the transgressors …" Matthew calls those executed with Jesus robbers, but normally mere robbers were not crucified. These two men were probably insurrectionists and were affiliated with Barabbas, who had formerly been destined to join them.

Scripture tells us that all who passed by mocked Him, some taunting Him to use His supernatural powers to save Himself. Even the chief priests and scribes derided Him, saying to one another that if He came down from the cross they would believe that He truly was the Son of God. They further said that if He trusts in God, let God deliver Him if His Father so desired to do so. After all, hadn't Jesus said that He was the Son of God? They were still asking for and seeking some heavenly and miraculous sign, and in a few short days, they will witness one in the rebuilding of His bodily temple. Everyone piled on the insults and recriminations, including the two robbers who were being crucified with Him. They all were mocking Him for His faithfulness and for being exactly who He said He was: our Savior and King, the everlasting Son of God.

What none of them could grasp, what none of them saw or heard in His teachings and now in His death, was that it wasn't Rome, the religious leaders, or the nails that kept Him on the cross. It was His passive obedience to the will of the Father to complete the destiny for which He was born, which was to be the propitiation and salvation for all that God had chosen from eternity past. Jesus chose to lay down His life, to set aside His glory and humble Himself in His incarnation, to suffer under the persecution of God's chosen people, and then to die upon the cross utterly alone, with even God the Father temporarily abandoning Him under the full wrath executed upon Him for the sin that was imputed to Him for our salvation.

VERSES 45–50

As we know, in the Roman reckoning of time, the first hour begins at six o'clock in the morning, which would mean that the hours delineated in scripture for the duration of this darkness would have taken place between twelve noon (the sixth hour), and three o'clock in the afternoon (or the ninth hour).

The Roman historian Phlegon in his documentation of this darkening wrote,

> In the fourth year of the 202nd Olympiad, there was an extraordinary eclipse of the sun: at the sixth hour, the day turned into dark night, so that the stars in heaven were seen; and there was an earthquake.

Although this historian called it an eclipse of the sun, this language was descriptive of the type or magnitude of the darkness that had ensued and not an astronomical explanation for the reason of the darkness. Passover always coincides with a full moon, and it is impossible to have a solar eclipse and a full moon at the same time. In his explanation, the late James Montgomery Boice, in *The Gospel according to Matthew,* wrote, "The darkness [cries] out against the blackness of our sin and [testifies] to the tremendous cost to God of our redemption."

Josephus, the ancient Jewish historian, reminds us that the ninth hour was traditionally the time that the Jews offered the evening sacrifice, and we can see that in God's providence, this was the exact time that the substitutional lamb of God gave up His spirit to atone for our sins. It was at about the same time that the darkness ebbed that Jesus cried with a loud voice, saying, Eli, Eli, lama sabachthani? that is to say, My God, my God, why hast thou forsaken me?

Although

> true, the scourging of the guards, the nails in Christ's hands, and the other physical pains Jesus suffered manifested God's wrath. Nevertheless, the most intense suffering Christ experienced was spiritual in nature, the hopelessness of losing the gaze of His Father's blessing and the torment of experiencing God's wrath for the sins of His people.[117]

The agony of the intense loneliness that Christ experienced as God's wrath was poured out on the sin that Jesus had been imputed with is an anguish that true Christians will never know, nor can the depth and the magnitude of it ever be imagined. For all of eternity past, present, and future, with this one exception as God cursed Jesus in our place, the unity of God the Father and God the Son had been, and always will be, unbroken. Even within this apparent separation between Father and Son, Their unity was not fully severed. Paul tells us in 2 Corinthians 5:19 (ESV) that "in Christ God was reconciling the world to himself, not counting their trespasses against them, and entrusting to us the message of reconciliation." During this moment in time, Jesus was in complete obedience to, and in unity with, His Father's will as He finished the work that they had eternally planned for: providing the only means for our salvation.

---

[117] *Tabletalk Magazine* (Sanford, FL, Ligonier Ministries, Inc., April 30, 2012).

Jesus's cry led some of the bystanders to misunderstand Him, and they thought that He was calling out for Elijah to come and rescue Him. Someone ran to get a sponge, filled it with sour wine, put it on a reed, and gave it to Jesus to drink. (See Matthew 27:48 and Psalm 69:21.) Jesus then cried out once more and gave up His spirit. Luke 23:46 tells us that this last cry was Jesus calling out to His Father, "Father, into thy hands I commend my spirit." In Jesus having committed His spirit into God's hand, He also commits ours as well. John Calvin comments on this when he wrote,

> Let us now remember that it was not in reference to himself alone that Christ committed his soul to the Father, but that he included, as it were, in one bundle all the souls of those who believe in him, that they may be preserved along with his own; and not only so, but by this prayer he obtained authority to save all souls, so that not only does the heavenly Father, for his sake, deign to take them into his custody, but, giving up the authority into his hands, commits them to him to be protected.

In addition to Matthew's brief comments, we find that John 19:30 tells us that Jesus cried loudly, "It is finished," and that He bowed His head and gave up His spirit. Once more, we see in these verses that no one took Jesus's life; He gave it up. Elsewhere in John's gospel, we see Jesus's own words to this effect when He teaches,

> I lay down my life, that I might take it again. No man taketh it from me, but I lay it down of myself. I have power to lay it down, and I have power to take it again. This commandment have I received of my Father. (John 10:17–18)

VERSES 51–56

The temple veil was a curtain that separated the Holy of Holies, the earthly dwelling place of God's presence, from the rest of the temple where men dwelt. This signified the separation between sinful man and our Holy God. Josephus records that the temple veil, although originally thirty cubits high (1 Kings 6:2), had been increased to forty cubits when Herod rebuilt the temple, which would have made the veil to be about sixty feet in height. In addition, early Jewish tradition says that the veil was about four inches thick, but there is no biblical record of that dimension. The height and thickness are mentioned to demonstrate that no man could have manipulated the tearing of such a massive curtain from the top to bottom let alone coordinated its rending with the timing of the death of our Savior. The picture or the symbology we get from this event, and its synchronization with the finished work of Christ, is that His sacrifice signified that the Holy of Holies was now accessible for all who believe in Him as He is the Way, the Truth, and the Life. No longer was the temple and the deadness of its religious system and traditions to be the center of worship. Through Jesus, our High Priest and King, we as believers can come before God because we have been declared justified as we are wrapped in the cloak of His righteousness. Hebrews 10:19–20 echoes this as we read,

> Having therefore, brethren, boldness to enter into the holiest by the blood of Jesus, By a new and living way, which he hath consecrated for us, through the veil, that is to say, his flesh.

Matthew tells of earthquakes and rocks being split apart, and Matthew Henry writes that this signifies "the mighty shock, indeed, the fatal blow now given to the devil's kingdom."

Some days later, when Christ was resurrected as the firstborn from the dead, tombs were opened, and many saints were raised and went into Jerusalem and were seen by many. This event is not covered in any other gospel, and Matthew has little to say of it. The ESV Study Bible footnotes say that these were probably

> pious Old Testament figures and godly intertestamental Jews, reembodied to witness to the new order of things that was now in the process of dawning.

John MacArthur's commentary says that

evidently these people were given glorified bodies; they appeared to many, enough to establish the reality of the miracle; and then they no doubt ascended to glory, a kind of foretaste of 1 Thessalonians 4:16.

R. C. Sproul in his commentary concedes that it is unknown whether or not those raised were given resurrection bodies or, like Lazarus, were given mortal bodies and a second term of life. Sproul states that the importance of their being raised was the significance of the promise that Jesus's death and resurrection had conquered death and revealed that a Christian's physical death was a transition to a better facet of life in Him, one that is everlasting and glorious.

The love, poise, and compassion of Jesus, as well as the cataclysmic events that transpired at Jesus's crucifixion, were so dramatically striking that even the battle-hardened Roman soldiers, who had likely seen many deaths both in combat and during executions, were filled with fear and awe. The centurion, undoubtably speaking on behalf of his men, was compelled by his own witness to conclude, "Truly this was the Son of God!" Their feelings of awe and the reverence of the words that were spoken were in stark contrast to the barbaric cruelty and contemptuously insulting taunts that had been heartlessly displayed earlier that morning.

Among those who had seen these last hours of Christ's life and crucifixion were many of the women who had traveled from Galilee in Jesus's entourage. It is said that they looked on from a distance, and perhaps they were torn between being by His side and wanting to flee from the dreadfulness of what was before them. Some of these faithful women will also be the among the first to witnesses His resurrection.

VERSES 57–61

Normally the corpses of those executed were thrown into the Valley of Hinnom, which was the garbage dump of Jerusalem, and then left to rot or to be devoured by wild animals. Whenever possible, Jewish custom was to have the bodies of the executed removed before sundown, especially on the Sabbath, and during the Passover season, the Jews did not want the horror of the executions to be on display.

Joseph of Arimathea, who was secretly a disciple of Jesus and a member of the Sanhedrin, went to Pilate and asked for the body of Jesus. Unlike the disciples who had fled, Joseph now exposed himself to the rage of the religious elite by his public display of honoring Christ, which was in direct opposition to their vehement hatred of Jesus.

Pilate ordered that Jesus's body be given to Joseph, who then, along with the Pharisee Nicodemus, took the body down from the cross and wrapped it in a clean linen shroud, along with about seventy-five pounds of myrrh and aloes. And then they laid it in Joseph's own tomb, which had been hewn out of rock and in which no man had ever been laid. This was all done in the short span of time between His death and before sunset so that they would not violate the Sabbath.

The respect and generosity of Joseph in placing Jesus's body in his personal tomb fulfilled Isaiah 53:9, where we read, "And he made his grave with the wicked, and with the rich in his death; because he had done no violence, neither was any deceit in his mouth." And then, as was the normal practice, a large stone was rolled across the entrance. As all this was happening, "There was Mary Magdalene, and the other Mary, sitting over against the sepulcher."

VERSES 62–66

Jesus had been executed and buried, but that wasn't enough to allow for a good night of sleep for the religious leaders. They had been kept awake tormented and vexed with continual thoughts of Jesus and the potential consequence of the fulfillment or the appearance of the fulfillment of His promise to rise again. They are so exasperated by these possibilities that they break the Sabbath by going to the Praetorium to meet with Pilate. They go before him in a feigned deference that doesn't really mask their true feelings, and with as much veneration toward him as they can gather, they call him sir and then relate to him that Jesus, while He was still alive, claimed that He would rise again in three days. They wanted Pilate to seal the tomb and told him that they feared that the disciples would steal Jesus's body and proclaim that He had risen. They were adamant that this fraud would be worse than the first one that He had perpetrated. Pilate told them to take the guard of soldiers that they had and to make the tomb secure by sealing it and posting sentries. Both the Roman governor and the religious leaders felt that it was imperative to guard the tomb, but their efforts would only give greater testimony to the miraculous reality of Christ's resurrection. Jerome, one of the early church fathers, wrote this: "The greater their precautionary care, the more fully is revealed the power of the resurrection."

Guards were in place, with a normal contingent being at least four, two who were actively watching while fully armed and two who would be at rest until the start of their watch, at which time the first two would rest. These guards were seasoned Roman soldiers and they couldn't care less about the religious and political intrigue that surrounded this tomb. Their job was to guard it as if their lives depended on it, and of course, they did.

The tomb was sealed with the large stone that blocked the entrance. The stone that sealed His grave was set on an incline in a channel cut in the rock, making it easier to cover the tomb's entrance by rolling the stone downhill. To gain access to the tomb, it would take several men to roll the stone back up the incline. To this, the Romans fastened a rope stretched taught across the stone and affixed to either side by a seal consisting of either a clay or wax that was imprinted with the Roman imperial signet that would be easily broken during any attempt to open the tomb. This final seal carried the weight and power of Roman authority, and if broken, it would signify defiance to that authority; a heavy reprisal would be swift.

CHAPTER 28

RESURRECTION, THE GUARD'S REPORT, GREAT COMMISSION

VERSES 1–3

At dawn on the morning after the Sabbath, Mary Magdalene and the other Mary went to the tomb to further prepare Jesus's body, and the other gospels indicate that they had brought additional spices with them to complete the anointing process. The other gospel writers tell us that the women had wondered among themselves how they would be able to open the tomb, but in their faith, they would find a way. So they continued toward the tomb. Matthew, the only gospel writer to do so, tells of a great earthquake and continues his narrative by describing the miraculous appearance of an angel of the Lord who had descended from heaven, rolled back the stone, and then sat on it. The angel is described as having an appearance like lightning, and his clothing was as white as snow. In Matthew's and Mark's gospels, they speak of one angel, while in Luke and John, we read that there were two. R. C. Sproul comments that this apparent contradiction is merely the style of the writers, some choosing to focus on the individual angel who spoke to them while other writers are more specific on the number of angels present. Sproul states that if there were two angels, there was certainly one, and the fact that two of the gospel writers chose to report the actions and words of only one angel does not mean he was the only angel present.

There are varied views of the earthquake, one that the earthquake occurred simultaneous to the appearance of the angel or that the angel used it as the means to open the tomb. It is said that the tomb was opened not to let Jesus out but to give access to the women and to the apostles. Jesus had no need for the tomb to be opened by anyone. He had the power to overcome death; a mere stone would not have impeded His exit from the tomb. With the rolling away of the door to the tomb, and with Christ's resurrection, our adoption was ratified. Simultaneously, the doors of heaven were opened to those of the new covenant who accept Him as the Lord and Savior of their lives.

VERSES 4–6

The steeled Roman soldiers have no fight left in them. Overwhelmed by dread, they trembled, became faint, and appeared to be like dead men. They were frozen with a fearful paralysis that rendered them dysfunctional, and they were in no condition to fulfill their duties. Ignoring the guards, the angel told the women not to be afraid, soothing them with a comfort found in the softness and demeanor of his communication, as he told them that he was aware that they had come to find the crucified Christ. He continued by relating to them that Jesus had risen and was no longer there, inviting them to see where He had been laid. In the angels' words, they were hearing what was lacking in their faith, what they should have expected, and that was Christ had risen. This was the first time that the reality of Jesus's teachings about His resurrection had been verbalized, and they were stunned at the now evident truth of what He had said.

Death had been conquered, and He was the firstborn from the dead.

VERSES 7–8

After inviting them to see where Jesus had been laid, the angel told them to go quickly and tell the other disciples that He had risen from the dead. He further tells them that Jesus was going to Galilee and that they would find Him there. Many of them would see Jesus before Galilee, but Galilee had been the hub of Jesus's ministry and it would have made perfect sense to the disciples that this is where Jesus would go and be with them. This gave the women the assurance that they would soon see Jesus again. Then they quickly left the tomb, and at the very core of their beings, they wavered between fear and their joy at the news of Jesus's resurrection. In obedience to the angels' command, they ran to tell the great news to the disciples who remained in hiding. "The doors were shut where the disciples were assembled for fear of the Jews" (John 20:19).

VERSES 9–10

As they went to tell the disciples Jesus met them and greeted them. Some versions say that He had said to them, "Rejoice," and this would have dissipated the fear that they had as the joy they were experiencing would have flooded them with such an intensity there would be no room for any emotion other than the overwhelming compulsion to worship Him that they displayed by kneeling at His feet and holding to Him tightly. God alone is to be worshipped, and in His acceptance of their worship, Jesus attests once more to His deity. Jesus continues to ease their anxiety with the words "Be not afraid," and He once again instructs them to "tell my brethren" to go to Galilee, where they would see Him. Jesus's words of endearment toward His disciples, and specifically the apostles, must have seemed like a soothing balm on the wounds of their hearts because of their past cowardice and infidelity.

God's love toward us is immutable, and no matter how we fail Him, He remains steadfast.

VERSES 11–15

The evil intent and their grasping for worldly power had so darkened the hearts of the priests that even though they knew the truth of the resurrection, they continued to reject both the Son of God and His heavenly Father.

The guards had gone to chief priests and told them exactly what had happened, and instead of repenting of their sin, they compounded it by concocting a story about the disciples having stolen Christ's body. And then they bribed the soldiers with enough money to have them agree to perjure themselves with these lies. The priests had allowed their own pride and arrogance to overshadow the truth and continued in their machinations to deceive all Israel.

As far as the disciples, at this point, they were just trying to keep from being taken into custody and being put on trial. John Chrysostom writes, "These were men hiding out to simply stay alive," not those who would risk arrest and execution for robbing a grave.[118]

The priests then tell the soldiers that "if" the governor hears about it, they will satisfy him and keep them out of trouble. There is so much wrong with this idea. First of all, the governor is bound to question them, and if they say they were asleep, they would be executed themselves. And how would they know that the disciples stole Christ's body if they were asleep?

These verses end with "And this saying has been commonly reported among the Jews until this day." Despite the overwhelming historical evidence and with eyewitness accounts, there are still those who reject the idea that Jesus is the Christ and even that there is a God who is supreme. We shouldn't be surprised as His Word is foolishness to the world, and we know that redemption and perdition are both a reality in God's eternal plan.

---

[118] Paraphrased from *Tabletalk Magazine* (Sanford, FL, Ligonier Ministries, Inc., December 29, 2008).

VERSES 16–17

As he is prone to do, Matthew skips some of the details and events that are found in the other gospels, such as Jesus meeting with some of the disciples in Jerusalem. His intent here seems to be focused on the promise Jesus had made earlier that Matthew had recorded in chapter 26:32, where He had said, "But after I am risen again, I will go before you into Galilee." Or perhaps he felt that their meeting in Galilee had the weight of their having received the Great Commission and it overshadowed other events that seemed to him to have less significance.

When the disciples arrived at the location where Jesus had instructed them to meet with Him, their natural inclination was to worship Him. Like the women at the tomb, these men did not just greet Jesus; they worshipped Him in full recognition of His deity.

But Matthew notes that some doubted, which some translate as them having been hesitant, as the Greek verb *distazein* that was used reflects hesitation and not a refusal of truth. Christ's rising was a supernatural event and would have seemed to be almost unbelievable. Combined with their own shame and guilt for abandoning Him, some were hesitant to fully embrace the moment. Some scholars are of the opinion that there was no doubt about Jesus being the Messiah; they were just unsure how to respond to Him. Any type of doubt attributed to the disciples should have erased the bogus theory of a mass hallucination that they were purportedly subjected to.

Some commentators attribute this doubt not to the apostles but to the other disciples who were present. We cannot be certain, but these may have been some of those that Paul referred to in 1 Corinthians 15:6, where he writes, "After that, he was seen of above five hundred brethren at once; of whom the greater part remain unto this present, but some are fallen asleep." In any event, doubt is a human reaction that would be hard to overcome. Even Thomas still carries the stigma associated with his lapse of faith, and those who are skeptical in our day are still referred to as a doubting Thomas.

Verses 18–20

In Christ's risen state, God the Father has given all power and dominion to Jesus, both in heaven and on the earth. He has sovereign control, and within the power of His authority, He has given a command to His disciples. This command is that they go forth and make disciples of all nations, calling upon them to accept Jesus as their Lord and Master.

Not only are they to go to all the nations to make disciples, but they are to baptize them under the auspices and in the name of the Father and of the Son and of the Holy Spirit. The sacrament of baptism is to be done under the backing and in the unity of each person of the Triune Godhead. In their being baptized, the new believers, men from all nations without distinction, are entering a new covenantal relationship with Jesus, and their hearts were to be circumcised.

Those who are to embark upon the Great Commission are commanded to teach all the nations the complete obedience that they are to adopt toward every command that Christ had previously given. This mandate to teach is not limited to the evangelism of new believers but includes the ongoing instruction necessary to promote spiritual growth in those who are already brothers and sisters in Christ.

The Jews, as God's chosen people, were the launching point of Christ's ministry, and now the gospel message will be proclaimed not only to the Jews but to the Gentiles as well, and it will be professed to every people of the earth.

Jesus, in the fullness and glory of His deity, has unconditional authority and demands unconditional obedience to His commands, and by this imperative, He has every expectation that the disciples will go forth, that they will teach, and that His Word and the requisite obedience to His Word will be carried out to the letter. The nations are not only to learn about the whole counsel of God's Word but are also to be taught it and learn it by the resurrected power of Christ Himself. They are to know that He is ever present and that He will be with them always. The fact of His being with them always is not just a nebulous presence but one that carries with it the promise of unconditional love, divine protection, comfort in times of trouble, and the power to abide in Him and to persevere through all the trials that life brings to them. He is Emmanuel, "God with us." This is a precious promise that goes beyond their fleeting transience but extends throughout all eternity as He presents them with glorified bodies that will enable them to worship Him throughout all eternity.

CPSIA information can be obtained
at www.ICGtesting.com
Printed in the USA
BVHW071532300720
585046BV00001B/27